Anthony Minghella

Plays: One

Whale Music, A Little Like Drowning, Two Planks and A Passion, Made in Bangkok

Anthony Minghella won the 1986 Plays & Players Best Play Award for *Made in Bangkok*. His work is distinguished by a 'breadth of scope, a seemingly unaffected style with an individual resonance, uncanny flashes of poetry and wild humour, great tenderness in treating sexual relations and intriguing mysteriousness of purpose.' *The Times*

Whale Music is 'genuinely tender, poignant and spikily anti-male all at once.' *Daily Mail*

A Little Like Drowning 'makes you laugh, makes you cry and makes you think.' *Guardian*

Two Planks and A Passion 'is one of the best new plays I have seen in the past decade.' *Financial Times*

Anthony Minghella is the author of *A Little Like Drowning, Made in Bangkok* (*Plays and Players* Best New Play 1986), *What if it's Raining?*, *The Storyteller* (Emmy and Bafta Awards 1987/88), *Hang Up* (Prix Italia 1988), *Cigarettes and Chocolate* (1988 Sony Award, 1988 Giles Cooper Award) and the screenplay *Truly, Madly, Deeply* (1991).

ANTHONY MINGHELLA

PLAYS: ONE

Whale Music
A Little Like Drowning
Two Planks and A Passion
Made in Bangkok

with an introduction by the author

Methuen Drama

METHUEN WORLD DRAMATISTS

This edition first published in Great Britain in 1992 by Methuen Drama, Michelin House, 81 Fulham Road, London SW3 6RB and distributed in the United States of America by HEB Inc., 361 Hanover Street, Portsmouth, New Hampshire NH 03801 3959.

Whale Music, A Little Like Drowning, Two Planks and A Passion first published in 1987 by Methuen London, copyright © 1987 by Anthony Minghella
Made in Bangkok first published in 1986 by Methuen London and revised in 1988, 1990 for the Samuel French, Inc. edition in the USA, copyright © 1986, 1988, 1990 by Anthony Minghella

This collection copyright © 1992 by Anthony Minghella
Introduction copyright © 1992 by Anthony Minghella
The author has asserted his moral rights.

A CIP catalogue record for this book is available from the British Library

ISBN 0 413 66580 1

Printed and bound in Great Britain
by Cox & Wyman Ltd, Reading, Berks

The front cover shows *La Musique*, 1939 by Henri Matisse, oil on canvas, 45⅜ × 45⅜ in, Albright-Knox Art Gallery, Buffalo, New York.
© Succession H Matisse/DACS 1992
The back cover photo of the author is by Paul Tozer

The lines from the *Insight Guide to Thailand* quoted in *Made in Bangkok*, page 203, are reprinted by kind permission of Apa Productions (HK) Ltd.

Contents

For my mother and father

A Chronology

of first productions in each medium

Child's Play, Humberside Theatre	1978
Whale Music, Leicester Haymarket	1981
Granada TV film 1983, and BBC Radio 4, 1985	
A Little Like Drowning, CV-One Touring Company	1982
and BBC Radio 4, 1989	
Two Planks and A Passion, Northcott Theatre,	1983
and BBC Radio 3, 1986	
Love Bites, Derby Playhouse	1984
Made in Bangkok, Aldwych Theatre, London	1986
What If It's Raining, Limehouse/Channel 4 TV	1986
The Storyteller, Jim Henson Productions/	1987
NBC/TVS/Channel 4 TV	
Hang Up, London Contemporary Dance Theatre	1987
and BBC Radio 3, 1987	
Cigarettes and Chocolate, BBC Radio 4	1988
Living with Dinosaurs,	1989
Jim Henson Productions/NBC/TVS/Channel 4 TV	
The Mathematics of a Kiss,	1989
short opera with Orlando Gough and John Lunn	
for Signals/Dancelines/Channel 4 TV	
Days Like These, short monologue for Comic Relief	1989
Second Thoughts, for Mel Smith and Griff Rhys Jones	1989
in Small Doses, Talkback/BBC TV	
Brick Wall, a commercial for Comic Relief	1991
Truly, Madly, Deeply, BBC Films/	1991
Samuel Goldwyn Co.	

Introduction

From another country and – I suppose – another life as a writer and now director of films, what concerns me most about this collection of plays is that it comprises (excepting some juvenilia and a much-loved but ultimately incomplete play from 1984) my entire output for the theatre. That the most recent, *Made in Bangkok*, was written over six years ago is especially salutary. Not so much *Minghella Plays: One* as *Minghella Plays: period*. What I have liked to defend as a temporary stutter threatens to become a silence.

The truth is that I have lost some confidence in the theatre. It feels rather like a loss of faith. I find myself in similar thrall to the theatre as I do to Catholicism. It informs a great deal of what I think and do – like it or not; I find it hard to practice, increasingly marginalised, excluding, often infuriating. Then once in a while I experience an epiphany, some small miracle, which excites a spate of consuming evangelism. Perhaps it is beyond the scope of a brief introductory note to wrestle with such dilemmas – what is theatre for? who is it for? what is the appropriate relationship between the dramatist and the community? But I do know that these lumbering and clumsy debates obscure my vision when I try to settle with a play as writer, and often as audience. Nevertheless, if these were my last plays for the theatre I should feel thoroughly dispirited.

It has often seemed to me that there are two kinds of writer at least: those who understand the world and tell us about it; and those who don't understand the world and share their confusion with the audience. I have always admired the first group and resided in the second. And I can identify in each of the plays in this volume a question or a problem or a puzzle which informs and orders the material. In *Whale Music* I tried to make sense in my own mind of some of the issues surrounding an unplanned and unwanted pregnancy. *A Little Like Drowning* was prompted by a conundrum in my family history, where my grandfather appeared to have maintained a loving relationship with two women over the larger part of his life. *Two Planks and a Passion* was an attempt to understand why the medieval Corpus Christi cycle, a collection of apparently innocuous religious plays, aroused so much political intrigue and civic rivalry. *Made in Bangkok*'s debate is more elusive – why have men so annexed their desires that they impose and abide by strict sexual constraints at home and then travel many thousands of miles to behave freely and badly?

But these issues, along with the perennial concerns of style and mechanism and beauty in play-making, exercised me less than the attempts, however rudimentary, to create a world of feeling, to emulate what I have most responded to in the work of others: moments of insight which enlarge upon the narrow range of direct experience possible for any of us. And here, with the obligation to be accurate, is where drama acquires something like a moral responsibility. The world offered back to the audience, be it magical, funny or tragic, had better be scrupulous: or else, like Flute's Thisbe in *A Midsummer Night's Dream*, we kiss the wall's hole and not the lips at all. Which is why the theatre – of all the dramatic media least disposed to adornment or mediation, roughest, live, and the harshest arena of judgement – is finally the one I most respect, most care for, and most fear.

Anthony Minghella
Los Angeles, March 1992

WHALE MUSIC

Whale Music was originally written for Eileen Ryan, Tina Perry, Jane Dale, Alison Watt, Alison Head, Audrey Middleton and Siv Jannsen who performed it at the Gulbenkian Centre, University of Hull, in June 1980.

The play received its first professional production at the Haymarket Theatre, Leicester in April 1981, with the following cast:

CAROLINE	Michele Copsey
STELLA	Carol Leader
FRAN	Camille Davis
KATE	Julie Legrand
D	Sadie Hamilton
VERONICA/WAITRESS	Mary Waterhouse
SHEELAGH O'BRIEN	Anne Jameson

Directed by Colin George

Setting: The Isle of Wight
Time: The present

This version of the play includes a NURSE and STAFF NURSE.

A television version of *Whale Music* was made by Granada Television in 1983, with Howard Baker producing and Pedr James directing. The play was also produced on BBC Radio 4, the first broadcast taking place in October 1985.

ACT ONE

Scene One

STELLA's *Flat. Winter.*

CAROLINE *has answered* STELLA's *advertisement for a lodger.*
STELLA *shows her the room.*

STELLA. This is it. Not enormous.

CAROLINE (*not looking at the room much; checking the window*).
No, it's fine. Do you want a deposit? I can write you a cheque.

STELLA. The wardrobe's full, I'm afraid. I'll clear it out tomorrow.

CAROLINE. That's OK. I don't have much with me.

STELLA. I use this as a dark room in the summer. There's a blind.
Great if you're into meditation.

CAROLINE *goes to the window.*

CAROLINE. The sea.

STELLA. Oh yeah. It's everywhere. The gulls will probably keep you
awake at first. You'll get used to them. They scream at the
weather.

CAROLINE. I was born here.

STELLA. Oh. That makes sense. You're either born in this place or
you come here to die. Listen, you couldn't manage cash, could
you? A cheque's a bit . . .

CAROLINE. Of course.

STELLA. Just, I don't work in the winter. I sign on as a beach
photographer. But the facts of life don't interest Social Security
much. They think it's my fault that nobody sunbathes in
November. But they DO pay the rent and they wouldn't like it if
they found out you did too. As it is I keep getting visits from
unpleasant men before breakfast, demanding to examine the
mattress for signs of cohabitation. Which is pretty absurd.
However high in protein sperm's supposed to be, it can hardly
amount to dependency. I keep telling them it would never stand up
in court. Did you tell me your name?

CAROLINE. It's Caroline.

STELLA. I'm Stella. Listen, forget the deposit – but you can give me
a week's rent in advance if you like.

CAROLINE. Thanks. Oh – is there a bathroom?

STELLA. Yeah. It's downstairs. If you want hot water there's a

meter – 10ps – you have to kick the coinbox. (*She takes the rent.*)
Great. If anyone asks, I'm going to say you're an old school friend
come to stay. Is that OK?

CAROLINE. Yes, that's fine.

STELLA. Tremendous. (*She offers her hand.*) Good to see you, old
school friend.

Pause.

Anything wrong?

CAROLINE. No. (*Pause.*) Why? (*Pause.*)

STELLA. Hey, do you cook?

CAROLINE. A little.

STELLA. A girl who cooks! I cook tins and packets. Oh – and I can
thaw frozen things.

CAROLINE. I reheat take-aways.

STELLA. Never touch them. I'm working hard at getting anorexia.

CAROLINE. Why's that?

STELLA. Oh, it's the fashion to be unhealthy. Anyone who's anyone
looks as if they could do with a good square meal. I've never lived
with another girl before. When you moving in?

CAROLINE. Now?

STELLA. I'll make some tea.

CAROLINE. Uh – no thanks.

STELLA. Coffee? Booze?

CAROLINE. No, I'm fine. But don't let me stop you.

STELLA. Is it a man?

CAROLINE. Is what a man?

STELLA. Why you're here?

CAROLINE. No.

STELLA. Sorry. I know. I ask too many questions.

CAROLINE. No. Depends what kind of reply you want. How are
you? – fine – or, how are you? – falling apart, suicidal. You know
– polite or honest. I'm fine on the polite.

STELLA. It's cold in here. I hate the winter. I try not to go outside.
The idea is to raid a supermarket in September and lock the door
until April. Go in a slug; emerge a butterfly.

CAROLINE. What do you do?

STELLA. Paint. No. Plan paintings. Think about them. In fact, nothing much. I mean preferably I find a man to lock in with me. Else I go maudlin. On balance I've been better off maudlin. I set one loose yesterday. There was something VERY wrong with him. He's left a smell. Did you notice? Musty. He's gone off to find a cave in Greece.

CAROLINE. Really?

STELLA. My dear, this is the dregs of the beautiful people you're moving in with. You know: record collection stops at Hendrix. South coast trying hard to be West coast. Marijuana and muesli.

CAROLINE. You don't sound very convinced.

STELLA. It pales like everything else. How long do you plan to stay?

CAROLINE. I don't know. Until the Spring.

STELLA. A fellow hibernator.

CAROLINE. Oh yes.

STELLA. There are some things I can't work out.

CAROLINE. Yes?

STELLA. Strictly polite questions. Like why not stay with parents? Where school friends?

CAROLINE. Easy. Parents not here. Moved to Derbyshire. School friend here. Has family. I want to see her but I wouldn't want to stay. I'd trip all over the acquisitions.

STELLA. I see. And what – have you been at college or something?

CAROLINE. Yes. Leeds. I'm taking a year off. That's my speciality. I took a year off before I went, too.

STELLA. Good?

CAROLINE. My year off? No. Well good, yes, to have . . . to get around. That was good. The bits in between were on the whole not good. At all.

STELLA. Where d'you go?

CAROLINE. Most places on the Underground, Islington the longest.

STELLA. Funny – you left here and went to London. With me it was the reverse. I came down here for a festival and never left.

CAROLINE. It's the air.

STELLA. It's laziness. Nobody minds here. It's a lazy place. If you give up in London, half the caring agencies in the world are fighting over you. Compared to the noise those vultures make, the seagulls sound terrific.

CAROLINE. I'm going to walk and walk and walk.

STELLA (*unimpressed*). Wonderful.

CAROLINE. We used to hate tourists. Grockles, we called them. Armies of little fat red people in vests collapsing on the beach, wobbling into the water. When I think of the Summer that's all I see. Now you can shoot a gun down the high street. You can walk for hours. You can breathe a bit. I want to get my lungs full. Throw some stones.

STELLA. Well, don't worry about me. I won't clutter up the landscape. I'll wobble about here. You haven't got a thing about mice, have you?

CAROLINE. No. Why?

STELLA. They've moved in too. I think the Greek god must have brought them with him. I went to make my toast this morning and it looked like a Polo mint.

CAROLINE. Perhaps you'd better get a trap or something.

STELLA. I've got a trap. I've got two traps. I've also got poison and I'm thinking of getting an air rifle. I tell you – it's them or me.

CAROLINE. A cat's more effective. (*She eyes Stella.*) You don't like cats.

STELLA. At least mice just nick food. Cats expect you to buy them the stuff. I adopted a cat once. I thought it was dying or something. I'm bloody certain it gave me worms. And it stank. AND it was permanently on heat. Hey, are you sure you're all right?

CAROLINE. It's nothing. I just feel a bit tired. I'll be OK in a second. Could I have some water?

CAROLINE *lies down on the bed. She suddenly retches and scrabbles for a tissue in her bag.*

CAROLINE. Oh. I'm sorry. Oh.

STELLA. Hey, don't die on me.

CAROLINE. I'm really sorry.

STELLA. Listen, have you seen a doctor?

CAROLINE. Yes. Thanks. I feel much better.

STELLA. Well, what did he say?

CAROLINE. It's a she and she said I was pregnant.

Scene Two

A café.

CAROLINE *is sitting at a table stirring coffee.* FRAN *enters, 'Clothkits' to the nines, carrying a couple of carrier bags.*

FRAN (*with genuine pleasure*). Hello!

FRAN *and* CAROLINE *embrace.*

CAROLINE (*with genuine pleasure*). Hello!

FRAN (*breathlessly*). I'm really sorry I'm late. I've had heaps to do. Absolutely mad. And I forgot to put the timer on the casserole. Do you know I haven't been to this café since, years, since school. It's great.

CAROLINE (*delighted*). It's awful. Where's Heidi?

FRAN. At mum's.

CAROLINE. What a shame. I'm dying to see her.

FRAN. Oh yes. She's a terror. Honestly, she's a real scream. She's crawling.

CAROLINE. Really.

FRAN. You should see the house. She can destroy a room in five minutes. She tried to eat the liquidizer this morning.

CAROLINE. Let me get you a cup of tea.

FRAN. Please. I'm parched. This is lovely. Five minutes' peace.

CAROLINE. Could we have two teas, please? (*To Fran.*) You hungry?

FRAN. I'd love a scone or something.

CAROLINE. And a scone, please.

FRAN. Well. I got your letter.

CAROLINE. Good.

FRAN. I think you're really brave. I really do.

CAROLINE. Oh Fran.

FRAN. No really. I mean if Heidi had come along and I hadn't been . . . What I mean to say is that so many girls, you know . . . just take the easy way out.

CAROLINE. I didn't know there was an easy way out. If there had been I would have grabbed it.

FRAN. No, I know, of course. And you look so well. I went all blotchy and cow-like and my hair fell out in chunks.

CAROLINE. I feel terrible.

FRAN. Oh love.

CAROLINE. I'm getting morning, afternoon and evening sickness.

FRAN. Ah, it'll be a girl. Have you done the needle test?

CAROLINE. What?

FRAN. Dangle a needle over your lump. It works. If it goes up and down it's a boy, and if it goes round and round in circles it's a girl. It's something to do with electricity.

A WAITRESS *brings tea and a scone. She is not a happy waitress.*

CAROLINE. Thanks.

FRAN. Let me get this.

WAITRESS. You pay at the counter.

The WAITRESS *goes.*

FRAN. I know her. You know who she is, don't you? She was in the third year when we were prefects. She was Maureen thing's friend – the one who pushed drugs.

CAROLINE. Is it? Anyway, you do exaggerate, Fran. She told you she'd smoked a joint once.

FRAN. Well. Do you know who else I saw recently? Launa Carter. Vast. Like the side of a house. She was a size eight in the sixth form. Poor thing. She looked really depressed. Do you see anyone?

CAROLINE. No. Just you.

FRAN. How's Miss Lawrence?

CAROLINE. OK. Don't call her Miss Lawrence, Fran. She doesn't teach us any more.

FRAN. I know. But I can't think of her as Kate, somehow. It seems blasphemous.

CAROLINE. Well don't call her Miss Lawrence when you see her. She'll have a fit.

FRAN. Why, is she here?

CAROLINE. No. Not yet. But she will be.

FRAN. Really?

CAROLINE. Don't know. She's coming for my birthday, definitely.

FRAN. That will be nice. She's so fond of you, isn't she? That must have been great when she got the job in Leeds.

CAROLINE. Yes, it was.

FRAN. I didn't realize you were actually sharing together.

CAROLINE. It's Kate's house. I just have a room.

FRAN. It's amazing how things work out. You couldn't have guessed, could you, that you'd both end up in Leeds together?

CAROLINE. And you a mum.

FRAN. Oh, come on, I was marked down as a breeder from the word go. All my brains are in my womb.

CAROLINE. Rubbish.

FRAN. It's true. When Heidi appeared, something in me went click. Into overdrive. (*Pause.*) I'm sorry Caroline, we're talking babies. I promised myself I wouldn't. She's got Graeme's hair. Not that she's got much.

CAROLINE. How is Graeme?

FRAN. Busy. He's fine. In and out like a maniac. They've made him a partner. Can you imagine? He wears a suit!

CAROLINE. Amazing.

FRAN. He said to say hello.

CAROLINE. Say hello back.

FRAN. Right (*Pause.*) I've brought you some things. Don't be insulted. Everything's so expensive.

CAROLINE. Stupid. What sort of things?

FRAN. Here. There's a couple of sleep bras. You'll need those. And a really nice smock and trouser thing from Clothkits. The trousers have an elasticated waist so they grow with you.

CAROLINE. You're a dear, Fran. Bless you. (*She looks in the bag. What she sees upsets her.*) Thank you.

FRAN. I hope I'll have to ask for them back soon. (*Quietly.*) Oh, Caroline. Why don't you come and stay with us? We'd love to have you. I'd be ever so useful – I'm encyclopaedic about pregnancy.

CAROLINE. I'm not good company just now. But thanks.

FRAN. Think about it. It's an open invitation. It would be nice to have a grown-up around.

CAROLINE. Grown-up! Anyway, doesn't Graeme qualify?

FRAN. When he's in. It's hard for men. They don't get so excited by feeds and nappies. And I believe in the family bed.

CAROLINE. The what? No, don't tell me. Heidi sleeps with the two of you. Right?

FRAN. You disapprove.

CAROLINE. Not at all. It's not my business.

FRAN. Graeme says it's ridiculous. But I think it'll make so much difference later on. Besides, it's marvellous. We all cuddle up and she can help herself if she gets hungry in the night.

CAROLINE. Yes, but what about you and Graeme?

FRAN. What about us?

CAROLINE. I mean, what if you have a second baby?

The WAITRESS *comes forward.*

WAITRESS. We're closing.

FRAN. Sorry. (*She devours the scone.*) Mmm. Just the job. (*Pause.*) It's so nice to see you again.

CAROLINE. Good old Fran. Constant as ever.

FRAN. What d'you mean?

CAROLINE. Nothing. It's just good to see you too.

FRAN. I'm a twit. I almost forgot. Two special pressies. (*She produces a record.*) Now, this is wonderful.

CAROLINE (*reading the back of the record sleeve*). Whale Music?

FRAN. Yes, they sing to each other. It's ever so strange. What you do is play it and relax. It's supposed to comfort the baby.

CAROLINE. Ta.

FRAN. No, really. It's tremendous. It's like being very deep under water. Womb-like.

CAROLINE. But it's already in the womb.

FRAN. Well, Heidi loved it. And there's simulated heart beats and things and some Purcell. Only that side's a bit scratched.

CAROLINE. I'll play it, I promise.

FRAN (*holding up a book*). And there's this. '*Essential exercises for the child-bearing year*'.

CAROLINE. Oh God, Fran.

FRAN. They're a must, Caroline. Otherwise you'll look like a deflated balloon afterwards. And it makes such a difference for your labour. Don't make that face. It's going to happen. It's no use pretending it won't.

CAROLINE. Fran, do you think we could change the subject for a minute?

FRAN. Oh, sugar! I'm sorry. I know, I'm like a steamroller when I get going. That's what Graeme says. I'm sorry love. Do you want to go for a walk? You must walk a lot.

CAROLINE. I'd like to go down to the beach.

FRAN. Lovely. You sit there and I'll pay this.

CAROLINE, *alone for a second, gathers up the things. She inspects them.*

FRAN (*to the* WAITRESS). It was a lovely scone. (*To* CAROLINE.) I wish I'd brought Heidi now. She loves sand. And you wouldn't have minded, would you?

CAROLINE. Of course not.

FRAN. I thought she might have upset you.

CAROLINE. Nobody's going to die, Fran.

FRAN. I know, I know. It's just I know how I'd feel.

CAROLINE. I feel like there's glass in my guts. That's all. Everything else is just numb.

FRAN. Well, I'm sure a walk will do you good.

WAITRESS. D'you think you might hurry up?

FRAN. I shouldn't bother with the Clearasil. It just joins the spots together.

CAROLINE. Oh Fran!

FRAN. Want to hear the noise the whales make? It's like this . . . (*She makes whale noises.*)

The WAITRESS *stacks chairs on table.*

WAITRESS (*to an unseen partner*). D'you know her trouble? The husband goes up every skirt in the town . . . except hers.

Scene Three

STELLA's *Flat.*

CAROLINE *and* FRAN *are doing an essential exercise for the child-bearing year.* STELLA *is in a chair, smoking and drinking.* FRAN *reads aloud an instruction from the manual.*

STELLA. That thing in there will be mentally disturbed by the time it drops out. It probably won't ever come out now. You can see it thinking bugger that, mate, if it's this bad in the padded cell you can forget the great outdoors.

CAROLINE. Stella's right. This is killing me. What about my twenty minutes' total relaxation, Fran?

FRAN. Once more.

CAROLINE. Once more.

FRAN. Come on. Big effort. (*She yells out instructions.*)

STELLA. I know what it is. It's the Karma Sutra done single-handed.

CAROLINE (*laughing*). I think I'm breaking something.

FRAN. That's good!

STELLA. That's good, Caroline. Break something!

CAROLINE. Oh come on, Stella. It's great for the anorexia.

STELLA. So's dying. (*Getting up.*) This bloody rain will drive me crazy. Who's for a drink?

    FRAN *and* CAROLINE *loll about, exhausted.*

FRAN. I've brought some Lucozade. Do you fancy some, Caroline?

CAROLINE (*laughing*). I do, actually.

STELLA. Terrific!

FRAN. Your day will come. Have you got a boyfriend?

STELLA. Oh yeah. He's in the wardrobe right now. I keep him in kit form. No, my day won't come. I don't have Caroline's scruples.

FRAN. Oh, I don't know. I think you might feel different if it happened. You see – well, this is my theory anyway – it's not just a question of giving house-room to an egg for a few months . . . no, all kinds of things – hormones and what have you – are rushing about, sort of educating you for motherhood. It's very animal, I think. I mean, it's like the way your milk suddenly comes, for instance.

CAROLINE (*bitterly*). Where does that leave me?

STELLA. Right.

FRAN. Well, I don't know. I don't know, but it's love I'm talking about really, isn't it? I mean, I don't think that can hurt you.

STELLA. Oh! Come on!

FRAN. I think Caroline knows what I mean.

CAROLINE. No, I don't.

FRAN. I wish I hadn't started this.

STELLA. It strikes me, Fran, you wouldn't have a problem if it came up and bit you. Well, love's great. I hear you can buy it from Habitat.

    FRAN *looks to* CAROLINE.

CAROLINE. Don't look at me. I lose both ways, don't I? Do you know, when I told my mother what had happened, she said, 'Only a whore would sleep in two men's beds.' No, not 'sleep in' – 'go to' – those were her words. 'Only a whore would go to two men's beds.' She was in the garden, pruning roses. She had a pair of those secateur things in her hand. She didn't look at me, she stared at the roses and told me it would kill my father. I know she didn't mean it. Basically she's kind. But those are the words that stick. Anyway, then we went indoors and everybody cried and then . . . then we had a cup of tea.

There is a pause

FRAN. You haven't drunk your Lucozade.

STELLA. I didn't realize there were two men involved.

CAROLINE. Oh, yes.

STELLA. Have you told them?

CAROLINE. They both think the other is the father. It seemed simplest.

FRAN. I think you're right. Tell a man he's going to be a father and you burst a door marked hero.

STELLA. You're really sold on the metaphysics, aren't you?

FRAN. I've seen it in action.

STELLA. Well I don't know if it's such a good idea. Why should they get off?

CAROLINE. I don't want to see them.

STELLA. Bugger seeing them. What about money? What about a bit of moral support? Why should you have to cope by yourself?

CAROLINE. I'm not. I'm here.

STELLA. What kind of set-up is this? What is it when we're all clucking about like hens with our Lucozade and knitting and sticking our bloody bums in the air? Can you see a man doing that?

FRAN. Are you saying you think men ought to have more to do with their families? Because if that's what you mean you don't know them. Have you seen men with babies? It's laughable. I think it's a crime to leave a child with a man.

CAROLINE. Come off it, Fran.

STELLA. That's just crap.

FRAN. Is it? I'm sorry. I wouldn't go out to work and leave Heidi with Graeme. I wouldn't trust him. They push prams – have you watched them? You'd think they were walking on nails. His idea of playing with Heidi is to sit her in the playroom and watch her through the newspaper. That's why it's a woman's job. Because men can't do it.

STELLA. You mean WON'T do it.

FRAN. No. It's just not in them with all the will in the world. A child goes to its mother. You don't have to tell it.

STELLA. What do you expect? Your husband isn't wearing milk bottles, is he?

FRAN. No, he isn't. And I don't think that's an accident.

CAROLINE. I don't think you believe it. But if you say it often enough you can live with it.

FRAN. Because it's always been that way doesn't make it wrong. Just unfashionable.

STELLA. Just bollocks.

FRAN. No! I'm sick and tired of women telling me I'm wasting my life. Envy thy husband's penis. No. I'm sorry. You have to cut it off now, don't you? There is something that neither of you can understand. You talk about love, Stella – you've got no idea – because it's not love, you're right. It's not love with men and women, it's necessity. Love is between the mother and her child. That's why you're so poisoned. That's why men work so hard at making everything else look more fulfilling, because it's not their magic, it's my magic. And what's so sad, is that women are abandoning what they have because they think men are hiding some miracle in their hands. But there's no miracle . . . This is it, you see there's no miracle.

STELLA. I've got to hand it to you – you can't be all bad if you hate men that much.

FRAN. I didn't mean to say I hated men. Is that what it sounds like?

STELLA. Maybe it's just your husband. I think you had him up against the wall there – along with me and the liberated lesbians.

CAROLINE. You didn't say lesbians.

FRAN. No, I didn't. Did you say there was drink going? I've finished this.

STELLA. That's more like it, have a proper drink, that stuff will rot your teeth.

FRAN. I was just thinking – I was beginning to sound like a grudging hausfrau.

STELLA. You were – and so what? A little grudge never hurt anyone. Which is more than can be said for hausfrauing.

FRAN. You get into this circle. Babies and mothers and your mothers' and baby-sitting circles and, you know, magazines and double-drainers, like – that's a good example – do you know I was the only wife in the Close without a double-drainer and it got to me so much I couldn't get to sleep thinking about it. But what I'm saying is, in that circle, well, no one talks about anything really, I mean you'd think to listen to us that nobody got depressed or frustrated. I mean, I'm not even talking about the bloody world, about a single bloody current event, I'm talking about our own lives. Not a murmur. It's like it's some dreadful treachery to admit you're fed up. And then someone turns up to a coffee morning and in the middle of what's new in Mothercare says, 'By the way, we're getting divorced' and bursts into tears. (*Pause.*) That actually happened.

There is a pause.

CAROLINE. In Leeds nobody talks about anything BUT themselves or orgasms, or Women Against Rape or, I don't know, Nicaragua, and I don't see that doing much to alleviate the general misery.

STELLA. This is awful! God! I think I preferred the exercises. In a minute we'll all be lying on the ground wailing, which reminds me – the whale record – wow!

FRAN. Oh, do you like it?

STELLA. No, it's absolutely horrendous, but it's got rid of the mice!

CAROLINE. Stella rigged up the stereo in the kitchen.

STELLA. They ran up the street waving white flags.

FRAN. It's not that bad.

STELLA *imitates whale music.*

CAROLINE. I'd like to go out.

STELLA. It's raining.

CAROLINE. I don't mean the beach. I mean US go out.

FRAN. Where?

CAROLINE. I don't know. What about a disco?

STELLA. You want to go dancing?

CAROLINE. I do. Come on, Fran, we could take the exercises.

FRAN. I haven't been to a disco since, oh, I don't know. Can't remember.

CAROLINE. Right. Where do we go? You're the expert Stella.

STELLA. At this time of year? There might be a late funeral.

CAROLINE. Boring. So where were you on Saturday?

STELLA. The Sixty-nine.

CAROLINE. What's wrong with that?

STELLA. We can't go there. It's really nasty. Besides, it's not a disco, it's a cattle market.

CAROLINE. We could ignore all that and just have a dance.

STELLA. Around our bags?

FRAN. I can't. I ought to get back.

CAROLINE. I thought Heidi was sleeping at your mum's.

FRAN. No, but Graeme will be there. The football club always go for a drink after training.

CAROLINE. Great. You can dance with Graeme.

STELLA. And we'll have the football club.

CAROLINE. That's settled then.

FRAN. What if he's dancing with someone else?

STELLA. I would think it's pretty unlikely he WON'T be dancing with someone else.

FRAN. I know.

STELLA. Well, look love, I've never met your husband but it strikes me it wouldn't hurt to remind him that you can wiggle your udders with the best of them.

FRAN. You're right. You've never met him.

CAROLINE. Well, OK, let's go somewhere else.

FRAN. No. We'll go there. Sod him. Can I borrow something to wear?

STELLA. A holster?

FRAN. Hmm. It's dangerous, isn't it? Talk – I mean, women talking. If we ever had a union the world would stop dead.

STELLA. Well, it certainly puts a whole new light on withdrawing labour.

CAROLINE *groans*.

FRAN. I'm enjoying this. I'm really enjoying myself.

Scene Four

STELLA's *Flat. Morning.*

CAROLINE *is alone, going through a bundle of letters and a parcel. She is wearing a dressing gown.*

STELLA *enters, dressed as the previous scene but rather the worse for wear.*

STELLA. Oh, you're up.

CAROLINE. D'you want coffee?

STELLA. No.

CAROLINE *makes a point of going through the letters.*

OK, I know what you're thinking.

CAROLINE. Do you?

STELLA. Look, have you got any money?

CAROLINE. Yes.

STELLA. I need a cigarette and a shower.

CAROLINE. I'll get my purse.

STELLA. We can take it off the rent.

CAROLINE. I've paid the rent.

CAROLINE *exits for her purse and returns immediately.*

STELLA. Next week's then. How did you get home?

CAROLINE. I walked.

STELLA. What happened to Fran?

CAROLINE. They left. I didn't hear what was said. But the headlines were plain enough.

STELLA. Not good.

CAROLINE. No.

STELLA. Well, it's her own fault. What did she expect?

CAROLINE. It's our fault. We should have gone somewhere else. We shouldn't have gone at all.

STELLA. That why you didn't stay?

CAROLINE. I was by myself.

STELLA. Not when I started dancing.

CAROLINE. Oh no, not then – then I was being massaged by a psychopath.

STELLA. I though that's what you went for.

CAROLINE. I thought I was going out with you and Fran. Anyway, let's forget it. (*Pointed.*) How was YOUR night?

STELLA. Oh, piss off.

CAROLINE (*looking in her purse*). Will five pounds do, Stella? (*Pause. Then, thawing.*) You don't have to feel guilty.

STELLA. No, I don't have to. Do you feel OK?

CAROLINE (*smiling*). Awful.

STELLA (*smiling*). Me too.

CAROLINE (*pointing to the parcel*). From my mother. Red Cross parcel. I've just eaten a pound bar of fruit and nut. I saved you a piece.

STELLA (*accepting it and sitting down*). I don't know why I did it. Reflex. Didn't even fancy him. D'you know what he does? You won't believe this – he works for Social Security.

CAROLINE (*laughing*). Was he on duty?

STELLA. He was barely conscious. Stupid, isn't it? But it was raining and he had a car, and I didn't fancy walking home much. And then, of course, this morning it's still raining and I had even further to walk. (*She sighs.*) I must have a shower. (*Looking at the pile of letters and the parcels.*) Someone's popular.

CAROLINE. Stella. Graeme . . .

STELLA. What about him?

CAROLINE. You know him, don't you?

STELLA. Yes, probably. It's a small place. I know everyone.

CAROLINE. That's not what I meant. I don't think it was reflex that made you go off so suddenly.

STELLA (*sighing*). I know him.

CAROLINE. I knew it – what a joke.

STELLA. I didn't find it funny.

CAROLINE. You've slept with him. Right?

STELLA. Yes, I've slept with him.

CAROLINE. So've I. So have I.

STELLA (*astounded*). When?

CAROLINE. That's pretty funny, isn't it? He was the first. When we were at school.

STELLA. Oh. Does Fran know?

CAROLINE. No.

STELLA. Well, you live and learn.

CAROLINE. You certainly do.

STELLA. Has he changed much?

CAROLINE. Look it was a farce – the whole thing. It was just . . . I don't know what it was.

STELLA. I just can't see it. You.

CAROLINE. It has happened. (*Referring to her stomach*.) Very much so.

STELLA. Means nothing to me. When I see a pregnant woman, sex seems a million miles away.

CAROLINE. I'm afraid there were no angels.

STELLA. Can I feel?

STELLA *gets up and puts her hand on* CAROLINE's *stomach.*

STELLA. Amazing. It's always amazing.(*She sits back in he own chair*.) When you think it's completely formed. (*Pause*.) Would you mind if I knit something for it? It could wear something for a week.

CAROLINE. I'd like that. Thanks.

STELLA. How do you feel? About the adoption?

CAROLINE. I don't feel anything. I don't feel a child inside me.

STELLA. No. (*Pause*.) I could take photographs. As you get bigger. You'll be bloody beautiful.

CAROLINE. You're different this morning.

STELLA. I'm wet.

CAROLINE. Yes, but nicely. Does it happen often? Like last night?

STELLA. I suppose so. (*She shrvgs*.) I pinched his socks. Look. Mine were sodden. Tell you a lot about him, don't they? (*Visualizing*.) Men's bedrooms. Someone should do a study of them. (*Laughs*.) Me, I suppose. (*Shrugs, perhaps only half serious*.) I'm quite terrifying you know. (*She gets out some eye make-up remover from her handbag, dabbing off her mascara*.) With men. It feels like lust, but it's loathing really. Quite cold.

CAROLINE. Why? What's the point?

STELLA. Because of the way they look at you. The way they sniff you about.

CAROLINE. Wow!

STELLA. They do exist, Caroline. It's not my imagination. There's something I do, have done before. If I land a really three-star macho man . . . you know, the whole image . . . never stops telling you what a great time he's going to give you. He's going to make you really cry out, you know, like drowning . . . and all this whispered or licked at you across his MG or yelled in your face on his Yamaha, a great gob full of, whatever, garlic or grease or fag smoke, and fucking Brut – always Brut or Prick or Stud or Come or whatever they can dream up to call that very unpleasant smell that hides that other very unpleasant smell which is the smell of them getting turned on to you – and they want to get it up through your tights in some car park so that they don't have to cope with you afterwards, you know, because they have no feeling, nothing . . . dead eyes, dead bodies. So what I do is this. I give him . . . Mr Godsgift . . . I give him the real Penthouse cliché, right. Lick my lips, touch myself, scream a bit, play scared when he steps out of his knickers, I mean – awestruck – and I get so very excited in the first number. I always try and break things in his bedroom – preferably something expensive – because I'm so wild for it – and I give out all the words. And I can get it done in a few minutes and, well, there he is, slack-jawed, grinning, notching me up on the barrel, three-quarters asleep. So I leave him for a few minutes, then kiss him like it was love – and then I get going on him for round two. Well! Bit of a laugh, bit nervous now, Mr Godsgift, bit sheepish . . . but it's going to be a great story for his pals in the morning: 'You should have seen this slag – she couldn't get enough of it!' And he makes ride number two, sometimes makes ride number three, perhaps, but he's losing and he's worried and he's sore and he's fucking terrified, and the NEXT time I make certain he falls apart. I'm surprised. I'm very disappointed he can't make it. I even get angry with him. And then I get dressed and come home and stand under the shower and scrub him off me and if I could stand boiling water I'd boil myself clean to the marrow.

CAROLINE. That's horrible.

STELLA. There are men doing it every day. It's my little bit to restore the balance. I mean, fuck it. If you're holding someone's hand you've only got one free to grab with.

CAROLINE. What's the point?

STELLA. That's why you're so nice, Caroline. Because you're still interested in finding out. I envy you. I really do.

CAROLINE. Is that why you do this? To harden me up?

STELLA (angrily). That's exactly what I mean; the social worker mentality. Poor Stella – there must be a jolly good reason why she's like this.

CAROLINE. I'm sure there is.

STELLA. You must tell me sometime.

CAROLINE. It doesn't matter.

STELLA. No, really, I'm fascinated.

CAROLINE. You and Kate'll get on like a house on fire.

STELLA. Is this your teacher friend?

CAROLINE. Yes.

STELLA. We'll have to compare notes.

CAROLINE. I didn't mean that. Kate has no notes to compare. She's gay.

STELLA. What? And you think I must be?

CAROLINE. No, but you both . . . you both forgive women but you won't forgive men.

STELLA. Oh, come off it. I mean, what does that mean? I forgive women but not men. I can't abide most women.

CAROLINE. It wasn't a criticism.

STELLA. Well, I'm not gay. That's one thing that can be said for Fran – she can't stomach all that Women's Movement crap. At least men laugh.

CAROLINE. So do women.

STELLA. Ach.

CAROLINE. It's true, I've laughed more with you than with any man.

Pause.

STELLA. What do you do? When you're down on the beach?

CAROLINE. Nothing. Walk.

STELLA. Are you going today?

CAROLINE. Probably. (*With an air of self-mockery.*) D'you know why I came back here? Why I go on the beach? I thought it was going to be romantic. To walk by the sea at night, tasting the salt on my tongue. But I don't like the cold! I spend a lot of time in cafés warming up and anyway, after all, being pregnant isn't very spectacular, is it? Just lots of days to fill up.

STELLA. Can I come with you today?

CAROLINE (*surprised*). Yes. (*Delighted.*) Yes!

STELLA. Right, I'll fetch the thermal underwear.

CAROLINE. Actually, what's strange is it never feels so cold if there's two of you.

Scene Five

STELLA *and* CAROLINE *are outside. They're on bicycles, enjoying themselves.*

STELLA. What about Max?

CAROLINE. What?

STELLA. If it's a boy: Max?

CAROLINE. Max what? Maxwell or Maximillian?

STELLA. Max! Max-Max.

CAROLINE. I like that. Does it get into the top three? Is it a one to watch?

STELLA. Well, what's there at the moment? Nathan . . . ugh!

CAROLINE. Joshua . . .

STELLA. Well it's better than those two!

CAROLINE. Max. Yes it's good. Okay – Max if it's a boy.

STELLA. And Stella if it's a girl. Definitely!

CAROLINE. Oh, definitely. And we'll come to visit once a year, and have wonderful times and eat sweets.

STELLA. Right, it's a deal. Wonderful times with Auntie Stella . . . only promise – no bike rides.

CAROLINE. Yes. Bike rides! He/she will be a cycling fanatic. He/she will have black hair possibly, or brownish hair or blond hair . . . black hair: all me; brownish: me/Robin; blond: me/John. And will laugh lots, little or not at all . . . that's Robin lots, John little and me not at all. I'll tell you . . . it's crucial what happens now, you know. By the time you're born, it's all decided. This child will love the sea, bicycles and the sound of women talking.

STELLA. And whale music!

CAROLINE. It would be nice, wouldn't it?

STELLA. Yes, it would be nice.

CAROLINE. Come on, slowcoach.

STELLA. Hang on. Caroline, I'm getting off.

CAROLINE. No, don't stop!

STELLA. I'm shattered!

CAROLINE. Oh come on, pathetic. I don't want to get off. It's extraordinary. (*Cycling off.*) I don't want to get off ever . . . ever . . . ever . . . ever . . . ever.

Scene Six

STELLA's *Flat.*

STELLA *is alone.* FRAN *enters.*

FRAN. Hello. I came as soon as I could dump Heidi. Is she upstairs?

STELLA. Yeah. I think she's asleep.

FRAN. What did the doctor say?

STELLA. Nothing much. He said she'd be okay. She's not going to lose it.

FRAN. Thank God for that.

STELLA. He didn't really want to know. He was very polite, but he kept saying 'miss', 'miss', and it stuck in his throat.

FRAN. Perhaps he thought she'd wanted to, that she'd . . . uh . . . done something to herself.

STELLA. Very likely. Anyway, at least she's stopped panicking.

FRAN. So, and what was it, she just started bleeding?

STELLA. Yes, apparently. But she's been down for days. I thought she was just pissed off, I mean, do you know that neither of those blokes write to her . . . she's had a couple of postcards! It's pathetic. It makes me bloody weep when I see the post.

FRAN. What, not even her mum?

STELLA. Oh, she writes, and the schoolteacher friend, but, well I don't know . . .

FRAN. That's what she wanted though, isn't it?

STELLA. She doesn't know what she wants. Nobody sane spends nine months lugging a spare tyre around and then gives it away to some self-righteous couple.

FRAN. They don't have to be self-righteous.

STELLA. Of course they do. You've got to be white, comfortable and self-righteous.

FRAN. So what do you suggest? And actually, Stella, you're wrong, actually, completely. So tell me, what do you suggest she does?

STELLA. OK – she's a really nice girl. She's lovely. It'll be a lovely kid. She ought to be able to keep it.

FRAN. She doesn't want to.

STELLA. How does she know?

FRAN. How do you?

STELLA. I don't, but Christ, Fran, she's got practically no choice, and that can't be right. It makes me go bloody reactionary, you know. I keep getting the urge to drag one of those men up the aisle with her. I know it's ridiculous.

FRAN. Well that's no use. If she's not up to keeping the child herself, marriage won't help. I mean, that's a really daft argument, it's like you get these couples who say they'll only get married if they have children, but that's rubbish because there's got to be something really tough there when a child comes along . . . because it really can destroy things . . . between people . . . that's what happened to me, Stella, isn't it? Because, I mean, you can ignore things – but a child – if there are cracks anywhere it'll force them apart. You can be sure of that . . . I think I'll go up, anyway, see if she's okay, poor old sod.

   CAROLINE *appears in the doorway.*

CAROLINE. Speak for yourself.

STELLA. You're supposed to be in bed.

CAROLINE. Yes, nurse.

STELLA. I'm serious.

CAROLINE. In a minute. Hello Fran.

FRAN. Hello love.

CAROLINE. I'm still here. (*Sitting down.*) Despite Mr Maloney and the instruments of torture. What's the matter with you two?

STELLA. There's nothing wrong with me

FRAN. There's nothing wrong with me either. Except I've left Graeme.

CAROLINE. You're joking.

FRAN. Do I mean left him? Yes, I think I do.

STELLA. Bloody hell!

CAROLINE. When?

FRAN. Sunday. Sunday was not a good day, apparently several

football teams had lost the previous afternoon. I was supposed to realize this . . . because that's why no appearance until sometime in the middle of the night. And then of course, Heidi and I are supposed to leave him alone all the next day and not talk, or you know, live much. And certainly expect no help or whatever else a man can contribute to family life. So I had a major wobbly. Oh, there was a classic – you'll love this, Stella – 'Why do you think Mothercare is called Mothercare?' . . . this is a question from my husband . . . 'Think about it' he said . . .

STELLA. I bet you did.

FRAN. I did not. I went to my own mother and she's caring for me!

STELLA. Terrific!

FRAN. Well, it's not permanent, I don't suppose. I'm waiting for signs of repentance. I know how many clean pairs of socks he's got left.

STELLA. How do you feel?

FRAN. All right, but my mum keeps crying. Anyway we'll sort it all out, I expect. Hey! I bought you some avocados! Any use?

CAROLINE. What a memory!

FRAN (*to* STELLA). The way to Caroline's heart . . . the avocado pear.

CAROLINE. This is absolutely true. Can I eat one now?

STELLA. I'll get a spoon.

CAROLINE. Get three spoons!

    STELLA *exits*.

FRAN. You okay?

CAROLINE. Yes, I'm okay. He said the baby's still going strong.

FRAN. Stella said. That's good.

    STELLA *enters with the spoons*.

STELLA. Three spoons.

CAROLINE. Wonderful. These must have cost you a fortune.

FRAN. They did!

STELLA. Well bloody hell, we're celebrating!

FRAN. Right. I've shown Graeme the yellow card.

CAROLINE. And I'm still pregnant.

    The three girls are close and relaxed. They continue to eat happily as the lights fade.

ACT TWO

Scene One

The Seafront. Spring.

KATE *and* D *are waiting for* CAROLINE *by a children's amusement park or playground, suggested by a climbing frame or slide, or both.* D *is seventeen and wearing a leather jacket decorated with political and feminist badges. She has just been spraying a poster with spray paint and has some over her hands.*

KATE. Now you've got paint all over your hands.

D. It'll come off.

KATE. Christ, it's freezing. Where is she?

D. I'm not cold. It's great, Kate, really exciting. It's so quiet but it's really noisy as well, isn't it?

KATE. What was so offensive about that poster?

D. It was sexist.

KATE. How? It was for gardening tools.

D. For whose garden?

KATE. How should I know? Just gardens.

D. Well, if it's for anyone's garden, how come you never see a woman in a gardening advert? Like on telly – who shows you how to cultivate the world's fattest potatoes? The man. And then who shows you how to peel them? His missus. That's sexist. My dad doesn't even know where our garden is. He never goes out the back door unless he's sneaking off to the pub.

KATE. I see. And that will be perfectly clear to passers-by, will it?

D. Yes. . . . Probably.

KATE. Mummy, mummy why has that got 'This is a sexist poster' written on it? Because D's dad never goes in their garden.

D (*sulkily*). You taught me to spray posters.

KATE. Did I?

D. You're sorry you brought me already.

KATE. I didn't bring you – I couldn't get you out of the van.

D. You said I could come.

KATE. Yes, I did, and here we are, getting cold. Happy?

D. You're like you are in class.

KATE. Really?

D. Sarcastic. Unfriendly. It's because you don't want the others to know.

KATE. Fine. There's nothing for them to know.

D. I've told you how I feel. Are we going to sleep together?

There is a pause. KATE *is flustered.*

I know you want to.

KATE. You don't know anything.

D. No Miss, sorry Miss. Can I play on the swings, please Miss?

KATE. Go to hell.

D *sulks.*

Oh, for God's sake. Look, I'm sorry. I can't stand long journeys. I get ratty.

D. It's not that. It's Caroline.

KATE. What about her?

D. You used to teach her too, didn't you?

KATE. So?

D. Whose baby is it?

KATE. Well, it certainly isn't mine.

D. No. (*Triumphantly.*) She's not gay then, is she? (*She slides down the slide or equivalent gymnastic apparatus.*) Wheee!

KATE. You're very naive, D. Apart from anything else, being lesbian doesn't stop you having children.

D. Must make it hard work though. But she's not, anyway, is she?

KATE. Ask her yourself.

D. Why did she come down here?

KATE. She was born here. It's her home.

D. She should have got rid of it. I would have. The guy just gets on with his life. Why can't she get on with hers? It's typical.

KATE. Well, it's also inescapable. You can change most things, you can't redistribute wombs.

D. The day will come.

KATE. I hope not.

D. She could've still got rid of it.

KATE. She didn't want to.

D. What, just so as to give it away? Stupid.

KATE. Don't act thirty. You're a very bright seventeen, you're a dim thirty.

D. My English teacher told me that when someone pulls rank on you in an argument it normally means they're losing.

KATE. I never said any such thing.

D. Anyway I'd hate to be thirty. I don't care if I'm dead before then.

KATE. You will.

D. I'm not talking about you. I'm talking about me. About my generation. Things are moving really quickly, really fast. Seven-year-olds are on the pill or they're winning Nobel prizes. Everything's speeded up. It's to do with technology. There's no room for age now. So you've got to get everything done, cram it in quick. I think soon everyone will die before they're twenty-one.

KATE. Fine – we'll have to warn Caroline she's only got a day left. Who's been telling you all this nonsense?

D. Actually, it's not nonsense. Lots of people know about it. It's got to happen because there's nothing left, there's not enough energy to go round anymore. (*She climbs to the top of the slide or frame.*) I can see Caroline. (*She waves.*) She's seen us.

KATE. Where? (*Scanning the landscape.*) She thinks she's Sylvia Plath, you know. That's why she wanders around here. She's living it all out.

D. Is she?

KATE. Look at her. She's inside some poem – you know? – and it's very sad.

D. She doesn't look sad to me. She looks bloody enormous.

KATE. Where are the things for her? Have you got the bag?

D. You left them in the van.

KATE. Oh, right.

CAROLINE *enters, heavily pregnant.*

Where've you been?

CAROLINE. Walking. Hello.

CAROLINE *and* KATE *kiss.*

Hello D.

D. I hid in the luggage.

D *looks to* KATE *for support, but does not get any.*

CAROLINE. Fine. I hope you don't mind the floor.

D. No. I can sleep anywhere.

CAROLINE (*smiling*). How was the journey?

D ⎱ All right.

KATE ⎰ A pain.

CAROLINE. You must be tired.

KATE. I'm frozen.

CAROLINE. You met Stella?

KATE. We said hello. How are you?

CAROLINE. Fine. Did I tell you? I've been seeing a lot of Fran?

KATE. Yes, you did.

CAROLINE. She's fine.

KATE. Are we going back?

CAROLINE. Sorry, you're cold.

KATE. Is there any food?

CAROLINE. Oh, I don't know. Probably.

KATE. We haven't eaten. I wanted to get here in daylight.

CAROLINE. Sorry, I'm not thinking. I should have made something.

KATE. We'll get a take-away.

CAROLINE (*to* D). How's D?

D (*simply*). Great. It's a great place.

CAROLINE (*gently*). What've you got on your hands?

KATE (*laughing*). She's been defacing posters.

CAROLINE. Ah.

KATE. You can tell her about it on the way. Along with your catastrophe theory.

D. No. You two go on. I'll catch up.

KATE. What are you doing?

D. Just going for a short walk. You two have a nice chat.

   D *exits*.

CAROLINE. What does that mean?

KATE. Search me. Oh, come on, I'm not going to run after her.

CAROLINE. Poor Kate.

KATE (*looking after* D). Poor Kate. (*Looking at* CAROLINE.) So . . . you look OK.

CAROLINE. I am OK.

KATE. I've missed you.

CAROLINE. Despite D? I've missed you too.

KATE. Oh yeah! I know what you miss . . . someone to wash your knickers . . . food.

CAROLINE. Don't start.

KATE. Did you get the cheque?

CAROLINE. I will pay you back,

KATE. I don't want it back.

CAROLINE. Then don't play the martyr.

KATE. Speak for yourself.

CAROLINE. Have you seen him?

KATE. Which him?

CAROLINE. John.

KATE. Yes

CAROLINE. And?

KATE. I've seen him. Look, neither of them want to know, Caroline.

CAROLINE. How do you know? (*She moves away.*)

KATE. You shouldn't have gone through with this. It's absurd.

CAROLINE. It moves. It kicks. I can feel it.

KATE. Yes. And you'll feel it afterwards too. It's conscience. And you can't have that adopted.

CAROLINE. But I could have killed it. Is that what you're saying?

KATE. No, that's not what I'm saying. (*Pause. Then angrily.*) Does it make it easier, Caroline? To use those words? To justify yourself? In which case, OK. Yes. You could have killed it. Or you could keep it. But neither of those is romantic, is it?

CAROLINE *is hurt. Stung. She moves away towards the water.* KATE *exhales sharply, frustratedly.*

(*Shouting after* CAROLINE.) Is this what you're going to live off . . . all the pain you've stored up over the Winter?

CAROLINE. I'm happy, Kate. I could stay here for ever.

KATE. Well, I'm cold, and I've got the van, and I'm driving back. Coming?

CAROLINE *turns. A beat. She smiles.* KATE *smiles.* CAROLINE *returns. They embrace.*

Scene Two

STELLA's *Flat*.

FRAN *and D are sitting together.* STELLA *has wet hair and is drying it with a hair dryer.* KATE *is apart from them, waiting for* CAROLINE *who is supposedly outside, making a telephone call to her mother.*

FRAN. Are you keen on motorbikes, then?

D. No, I just like leather jackets.

FRAN. Oh, I see . . . I love the badges. Is that the fashion now?

D. I don't know anything about fashion. Fashion stinks.

STELLA. Why?

D. Well, for a start . . . shaving your armpits or your legs or something . . . or painting your bloody face up. It's all rubbish.

STELLA. You won't mind if I dry my hair?

FRAN. Long phone call.

STELLA *turns off the dryer.*

STELLA. What?

FRAN. No. I was just saying to Kate – Caroline's been gone a long time.

STELLA. Oh?

KATE. I don't know why her mother couldn't have come down. You'd think she might have made the effort.

FRAN. Well, it's quite a way, isn't it?

KATE. So's Leeds. They don't want to see her, do they? Then Caroline can turn up in April with a flat stomach and they can all pretend it never happened.

STELLA. They might be in for a shock. I don't think she'll give it away.

FRAN. Nor do I.

KATE. Nothing to be smug about, really, is it? Who's going to look after this baby?

FRAN. Lots of girls manage.

KATE. Caroline can't manage herself.

STELLA. How do you know?

KATE. I live with her. I make her bed.

STELLA (*acidly*). She makes her own bed here. Perhaps she thinks you like doing it.

KATE. You see, I don't think knitting matinée jackets is caring, particularly. I think that's easy. It's like buying a child a pet.

STELLA. No one's encouraging her to do anything.

KATE. No? Oh, Christ, D, do you have to pick your nails!

D. Great party. Who died?

FRAN. You're right, D. It's Caroline's birthday. It won't be much of a party at this rate.

STELLA. It won't be much of a party anyway. Without any men.

KATE. Well, that's a start.

FRAN (*cheerfully*). We'll have to play some games.

STELLA. We'll have to get some drinks in.

D. Why?

STELLA. Why what?

D. Why do we have to get drunk, or play games?

KATE. What do you suggest then?

There is a pause.

D. I'll go to the off-licence.

KATE. No . . . I'll go. I've got the van.

D makes as if to go with her but KATE turns at the door pointedly.

See you in a minute.

Scene Three

The Promenade. Night. The sound of gulls is heard.

CAROLINE is alone. KATE enters, looking for her.

KATE. Where've you been?

CAROLINE. Ringing my mother.

KATE. For an hour? Oh Caroline.

CAROLINE. I don't feel much like parties.

KATE. No. Me neither. Let's go somewhere . . . in the van.

CAROLINE. Where's there to go?

KATE. Well, we don't have to GO anywhere. We could just get in the back and have our own party. I bought this in case. (*She produces a bottle of Martini.*)

CAROLINE. No thanks, Kate.

KATE. Why not?

CAROLINE. I don't want to.

KATE. Why not?

CAROLINE. And I rang John.

KATE. And what did John have to say?

CAROLINE. He played Happy Birthday on his mouth-organ.

KATE. Was that instead of a card?

CAROLINE. Oh, probably, Kate. But he's sweet.

There is a pause.

D'you know what? I keep finding myself talking to my stomach. Extraordinary. But it's really nice because it's not like . . . it's not the same as talking to yourself, is it?

KATE. No, it's not the same. I want to kiss you for your birthday.

CAROLINE *kisses* KATE *quickly on the cheek.*

CAROLINE. Thanks . . . I think we'd better go back now.

Black-out.

Scene Four

STELLA's *Flat.*

CAROLINE *is standing in the middle of the room. A game of charades is in progress and* CAROLINE *is holding up four fingers.* STELLA, KATE, FRAN *and* D *are sitting around.*

STELLA. Four words.

KATE. What is it? Book, film or play?

CAROLINE *shakes her head.*

It's got to be.

FRAN (*who has chosen the charade*). Or a well-known phrase or saying.

KATE. Typical. OK, four words.

CAROLINE *shows her third finger, and makes the 'small word' sign.*

STELLA. Third word, small. An? At?

KATE. In? With?

D. To?

STELLA. On? Of? Off?

CAROLINE *nods furiously*

KATE. Of?

CAROLINE *shakes her head.*

On!

CAROLINE *points at D.*

STELLA. To! Something something to something.

CAROLINE *nods, raises her fourth finger and points to herself.*

KATE. Fourth word. You?

CAROLINE *encourages her.*

You? Run?

CAROLINE *indicates 'no'.*

STELLA. Girl?

D. Woman? Baby? Mother?

There are 'looks' all round.

CAROLINE. No.

STELLA. Not you. Uh . . . body? No. Uh . . . Caroline?

CAROLINE *nods, encouraging, and does the 'whole phrase' sign.*

KATE. Whole something. Something – Caroline? Not Caroline?

CAROLINE *shakes her head. Makes 'second word' sign.*

KATE. OK. Second word.

CAROLINE *shows 'two syllables' sign.*

Two syllables . . . first syllable . . .

CAROLINE *points to her stomach.*

D. Tum? Stomach? Belly? Stupid?

CAROLINE *nods, lies down on the floor, enacts a thirty second labour, pulls out an imaginary child, slaps its bottom. 'It' cries.*

KATE. Baby

CAROLINE *nods. There is silence.*

FRAN. Oh come on, it's obvious.

KATE. Something . . . not baby . . . to . . . you, Caroline, something.

FRAN. No! Do the first word, Caroline.

CAROLINE *is upset but tries hard to look happy.*

STELLA. Pleased. Smiling. Joy. Happy!

CAROLINE *nods.*

STELLA. Happy! Happy nearly baby to? Where does baby come into it?

KATE. Birthday! Happy Birthday to . . .

CAROLINE. Me.

A pause. Everyone is strained.

FRAN. Right! Happy birthday to you. . . . Come on (*singing.*) 'Happy Birthday' . . .

The others join in the singing.

CAROLINE. Thanks. (*At a loss.*) Uh, whose turn is it?

Scene Five

STELLA's *Flat. Night.*

KATE *and D are sleeping together in a narrow single bed.* CAROLINE *enters but seeing the situation starts to leave.*

CAROLINE. Oh.

KATE (*half voice*). I'm awake Caroline. Caroline. I'm not asleep.

CAROLINE. We'll wake D up.

KATE. No, we won't. Put the light on.

CAROLINE switches a lamp on.

What are you doing?

CAROLINE. I couldn't sleep?

KATE. What's the matter?

CAROLINE. Can't get comfortable.

KATE. The baby?

CAROLINE. It's taking me over. There's no room in the bed for me. Now it's got hiccups. I'm not joking.

KATE. What time is it?

CAROLINE. I don't know. Late. Early. (*She looks at* D.) She's remarkable.

KATE. What? Not waking up? She doesn't sleep at night, she dies.

CAROLINE. You're much closer, aren't you?

KATE. It's a very small bed.

CAROLINE. You know what I mean. Since I left.

KATE. What do you want me to say? Look . . . I started off teaching her English, now I'm teaching her this.

CAROLINE. God, you're patronizing.

KATE. I don't think so. I'm trying to get with it. Otherwise I get hurt when lessons finish . . . you know?

CAROLINE. It's your own doing, Kate.

KATE. I'm sure it is. Well you know us gays . . . We like getting hurt. Oh, and corrupting minors, let's not forget that . . .

CAROLINE (*cheerfully*). Oh, shut up.

KATE. Why did Stella put out that sleeping bag for us? Was she embarrassed?

CAROLINE. I don't know.

KATE. Do you talk to her?

CAROLINE. Of course I talk to her. What do you mean?

KATE. No, I mean TALK to her. Confide in her.

CAROLINE. I suppose so. A little. Yes.

KATE. Because you won't with me, will you?

There is a pause.

CAROLINE. I haven't seen you, Kate. I'm getting used to you being around again. And anyway there's D.

KATE. So . . . (*She looks at* D.) What's happening then? What are you going to do?

CAROLINE. I don't know. Have the baby.

KATE. And then?

CAROLINE. And then? I don't know.

KATE. Are you coming back to my house? Well what?

CAROLINE *does not respond.*

You can't stay here.

CAROLINE. Probably not, no.

KATE. What have you been doing? What do you do with your days?

CAROLINE. Walk. Think.

KATE. Have you thought about me much?

CAROLINE. Oh, Kate. I have written to you.

KATE. I've thought about you, Caroline. All the time. I've been sleeping in your bed at home . . . We could bring the child up together. I've thought about that, too. I've got enough money. We could manage.

CAROLINE. No.

KATE. I'd love her – I'd love both of you. I could look after you both, please.

CAROLINE. I don't want to.

KATE. The house is empty without you. Haven't you missed it? Haven't you missed Leeds at all?

CAROLINE. Look, this is impossible. Yes, I've missed Leeds. For God's sake, Kate, you're in bed with D, you've got someone. I haven't missed you, Kate, if that's what you're asking me . . . I mean, of course I have, but not in the way you want. I just don't have those feelings for you. I never have had.

KATE. Never?

CAROLINE. I'm pregnant – look! – a man did this, and I miss HIM desperately.

KATE. Oh, so you *do* know who the father is?

CAROLINE. I know who I'd like it to be. There was never anything between me and Robin. I was flattered. That he would be prepared to leave someone for me. I wasn't attracted to him. I was attracted to that.

KATE. But you had sex with him.

CAROLINE. The world doesn't stop.

KATE. I wouldn't know.

CAROLINE. No.

KATE (*bitterly*). Still, we'll be able to tell by the colour of its hair, won't we?

CAROLINE. That's the point. That's why I can't talk to you. Because you don't want to hear really, do you?

KATE. Not about you with men. No, not particularly. Why is that the point?

CAROLINE. Because we can never discuss the fact that I wanted a man, Kate. Can we? And I did. Not furtively. Not cluttered. Not ashamed of it. Not . . . it was like an ache . . . it was an ache. Sounds like dogs, doesn't it? But it was so good with John and me. Grabbing each other all the time. Just grabbing. And then we started to trade that in for a whole lot of crap like the future and what it meant and what we, and I . . . because you see all these people, these couples, and they can tell you about their relationship and what it means and you can see this energy totally strangled. They sit facing each other over tables when they really want to be grabbing, under the tables, grabbing. I'm not talking about orgies, I'm talking about honesty between people. And I'm angry because we had that and then we swapped it. So you see, Kate, it's hopeless, isn't it? I mean, look at us. D's dreaming and you're dreaming and I'm dreaming and it's hopeless. I end up with Happy Birthday played down the telephone. (*Pause.*) I'm sorry, but sometime you had to hear that.

There is a long pause.

KATE. Yes, I did need to hear that Caroline. But why now? Why not a month ago? A year ago? (*She pauses.*) You've always reeled me in a bit, haven't you? A look, a word, just enough to keep me there, hanging, foolish. Well, thanks. Thanks a lot.

CAROLINE. I'm going to bed now. Goodnight.

KATE. Goodnight, Caroline.

CAROLINE (*touching* KATE). You're my dear friend, Kate, and your letters have kept me going. Sleep tightly.

KATE. You too.

CAROLINE *goes out, turning off the light.*
A beat.

D. Kate?

KATE. Yes?

D. I wasn't asleep.

Scene Six

The Beach. Late Afternoon.

Everyone – CAROLINE, STELLA, KATE, D, FRAN – *is in a very loony mood. It is the late afternoon of a silly, wonderful day. They are all wearing cowboy hats and flowers and a picnic hamper is in evidence. There is a lot of fooling about and screaming. FRAN has a plastic bundle – a kite.*

CAROLINE. People were looking at us.

FRAN. I don't care.

STELLA. I do. I've got my image to think of. I'm not supposed to have fun in public.

FRAN. Shut up.

STELLA. And a for you Kate, you are an embarrassment.

KATE. This is true.

STELLA. Roll your trousers down.

KATE. Absolutely not.

STELLA. In that case I'll roll mine up!

FRAN. Now I'll have to roll mine up. C'mon Caroline.

CAROLINE. Must I!

D. Yeah. Go on Caroline.

CAROLINE. Okay. How do I look?

STELLA. Ludicrous.

KATE. Wonderful.

STELLA. Wonderful *and* ludicrous.

KATE. Are we going to hop?

STELLA. No!

FRAN. Yes!

STELLA. This is false pretences. You said picnic. You said fun day on the beach. You said as one with nature. You did not mention hopping.

KATE. Hop!

STELLA *hops*.

D. Yeah!

KATE. That is an impressive hop Stella. That is a hop you have kept under a bushel.

FRAN. What about my hop? C'mon! Give me marks out of ten!

KATE. Okay sisters. Stop hopping. Hop not and assess. We're looking for bounce, we're looking for style and we're looking for stamina . . .

FRAN. Hurry up.

KATE. Stella?

STELLA. Well . . .

FRAN. Hurry up! I'm knackered. (*She keeps hopping.*)

STELLA. It *is* difficult.

KATE. Caroline?

CAROLINE. Great, Fran.

FRAN. Great is not a mark! Are we talking 8? Are we talking 9?

KATE. What are we talking girlies?

D. Foot down!

FRAN. No!

STELLA. Definitely!

KATE. I'm sorry Fran. That was a foot down.

STELLA (*tragic*). Shame.

FRAN. I'm sitting down. I may sulk.

CAROLINE. You're all crazy.

FRAN. Come on love. Sit down.

CAROLINE. I think I'll lie down.

KATE. Oh no. Out of the way! Clear the runway!

D. Yeah! The kite.

KATE. Come on. Shift your bums. We're having a test drive. Out of the way weedies or I'll kick sand in your face!

FRAN. School bully.

KATE. The very same. Okay! Here we go!

She runs away from the group. The kite remains earthbound. Great applause.

STELLA. Rubbish!

KATE. It's off the ground! It's off . . . It's . . . There can't be any wind.

STELLA. You're joking. (*It's windy.*)

FRAN. I think we're struggling on the skill front here.

KATE. You'll eat your words, shitbags. I give up. I'm dying. Argh! Minister to me. Gorge my fat carcass with cake, you hussies!

STELLA. We come, your majesty!

STELLA *and* FRAN *attack* KATE *and stuff cake in her mouth.*

KATE. Get off! Argh! Help! Help! Gay-bashers!

D (*to* CAROLINE). How are you feeling?

CAROLINE. Fine. Exhausted. My stomach hurts from laughing. (*Looking at the cavorting.*) Watch out, Fran, she bites!

KATE. Yes, I do!

D. It's been a really silly day.

CAROLINE. Yes, lovely.

KATE *and* STELLA *are now tickling* FRAN *who makes groaning, hysterical noises.*

STELLA. It's a whale! (*She accompanies* FRAN *with whale music.*)

D (*to* CAROLINE). I'll be back in a minute. I'm going to find some shells.

KATE. Where are you going, D?

D. I'm going hunting for shells and things. Maybe have a paddle.

KATE. We're just going to eat. What's the matter?

D. Nothing. (*Truthfully.*) I'm happy. You coming?

KATE. Yeah. Sure. I'm stupid. A paddle! God! If I die, Fran, you can have my back copies of *Spare Rib*.

FRAN. Well hurry up – I'm ravenous.

D (*picking up the kite*). And I'm going to get this bloody thing to fly if it kills me.

KATE. Don't you dare scoff all the doughnuts.

KATE *and* D *exit.*

STELLA. Who wants some coffee?

FRAN. Please.

CAROLINE. Not me. Ugh, this yoghurt's leaking! It's all over the sandwiches.

STELLA. What flavour?

CAROLINE. Uh . . . muesli.

STELLA. Oh, that's all right then.

FRAN (*examining her damaged flower*). My flower's not very well.

STELLA. Actually, they're really nice, aren't they?

FRAN. What?

STELLA. Those two lunatics.

CAROLINE. Yes, they are.

FRAN. Kate's really different . . . you know . . . from school. Funny, isn't it? Like you expect, well I've always sort of thought that if you're . . . you know, if you don't like men, that you'd be –

STELLA. What are you wittering on about?

FRAN. Well, they're just nice, aren't they?

STELLA (*laughing*). That's really deep, Fran.

FRAN. You know what I mean. We've had a lovely day, haven't we?

STELLA *starts off singing 'Didn't we have a lovely time, the day we went to the seaside'.* FRAN *chimes in with whale music.*

CAROLINE (*a bit pale, peaked, lying down but speaking happily*). I'm so tired! I'm going to close my eyes and when I wake up I want it to be morning and we can start today all over again.

FRAN *and* STELLA *tuck into the picnic.*

FRAN. Do you know – I've never won anything before.

STELLA. Me neither.

CAROLINE. You won Space Invaders.

STELLA. This is true. Was I brilliant?

CAROLINE. Devastating.

FRAN. I didn't hit anything. I don't like the noise it makes when you do. (*To* CAROLINE, *indicating a coat.*) Do you want this over you, love?

CAROLINE. Please.

STELLA. How are things with Graeme?

FRAN. Oh, okay. He's taken Heidi to his sister's today. (*She bites into a doughnut.*) Yes, all right, it'll never be marvellous. Um . . . this is obscene. The thing is I can't talk to him. He has made an effort . . . sort of . . . you know, after I went back, but we can't have fun . . . not like this. I never laugh. I haven't laughed like this since I was at school. Sad, isn't it?

STELLA. Yeah.

FRAN. For him too. Half the time he doesn't know why he infuriates me. Neither do I really.

STELLA. But you think it will last?

FRAN. I don't know. I know him. I'm not dim, I know what he's like . . . you know – other women and things. But then you see at the end of the day he's still my husband. He's still Heidi's dad. Does that make any sense?

STELLA. Yes . . . Hey! They've got it up, look!

FRAN. Yeah!

STELLA. Look at Kate! She's an absolute maniac. They're getting soaked!

FRAN (*to* CAROLINE). Do you want something to eat?

CAROLINE. Oh, no thanks . . . my stomach hurts. I've been laughing too much.

STELLA. You'd better take it easy you nut. We don't want you going into bloody labour on the beach.

KATE *rushes on, kicking her wet legs at the others.*

STELLA. Get off!

KATE. We got it working! Good, eh? I'm freezing! Ach, give me a doughnut before I die. Is there any coffee left? Look at D. She's like a little kid. (*Yelling.*) Come in number fourteen – your time is up! (*Shaking her head.*) Mad as a hatter. You asleep, Caroline?

CAROLINE. Hardly.

KATE. Oh I'm so bloody wet! What am I doing? (*Lying down beside* CAROLINE.) Well that's it. I've had it. God!

D *comes on, looking mischievous, with a bucket and a spade.*

D. Mummy, mummy – I've found a contraceptive on the beach.

KATE. What's a beach?

FRAN. O God . . . she really has! Don't be bloody revolting . . . let's have a look.

D *displays the bucket.*

STELLA. Ugh, I can't stand those things. Look at it. Christ!

FRAN. It's a drowned semen.

STELLA. I thought it was supposed to be impossible underwater.

D. I've decided – it's a message in a bottle.

STELLA. She's absolutely right. Can't read it though – it's in French!

KATE. Don't show it to me, you perverts, it's probably poisonous.

D *teases* KATE *with the bucket.*

KATE. Go away! Ugh, how gross! Girls . . . this bag has been raped.

FRAN. No, no, of course! It's a silly fish!

There is general laughter.

STELLA. Silly fish! Well, that's it . . . can you imagine . . . next time you're in Boots: 'Excuse me, I'd like a packet of three silly fish, please!'

FRAN. I don't know how it happened, Doctor, we HAVE been using silly fish.

KATE. O throw it away, D. It makes me feel sick.

CAROLINE (*urgently*). Fran . . . I think something's happening. O God, Fran, what's happening?

KATE. Caroline! What's the matter?

STELLA. Caroline?

CAROLINE. Oh, my God.

FRAN. We'd better get the van, Kate. Stella – you ring the hospital. Tell them we're coming in. (*To* CAROLINE.) You're going to be all right, lovely. Just relax. Come on . . . remember your breathing.

CAROLINE. What?

FRAN. I think you're probably going to have your baby, love. Don't worry, it's all going to be fine.

Scene Seven

A hospital side room. There is a right angle of connected grey plastic seats. One table, with a pile of magazines on it. FRAN, STELLA, KATE and D are there. It is late. D is asleep with her jacket over her.

FRAN. Now I know what men feel like.

There is a pause.

STELLA. Why do hospitals always smell the same?

There is a pause.

KATE *puts down a magazine, gets up and walks about.*

KATE. This is ridiculous. What's going on?

FRAN. She'll be a while yet, I expect.

KATE. I think they should have let one of us stay with her.

FRAN. Oh come on. They've been ever so good. We might have been downstairs with the dads.

KATE. You're joking.

STELLA. Look at D.

KATE. Will it be all right? I mean why is it so early?

FRAN. It's not that bad. A few weeks. She should be okay. They've got babies in here two months premature – perfect. It's ever such a good hospital.

KATE. I didn't like that doctor.

FRAN. He didn't like you.

KATE. Well, they're so bloody clinical. She didn't know what was going on. They should have let one of us stay with her. I mean, there's no bloody father on the scene. If there had been they would have had him in holding a leg or whatever it is they do. I could have done that.

FRAN. He did explain, Kate. If her mum comes in time then she'll be with her and if not then one of us can go in.

KATE. Why one? Why not all of us?

STELLA. Christ, Kate, forget it will you? There's no point. Fran's right. Things could have been a lot worse. At least they treated her like a human being. They don't always.

FRAN. What do you mean?

STELLA. Well (a) she's not married, and (b) she's giving the kid away. She's not normal is she? I don't mean the nurses. It's the other women. They can be so bloody cruel. I've seen it. The way they say Miss. Miss.

FRAN. Oh I don't know. I don't think that's fair.

STELLA. Well . . . perhaps things have changed.

KATE. Since when?

STELLA. Since a long time ago. (*She gets up.*) Doesn't that smell get to you? That certainly hasn't changed. It's ten years since I went inside a hospital. I was pregnant. (*Very quietly.*) I got pregnant when I was seventeen. Before I came down here. One fuck! I was actually in love with the bloke . . . he's married now . . . really nice guy . . .

KATE. And what – did you have an abortion?

STELLA. No, I didn't, I was going to have the baby, that was the idea. (*Pause.*) But anyway, I started to lose it. I didn't really know, but I was at home, not actually at home, round my uncle's – in the kitchen – and I was really pathetically naive. And I was sitting in this chair, and feeling lousy, and not knowing what to do about it or what, you know, how to say anything – because, I mean, obviously my uncle didn't know what was going on. So I just sat there, and I knew I was in this pool of blood, and I just waited until he left the room, whatever he was doing, can't remember, and then just got up and rang the hospital. I mean I can't remember all the details, but they said it was hopeless, and my mother was there for a bit, and then I was in this bed, and I'd been knitting a little jacket for it, and the nurse had come round to give me a wash, and she came back and said I shouldn't bother with knitting, but I thought bugger that, and then you know, literally minutes later, I'd sort of passed it into the bedpan. I felt like a little girl. And they got a priest and he did a kind of baptism and he gave it a name. I mean I didn't, I hadn't thought of names or anything and he said best to call it Frances, because it was impossible to say, you know, if it was a girl or a boy, so I did. Well I just said okay Frances is fine. Anyway, anyway, why am I telling you all this? . . . Oh yeah, . . . the smell, that's what reminded me. And the other women . . . smug with their rings on their fingers and their stupid husbands.

FRAN. That's where the matinée jacket came from for Caroline, isn't it?

STELLA. Yeah, I thought I might as well finish it off.

FRAN. You kept the wool.

STELLA. Oh me – I'm a right hoarder.

KATE. Is it upsetting you? Being here? I could run you home, love.

STELLA. No, don't be daft. It's all water under the bridge. Besides, got to see it through: a bit of the old solidarity.

KATE. That's it. A bit of the old solidarity.

The NURSE *enters.*

NURSE. You've got company. (*Off.*) Here we are. Shall I get you a cup of coffee?

SHEELAGH O'BRIEN, CAROLINE's *mother, enters. She is drawn, anxious.*

SHEELAGH. Thank you. Uh, no thanks. No coffee thank you.

NURSE. Okay. Right, I'll leave you to it.

SHEELAGH. Thanks. Hello Kate. Hello Fran.

FRAN. Hello. Uh, Stella, this is Caroline's mother. This is Stella.

KATE. And this is D. Wake up love.

SHEELAGH. Oh no, don't worry . . .

D. What? I was asleep.

KATE. This is Caroline's mother.

There are hellos all round. SHEELAGH *replies with 'pleased to meet you'.*

SHEELAGH. Caroline's told me how kind you've been.

KATE (*sharply*). Have you seen her?

SHEELAGH. They let me look in. Just for a second.

KATE. Did they.

SHEELAGH. She wasn't really aware of what was happening, I don't think. They've given her some Pethadin.

FRAN (*disappointed*). Oh why?

SHEELAGH. I don't know. I should think they know what's best though, don't you? They've got one of those monitor machines on her that measures the contractions . . . and one for the baby's heartbeat. Anyway, the doctor told me they're very happy with her . . . Do you mind if I sit down? It's quite a drive.

KATE (*sharply*). Are you not going back in then?

SHEELAGH. Uh, yes. I said I'd come and give you a weather report. Yes. I just thought I'd . . .

SHEELAGH gives the impression that she is near breaking point. The girls generate an atmosphere that veers between sympathy and hostility.

You've all been so good to Caroline. We're very grateful.

FRAN. Is Mr O'Brien not with you?

SHEELAGH. No, he, uh, well, he's not as well as he might be. He gets very agitated, you know, if there's any stress. I don't think he'd be much help just now. No, but you must all be exhausted. Have you not been home or anything?

FRAN (*after a beat*). We've just been saying . . . it must be quite a novelty here to have a pile of women pacing up and down outside the delivery room.

SHEELAGH. Yes, that's right. (*Compulsively putting her hand to her face.*) Goodness, I think I must be more tired than I thought. Oh, I've got some chocolate. Would anybody like some?

FRAN. No, thank you.

STELLA. Not for me, thanks.

SHEELAGH. Are you sure? Go on, do have some please.

STELLA. Oh all right then.

SHEELAGH. Fran?

FRAN. Okay. Thanks.

SHEELAGH. Pass it round. Do.

KATE. Thanks.

They munch the chocolate in silence. The atmosphere is very strained now.

SHEELAGH. You must understand – I shall be fifty soon, and Caroline's my only child, and my husband's too, and then you see, you only want what's best, don't you? What's for the best . . .

FRAN. You don't have to explain to us, Mrs O'Brien.

SHEELAGH. No – but I don't want you to think that we don't love her, because we do, we do love her. She's our daughter.

There is no response.

She asked us not to come down, you know . . . Did she tell you that? *Several* times. But it's the same, as I said to my husband – when all's said and done . . . it's our grandchild, isn't it?

KATE. Well, don't try and persuade her to keep the baby . . . not because of your guilt . . . not when she's so vulnerable. She's already wasted getting on for a year. Don't ask her to waste the rest of her life.

SHEELAGH. And is that what you think families are? A waste?

KATE. I'm not talking about families. I'm talking about a single girl with a course to finish and no help, no father. It's not fair . . . on Caroline or the child.

FRAN. Kate . . .

KATE. Well, I'm angry. I'm bloody angry. You couldn't even teach Caroline to look after herself and then you talk about families.

SHEELAGH. And what have you taught her? She lives in your house. Don't you feel responsible?

KATE (*the irony not lost on her*). Oh, Christ . . . (*She sighs.*) Yes, I do, actually. I do feel pretty bad about it.

STELLA. I'm sorry. I don't see the point of all this.

FRAN. Neither do I. Blame . . . what does it matter? It won't change anything. That baby up there in the delivery room – Caroline's baby – somewhere around there's a couple, a woman who's been waiting for this moment. And it's going to make them so happy. I wish people would stop talking like the whole thing was a tragedy. No one's died.

KATE *goes over to* SHEELAGH *and touches her.*

KATE. I'm sorry. You start thinking of people only by their title: woman; mother; teacher . . . I'm always shouting off about that, but I do it myself all the time.

D. I've got a headache. Anyone got an aspirin?

STELLA. Sorry.

FRAN. No, sorry love.

KATE. We're in a hospital, and no one's got an aspirin.

SHEELAGH. Hang on, I should have some in my bag . . . somewhere . . . (*She fishes out a box of mints.*) I stopped at one those service places on the way down, and I bought these for Caroline . . . she doesn't like mints.

FRAN. Well I do.

STELLA (*smiling*). You're a bloody dustbin, Fran.

FRAN (*smiling*). Yeah.

The NURSE *comes in.*

NURSE. Would you like to come back in, Mrs O'Brien? The head's appeared. It won't be long now.

Scene Eight

The hospital ward. CAROLINE is in bed, surrounded by flowers. Her mother is visiting her.

SHEELAGH. I'd better go. Kate's waiting to come in.

CAROLINE. Yes.

SHEELAGH. Did I tell you? I spoke to Daddy. He thought we might try and go on holiday together.

CAROLINE. He hates holidays.

SHEELAGH. He wants to do something for you.

CAROLINE. Yes.

SHEELAGH. Well, you don't have to say yet.

CAROLINE. Right. You'd better get off. It's a long drive.

SHEELAGH. It's not too bad. I surprised myself, you know, coming down. Perhaps I'll feel less nervous now about the roads to Leeds.

   CAROLINE *nods.*

   I wish I could stay.

CAROLINE. There's nothing for you to do. I'm fine. Fran and Stella will supervise.

SHEELAGH. I used to think Fran was such a scatty girl . . .

CAROLINE. Oh no.

SHEELAGH. Oh, I realize now. Anyway, I'll go . . . (*She sighs.*) . . . you know before I come in I keep thinking of all the things I want to say . . .

CAROLINE. There's no need, Mum.

SHEELAGH. I think there is, darling . . . (*Abruptly.*) So – can I tell Daddy you'll think about where you'd like to go.

CAROLINE. Did you see him, Mum?

SHEELAGH. Daddy?

CAROLINE. My baby. Did you?

SHEELAGH. Yes.

CAROLINE. I wanted you to.

SHEELAGH. Caroline – it's not too late if –

CAROLINE. Don't . . .

The NURSE *bustles by.*

Nurse, Nurse, how's my baby?

NURSE (*in a hurry*). Fine.

CAROLINE. Because Sister mentioned he was a bit grizzly last night.

NURSE. No, he's fine. He's bonny. All right?

CAROLINE. Yes. Thanks. I just wondered.

The NURSE *is going.*

(*Stopping her.*) Nurse, yesterday they brought him up to me . . . you know, in the, it's not the incubator, uh . . .

NURSE. Baby trolley.

CAROLINE. Yes, the baby trolley. I just wondered whether I could, you could, whether I could see him this afternoon?

NURSE. I expect that'll be all right. I'll ask Staff. OK?

CAROLINE. Thanks. Sorry to . . .

SHEELAGH (*to the* NURSE). Thanks. (*To* CAROLINE.) That'll be nice.

CAROLINE. Yes.

SHEELAGH. Everybody seems very nice. You mustn't worry about him crying. It's perfectly natural.

CAROLINE. I know.

SHEELAGH. You cried all the time. Your lip always stuck out. (*She demonstrates.*) Your father used to say he could sit on it. Shall I send Kate in?

CAROLINE. Please.

SHEELAGH. I was thinking. It's a shame neither of your friends turned up.

CAROLINE. Which friends?

SHEELAGH. I'm afraid I don't know their names . . . uh. (*She thinks, cannot remember and gives a short laugh, shaking her head.*) The boys from Leeds.

CAROLINE (*nodding*). Oh yes. It's a shame. Whatever happens . . . we'll talk, eh?

SHEELAGH (*nodding*). Yes, that's right. Bye bye, darling.

CAROLINE. Bye, Mum.

SHEELAGH (*very quietly*). Bye.

SHEELAGH *exits.*
KATE *enters.*

KATE. Hello.

A buzzer sounds.

Goodbye!

CAROLINE. I'm sorry. There's no time.

KATE. Well, I'll see you next week, won't I?

CAROLINE. I'm only going to stop a day or two, Kate. I think I ought to go home for a while.

KATE. Right . . . I rang John.

CAROLINE. Yes. These came. (*She indicates some flowers.*)

KATE. He said he'd come down – if I thought it would help.

CAROLINE. It wouldn't.

KATE. That's what I said.

CAROLINE (*wryly*). Say it with flowers! Where's D?

KATE. In the van. She says goodbye.

CAROLINE. Well, I'll see her in Leeds won't I?

KATE. I expect so.

CAROLINE. Right. I'm glad you came. I'm glad you were here, Katie.

KATE. So am I.

CAROLINE. Have I been a fool? Is that what you think? (*Pause.*) I have, haven't I?

KATE. I don't know, sugar. Whatever you do, you lose. Whatever you'd done. Whatever you'd done, there's loss. It's a bugger, isn't it?

CAROLINE. Yeah.

KATE. Well hurry up and get out. You'll get soft in that bed.

CAROLINE. My milk's come through, Kate.

KATE *sighs. A pause. They embrace.*

KATE. Every day something will happen, won't it? Today it's your milk, then there'll be birthdays and reminders and . . . for ages . . . you'll have to get tough, won't you?

They just sit there on the bed, embracing. CAROLINE *starts beating* KATE *on the back.*

What are you doing?

CAROLINE. Getting tough.

KATE. You! (*She gets up, smiling.*) See, you, shitbag.

CAROLINE. Yeah. See you.

STAFF (*off*). Come along, fathers. Out, out, out. The buzzer's gone.

KATE *exits*.

The STAFF NURSE enters.

STAFF. Nurse says you'd like to see baby.

CAROLINE. Please, if that's OK?

STAFF. Well you can, but I'm afraid it can only be for a few minutes because I know that uh, Doctor Minareau and Mrs Holden have arranged for his new, for the adoptive parents to meet him today.

CAROLINE. Ah.

STAFF. I think you knew that, Caroline, didn't you?

CAROLINE. I don't know. Yes, probably, you lose track of what day it is. Oh, never mind then.

STAFF. I said you can see him for a few minutes now, and then later on if you want.

CAROLINE. Lovely. Thanks. That would be lovely.

STAFF. So, I'll get Nurse to bring him up. Now, are you still leaking a bit or is the injection taking care of it? (*She means* CAROLINE's *milk.*)

CAROLINE. It's all right I think.

STAFF NURSE *exits*.

STAFF (*off*). Mrs Fitzgerald, there's no need to walk like that. Goodness me! It's a baby you've had not an elephant.

MRS FITZGERALD (*off*). It felt like an elephant.

STAFF (*off*). I'm going to tell that nice husband of yours you're being an old misery guts.

We watch CAROLINE *in bed for as long as the moment can be held whilst she faces the reality of losing her baby.*
The NURSE *pops her head round.*

NURSE. Caroline, I'm sorry but they're already here.

CAROLINE. Never mind. What a bore.

NURSE. Look, I'll make sure he's brought up to you as soon as we can. Sorry. (*Pause.*) Have you got enough books?

CAROLINE. Oh yes.

NURSE. It's good isn't it? So many of your friends come to see you. We were just saying. Really nice.

CAROLINE. Right.

NURSE (*at the door*). Shout if . . .

CAROLINE. Do they seem nice? His new mum and dad?

NURSE. I don't know Caroline. I haven't met them.

CAROLINE. But they looked nice, did they?

NURSE. Uh, yes. Of course.

CAROLINE. Can't I ask that? I'm not allowed to ask if they look nice?

NURSE. I honestly have hardly seen them, but yes they seemed very nice.

CAROLINE. I just wish people would stop treating me as if I were a martian. You know?

NURSE. Uh.

CAROLINE. Forget it. Really just forget it. Could you draw the curtains please? I'm tired. I think I'd like to sleep.

The NURSE *draws the curtains and the room goes dark.*

Scene Nine

The Seafront.

FRAN, STELLA *and* CAROLINE (*with* HEIDI *in her pram*). STELLA *is carrying* CAROLINE's *haversack.*

FRAN (*referring to* HEIDI). Look at her face! And this was clean on this morning. I don't know, madam.

STELLA (*laughing*). She's great.

FRAN. When she's asleep. (*To* HEIDI). Hey, how could you manage to get choc-ice up your nose?

STELLA. Easy, isn't it Heidi?

FRAN. And she's finished it, little sod, I'm starving! (*To* HEIDI.) Hey, I'm starving.

STELLA. Christ, Fran, you should be enormous.

FRAN. I am. I've just got a tight skin.

STELLA. Twit.

FRAN. Yeah. Holds it all in. (*To* CAROLINE.) All right love?

CAROLINE. Yes. I'm just having a good breathe. Souvenir.

FRAN. Oh, don't say that.

STELLA. Hey no drama, right? If you're going to get weepy, either of you, you can piss off.

FRAN. Hark at tough tits.

STELLA. Too right. When she goes I'm going to have to get a job.

CAROLINE. I haven't gone yet.

STELLA. Well, you're not staying with me. It's Spring. I'm getting out my butterfly outfit.

CAROLINE. Wow the tourists.

STELLA. The idea is to frighten them off. (*Referring to* CAROLINE's *haversack.*) What's in this Caroline? Bricks? You're never going to manage it yourself. Is Kate going to meet you?

CAROLINE. Yes. Oh, listen, Fran I've left all the things, the clothes, and the books and things. Stella's got them.

FRAN. Lovely.

STELLA. And the Whale Music.

CAROLINE. Uh, no. I kept that. I mean, I'd like to keep that if that's OK?

FRAN. Sure.

A woman, VERONICA, *walks by with a very young baby in a pram.*

VERONICA (*to* FRAN). Hello, how are you?

FRAN (*uncomfortable*). OK. Just dashing.

VERONICA (*to* HEIDI). Isn't she a beauty? Hello fishface.

FRAN. She's a monster. You can have her. (*She wants to keep going.*)

VERONICA. You're joking. (*Indicating her pram.*) Yes, I'll do a swap. This one . . . no one told him about sleep.

FRAN. Ha! Listen, I'll give you a call . . . or pop in or something?

VERONICA. Smashing.

CAROLINE *goes up to* VERONICA's *pram.*

CAROLINE. How old is he?

VERONICA. He's new. He'll be three weeks tomorrow.

CAROLINE. What do you call him?

VERONICA. What do we call him? Oh . . . rat . . . pig. His name is Josh.

STELLA. Caroline. The boat.

CAROLINE. Right.

VERONICA (*to* FRAN). Bye now. Pop in.

FRAN. I will. Bye.

They walk on.

I'm sorry. I couldn't ignore her.

CAROLINE. Doesn't matter. Really. (*To* STELLA.) Josh!

STELLA. Urgh!

CAROLINE (*sighing*). Oh.

They walk on.

STELLA. So, when shall we three meet again?

FRAN. Four.

STELLA. What? Oh, yes, four.

They reach the boat.

CAROLINE. You must come up to Leeds.

STELLA. Yeah.

CAROLINE. Fat chance.

STELLA. I'll surprise you. Look, I'm going now. I'm a lousy waver. (*She walks away.*)

FRAN. You'd better get on love.

CAROLINE. Yes. I'd better . . . look, I'll . . . uh . . . you know.

FRAN. I know.

CAROLINE. I want to say sorry, but I'm not sure what for.

FRAN. Then don't.

STELLA (*walking back*). Right. Push off, I'll see you in Leeds.

CAROLINE (*she looks at them both*). Hey . . .

STELLA. What?

CAROLINE (*thinking; shrugging*). Just hey. (*She starts to go, then turns.*) See you.

FRAN. Yeah.

CAROLINE *exits.*

The lights fade as STELLA *and* FRAN *watch her go.*

A LITTLE LIKE DROWNING

A Little Like Drowning was first performed by the CV-One Theatre Company in March 1982 at the start of a national tour. The cast was as follows:

NONNA MARE	Jenny Howe
LEONORA MARE *Nonna as a younger woman*	
ALFREDO MARE	Haluk Bilginer
JULIET JARRETT	Rosalind March
GIOIA	Peta Masters
THERESA	Rosalind March
PETER	Haluk Bilginer
ANASTASIA	Peta Masters
GIANNA	Rosalind March
GRAEME	
FATHER DAVID	
BRUNO	
EDUARDO	Bob Hewis

Directed by Bob Lewis
Designed by Bernard Culshaw
and Vickie Le Saché
Lighting by Peter Gilbert

The play is set in England, Ireland and Italy between 1920 and the present.

N.B. The writing allows for some doubling, not least in the case of LEONORA and NONNA, PETER and ALFREDO.

The play was broadcast in March 1989 on BBC Radio 4.

ACT ONE

Scene One

The present. England.

OLD LEONORA (*known as* NONNA) *is in a rocking chair. There is a Giuseppe Di Stefano record playing.* LEONORA *is seventy-two.*
ANASTASIA *is a small girl,* LEONORA's *granddaughter.*
ANASTASIA *struggles in with pitcher, bowl and towel.*

NONNA. Thank you darling.
NONNA *kicks off her sandals,*
ANASTASIA *pours water into the bowl, and she plunges her feet in, sighing.* ALFREDO *appears as for the wedding night, 1926, with an identical toilet, same jug and bowl and takes off his shirt – not in the light – and begins washing, humming the Giuseppe Di Stefano.*
NONNA *and* ANASTASIA *do not see* ALFREDO.

NONNA (*to* ANASTASIA). I love this music. Don't you love it?

ANASTASIA (*shrugs*). It's all right. No. Not really. I don't understand it.

NONNA. It's a crime that none of you speak Italian. Will you cut my toenails for me this evening, Anastasia?

ANASTASIA. OK.

NONNA. My feet are so ugly aren't they, and my legs, hands, everything. Look at my hands and look at yours . . .

ANASTASIA. I'll get the scissors.

NONNA. Thank you darling. (*Sharp.*) Where is your sister? What are they doing?

ANASTASIA. Don't know. They're in the other room, I expect.

NONNA. Is that boy still here?

ANASTASIA. Expect so.

NONNA. Puttanas! Licking each other's backsides. Tell her it's time they packed up, she sent her – (*Makes a distasteful sound.*) – tell her to come in here! Wouldn't be any of this if your parents were in. Can't even get them to make me a cup of tea.

ANASTASIA. OK

She exits. NONNA *pours on more water. Remembers.*

Scene Two

The past. Italy, 1926.

The wedding night. LEONORA-ALFREDO. *Candlelight.*
LEONORA *brushing out her hair.* ALFREDO *takes off his shirt.*
Wears trousers with the braces dangling. LEONORA *wears a white*
cotton nightdress. She is 16.

ALFREDO. Think I'm drunk.

> *He comes up behind her, puts a hand to her breast.* LEONORA
> *flinches.*

ALFREDO (*admonishing her*). Hey! Hey! We're married,
remember?

LEONORA. I'm just getting ready to come to bed, Alfredo.

ALFREDO. And I was just trying to help.

> *Pause. He watches her.*

ALFREDO (*proudly*). Signora Mare.

NONNA. Signor Mare.

ALFREDO (*great sentimentality. Kisses her fingers. Sucks on the*
wedding finger down to the ring). With this ring I thee wed. With
my body I thee worship.

LEONORA (*holding on to his hand*). With this ring I thee wed. With
my body I thee worship.

ALFREDO. Is that what we actually said?

LEONORA. Yes, of course.

ALFREDO. Didn't understand it properly. I still don't see why we
couldn't have been married in England.

LEONORA. This is our village.

ALFREDO. Our village! I've never lived here.

LEONORA. Your family. Your family's village.

ALFREDO. Half the time I didn't understand what anybody was
saying. They talk so bloody quickly. Too much time in England I
suppose. My Italian's rotten.

LEONORA. You should let me translate.

ALFREDO (*defensive*). I can understand most of it. Just takes me
time to speak it, that's all. I'll be all right in a day or two. It's not
good Italian they speak here. Your Italian. Terrible dialect.

> *He goes to a bottle of wine and pours himself a drink.*

LEONORA. Siamo paesani. That's what you married. You know that

ALFREDO. I wasn't criticizing you. You're not real paesan. You're brighter than anybody in this place.

LEONORA. I don't think so.

ALFREDO. You want some wine?

LEONORA. No thank you. Oh yes. From your glass.

She drinks from his glass.

ALFREDO. I love it when you talk like that.

LEONORA. Like what?

ALFREDO. You're like a little girl.

LEONORA. I am a girl. (*Looks up at him. Simply.*) I'm a bit nervous.

ALFREDO. Have some more wine.

LEONORA. No. It makes me queasy.

ALFREDO. Don't worry. (*Pause.*) Stuffy in here, isn't it? Terrible.

LEONORA. I don't mind.

ALFREDO. I hate this country. If you close the windows you can't breathe and if you open them you get bitten to death.

LEONORA. It's your cologne. The mosquitos like it!

ALFREDO. It's got nothing to do with my cologne.

LEONORA. I remember when you came here for a holiday. I was twelve. (*Mischievously.*) Yes, because you were thirteen and fat! And I saw you walking up past the olives to this house. Your brother was with you and you were wearing a sailor's outfit. White with stripes. I wanted you to notice me but you didn't. Not that there was anything to see. I went home and said a whole rosary that one day you would marry me.

ALFREDO. Is that true?

LEONORA. Yes, it's true.

ALFREDO. So you had God organizing this, did you? Or was it the Madonna?

LEONORA. Alfredo, don't!

ALFREDO (*smiles, pleased with himself*). I remember that suit. To think you thought about me all that time ago, and I didn't know you existed and were growing up in Valvori – sleeping and waking and growing up to become my wife. I'm glad you said your rosary.

LEONORA. Are you really?

ALFREDO. Yes . . . and you see God gave you those eyes and that hair so I'd notice you. And those breasts. Shall we go to bed now?

LEONORA. Yes.

They blow out the candles.

Morning. Warm shafts of light through the shutter. The eiderdown stripped off the bed. ALFREDO, braces and trousers, with bowl and jug, preparing to shave. LEONORA kneels, her head on the sheet.

ALFREDO (*defensive*). Ma che fai?

Silence. He washes.

ALFREDO. Look. I hope you're not going to judge me on last night. I was drunk. It's no use crying.

Silence. He lathers his face.

ALFREDO. Besides. You seemed, well, oddly-shaped. Maybe not. We'll have to get used to each other, that's all. Put it down to experience shall we? Andiamo eh! Now, stop crying and come here and kiss your husband good morning. It's beautiful. Warm. Marvellous.

He goes to the windows. Opens the shutters. Strong light on them both. ALFREDO looks down.

ALFREDO. Funny. What are those people doing? Why are all those people down there? Your mother! Your family! What's going on?

LEONORA (*not looking up*). We must show them the sheet.

ALFREDO. What!

LEONORA. We must show them the sheet from our bed. With blood.

ALFREDO. They can piss off!

LEONORA. No! They want to see that I was pure. It was the same for my mother. And your mother.

ALFREDO. Well, how can we?

LEONORA. Wait.

She gets up and takes the water jug and spills a little of the water on to the sheet.

LEONORA. Give me your razor.

ALFREDO *hands her his razor. He snatches it back.*

ALFREDO. No!

He looks at her then quickly slices across his finger. He pulls the sheet off the bed and stains the damp patch with his blood. Then, together, he and LEONORA step out onto the balcony and hold

the stained sheet aloft like a flag. There is a cheer from below.
ALFREDO *looks at* LEONORA. *They smile foolishly.*

ALFREDO (*quietly to* LEONORA). Thank you.

Applause.

ALFREDO (*proudly*). Thank you! Thank you!

They kiss. More applause.

Scene Three

The present. England.

GIANNA *comes in. She is around seventeen.*

GIANNA. What is it, Gran?

NONNA. What are you doing?

GIANNA. Nothing much. Talking. Having coffee.

NONNA. You make yourselves coffee. What about my tea?

GIANNA. Can't Stacey make it? Graeme's got to go soon.

NONNA. Ach Graeme! I want you to come in here please. Tell him
to do up his trousers and come in here.

GIANNA. O Gran, really! Why do you talk like that? It's horrible.

NONNA. Is it? So are abortions.

GIANNA. Oh Christ.

NONNA. That's right.

GIANNA. Honestly Gran, I don't know what you think we're doing
when the door's open and Stacey's barging in every five minutes.

NONNA. Oh yes . . . little innocent.

ANASTASIA *comes back with scissors.*

GIANNA. Gran thinks we're having group sex in the dining-room.

NONNA. If you're not doing anything wrong then it won't hurt to
sit here, will it?

GIANNA. Oh come on, we're not children . . . it's so embarassing to
have to sit here with you and Stacey.

ANASTASIA. Thanks.

GIANNA. You know what I mean. You don't like it when, I don't
know, Chris comes round, do you, and you have to play in here?

ANASTASIA. Don't mind.

GIANNA (*sarcastic*). Course not.

ANASTASIA. I don't

GIANNA. Tch. Well, can we at least listen to some decent music? This stuff's out of the ark. (*To* LEONORA.) And please don't start taking your corsets off in front of everyone.

NONNA. Oh goodness! Don't think you're so high and mighty, madam. I've seen you do a wee-wee on this carpet.

ANASTASIA *giggles*.

GIANNA. Well, how nice for you. I mean I suppose I must have been nearly two. Sorry to be so weak-bladdered.

NONNA. Well I'm over seventy-two. Sorry to be so old.

GIANNA. It's much better, Gran, when you have your room and we have ours. Then we can all do and say what we want without rubbing each other up the wrong way.

NONNA. I thought that was what you were doing . . . rubbing each other up the wrong way!

NONNA *and* ANASTASIA *laugh*.

GIANNA. You've got such a dirty mind!

NONNA. When you've had your mind as long as I've had mine, yours will be dirty too. And I'll tell you something else for nothing. Experience! You can't take that to the launderette. It doesn't wash out. It's like always drinking from the same cup – coffee, tea, soup, wine – in the end everything tastes the same. And bitter.

GIANNA. I have absolutely no idea what you're talking about.

NONNA (*bitter*). No – of course not.

GRAEME (*from the doorway*). What's going on? You coming back in or what?

GIANNA. We've been summoned. Sorry.

GRAEME. I don't mind. I'm really into opera. Who is it?

GIANNA (*sardonic*). Terrific!

GRAEME. Evening Mrs M.

NONNA (*to* GIANNA *of* GRAEME). Why don't you make him a cup of tea?

GRAEME. I'm fine thanks. Just had some coffee.

NONNA. I'd like a cup of tea.

GIANNA. Stacey's not doing anything.

ANASTASIA. Nor are you. I've got homework to do.

GIANNA. Well, I've got A levels to do!

GRAEME (*chiding gently*). Have you? This year?

GIANNA. Next year. And she gets away without serving in the café.

GRAEME. Oh come on. She's only a kid.

GIANNA. So were we only kids and we had to do it.

NONNA. Poor you.

GIANNA. Yes, poor me!

GRAEME. You could still make your Gran a cup of tea. You should be good at it.

GIANNA. Don't you start! Don't be taken in by her. (*Referring to* ANASTASIA.) I have to pick up her smelly knickers and her smelly bloody socks and iron her smelly gymslips and . . .

ANASTASIA (*cutting in*). Mum irons my gymslips, actually!

GIANNA. Oh! That's all right then, if Mum does it.

ANASTASIA (*sulkily*). Yeah.

GRAEME. Gianna!

GIANNA (*to* GRAEME *as she exits*). You could at least offer to come with me . . .

GRAEME. In a minute. This is really nice. (*Referring to the music.*)

NONNA. The other side's beautiful. Puccini.

GRAEME (*nodding inanely*). Italian. Really nice.

NONNA. You're a bit fat. (*Laughs.*) Do you like a macaroni?

GRAEME (*taken aback*). Uh . . .

NONNA. Why doesn't Gianna bring you to supper? I make lovely gnocchi.

ANASTASIA. He's not fat. (*To* GRAEME.) You're not.

GRAEME. I don't mind.

NONNA. I'll tell you something – when I was Gianna's age, I was thin, terrible thin! Had to cut my wedding ring in half – really! – and join it back together. My fingers were so thin. And then babies . . . (*sighs.*) Had to have the ring sawn off my finger and the bits put back, baby by baby, bit by bit, until the original size. See? (*Shows ring finger.*)

ANASTASIA. That photograph of you in the hall – the coloured-in one. You're really pretty in that.

GRAEME. What photograph's this?

ANASTASIA. Come on, I'll show you. (*To* LEONORA.) Can I show him the wedding photograph too? From your bedroom? (*Going out.*)

GRAEME. When was that?

NONNA. 1926. In Italy. Valvori.

GRAEME. I bet it was an incredibly long exposure. (*To* NONNA.) Can you remember how long you had to keep still? I bet the photographer counted – oh twenty. Can you remember?

NONNA. No.

GRAEME. Pity. (*Going out.*)

ANASTASIA. Graeme!

GRAEME. Excuse me.

Alone NONNA *takes a swig from a sherry bottle, and then, settling herself into a relaxed position, falls asleep. The music continues.* GIANNA *comes in with tea tray. Sees* NONNA *asleep.*

GIANNA (*cheerfully*). Typical.

She sits down and drinks the tea herself. GRAEME *comes back in.*

GRAEME. Hi.

GIANNA (*referring to* NONNA). So much for the tea.

GRAEME. We've just been looking at those old photographs of her. Everybody in your family looks exactly the same. There's one with your Gran and Grandad dancing and he's all in black, little white tie, straight out of the Godfather.

GIANNA. Tell her. She'll love that.

GRAEME. And I really fancy her in it. Dead sexy.

GIANNA. Is she? What? More than me?

GRAEME. Dunno. Can't remember. Let's see now.

He starts kissing her. ANASTASIA *enters.*

ANASTASIA. Yuk!

GIANNA *pushing* GRAEME *off.*

ANASTASIA. She's got a cold, you know.

GIANNA. I love you too.

ANASTASIA (*giggling*). Gran's showing her drawers again.

GIANNA. Well at least she's wearing some. (*Laughs.*) Honestly, she's an absolute liability. Was she smoking do you know? You've got to watch for that. She's always practically setting herself on fire. It's a miracle she doesn't – the amount of alcohol she consumes – really! – she's a highly inflammable lady. (*Laughs.*) I'd better cover her up.

ANASTASIA. I'll do it.

GIANNA. The thing is, Stacey, if you think you're being good it doesn't count.

ANASTASIA. It does! (*Goes over to the sleeping* LEONORA.)

GIANNA. Fine. (*To* GRAEME.) She thinks doing that will get her two weeks off purgatory.

ANASTASIA. It might! I got Grandfather ten years off yesterday. With one decade of the rosary. It's in my missal.

GIANNA (*shaking her head. To* GRAEME). The Catholic Church! Actually, while you're at it you'd better wake her up. She'll be annoyed if she misses her tea.

ANASTASIA. OK. (ANASTASIA *is looking to prove she's mischievous. She takes a jug of water and holds it over* NONNA's *head.*) Shall I?

GIANNA. Stacey!

ANASTASIA *dips her finger into the jug and flicks water at the sleeping* NONNA *who wakes with a start. Her shawl slips from her shoulder. She's furious.* ANASTASIA *giggles stupidly.*

NONNA. Eh! Aiee! Anastasia! Bitch! You come here! I'll bash you! Bagasce!

GIANNA. Stacey, say sorry, you idiot!

NONNA. Get her! I'm wet! Catch her!

ANASTASIA *still giggling, embarrassed, runs out of the room.*

NONNA. I'm wet. Cow. Bitch.

GIANNA. It's OK Gran. She was just showing off. It wasn't much. A few drops. Come on, I'll dry you off.

NONNA (*tearful*). My scarf's wet. Why did she do that? I was asleep.

GIANNA. She was just showing off in front of Graeme. Here's your tea. Relax.

GRAEME. Shall I go and tell her off or something?

GIANNA (*sharp*). No, you should go home. It's late.

NONNA *starts wiping her face with the red scarf, muttering to herself.*

GRAEME (*offended*). And what's that supposed to mean? God! (*Sighs.*) Night then Mrs M.

GIANNA. Drink your tea, Gran, it'll get cold.

They exit.
NONNA *ties the scarf around her head.*

Scene Four

The past. England, 1929. Outside the Mare house.

ALFREDO *leads* LEONORA, *pregnant, down the steps. She is blindfolded with a bright handkerchief.*

LEONORA. Can I look?

ALFREDO. Not yet.

LEONORA. We're outside! Why have you brought me outside?

ALFREDO. Don't be so impatient.

LEONORA. The baby. Alfredo!

ALFREDO. Don't worry. I've got you. I won't let you fall.

LEONORA. Not this baby stupid. Theresa. What if she wakes up and we're both outside?

ALFREDO. A minute. She'll be all right. Anyway, shut up, we're here. Now, I'm going to take off your blindfold but don't open your eyes until I say. (*Does so.*) Right. Now, ready?

LEONORA. Yes. Can I open my eyes?

ALFREDO. Yes!

She does so.

LEONORA. It's dark. It's night. What am I supposed to be looking at?

ALFREDO. This.

LEONORA. What's this?

ALFREDO. The car, mamma! The car!

LEONORA. What car? This car?

ALFREDO (*waving his arms in a flapping gesture of impatience*). Aiee! Which car, which car! Questa macchina qui! Questa stupenda favolosa Alfa Romeo! Which car!

LEONORA. Ah that car! The one you drove home in. And?

She pinches his cheek, teasingly.

ALFREDO. How did you know?

LEONORA. I told you. I saw you drive home in it.

ALFREDO. How did you know to look?

LEONORA. Because you were late. Because I stood in the window waiting for you to come. Because I miss you.

ALFREDO. Okay.

LEONORA. Because you're always late home these days.

ALFREDO. Okay, okay. You can smell the leather, Leonora. So soft.

LEONORA. It's a beautiful car.

ALFREDO (*grunts irritated*). I knew you would be like this.

LEONORA. Like what?

ALFREDO. Criticizing me. You can never let me enjoy anything. I work and I struggle. And I mean why do you think I'm late home?

LEONORA. I don't know. Remind me.

ALFREDO. And what does that mean I'd like to know?

LEONORA. It means good you've got a new car.

ALFREDO. We've! We've!

LEONORA. Yes – we've got a new car. And I'm pleased we can afford it because I'm sure I don't know where the money came from to pay for it. Anyway, yes, good, fine. I have to go in now. Your daughter's crying.

ALFREDO. I can't hear anything.

LEONORA. No. You never can.

She turns to go back in.

ALFREDO. Aiee. Leonora. Leonora!

She comes back.

LEONORA. What?

ALFREDO. Mamma. Let's go for a ride, huh? Scusi, eh? Come on. We can put Theresa in the carry cradle.

LEONORA. It's too late. It's too dark.

ALFREDO. Come on.

LEONORA. It's too cold.

ALFREDO. This car has heating. It's an oven with the heater on.

LEONORA. Then it'll be too hot.

ALFREDO. Da mi pazienza!

LEONORA (*relenting*). Okay. (*Laughs suddenly*). Hey, your face!

ALFRED (*sulkily*). What's wrong with my face?

LEONORA (*putting her finger to his mouth*). I'll sit the baby on your lip.

ALFREDO. It's important for me to have a good car. Who's impressed – in this country – gl'inglesi – who's impressed with a man comes to do business with you driving a jalopy? Now I'm a serious proposition.

LEONORA. OK, Mr Serious Proposition, take us for a ride and don't spare the horses.

ALFREDO. OK, wife.

LEONORA. OK, husband.

She turns to go back in.

ALFREDO. I'll take you up on the hill and show you the city at night. Eh Leonora, che meraviglia! Hundreds of tiny lights, each one a house.

LEONORA. Oh no. We want to go to the seaside. And don't say it's too dark –

ALFREDO. But that's miles.

LEONORA. And this car can't go for miles or what? I want to walk on a beach with you. Like when we were courting.

ALFREDO. Right. We'll go to the beach. What the hell!

LEONORA. I'll get Theresa.

ALFREDO. And get a coat! For me, too. We'll freeze to death. (*Shakes his head, then looks admiringly at the car. Walks its length proudly, breathing in the smell of paint and leather.*)

LEONORA *puts on a coat or shawl or both.* ALFREDO *puts on a trenchcoat.*

The Beach. They walk for a bit, arms round each other, LEONORA *pulls them to one side suddenly, mischievously.*

ALFREDO. Eh! What are you doing?

LEONORA. I want to get my dress wet again! Do you remember?

ALFREDO. I remember. Lunatic!

LEONORA. I remember standing – this is afterwards – standing in your bedroom, in your dressing-gown – pinned up to the throat, ha!, with you pressing my dress, getting the creases out, that terrible old iron, and you telling me to stop howling.

ALFREDO. Which you didn't.

LEONORA. Imagine you ironing now!

ALFREDO. It had flowers along the bottom.

LEONORA. Yes.

ALFREDO. Tiny embroidered flowers. Lovely.

LEONORA. How do you remember that?

ALFREDO. Kissing the hem of your dress. I remember that vividly.

LEONORA. Getting home late thinking my mother would notice.

ALFREDO. Why? Nothing had happened.

He tries to kiss her legs as he holds the hem of her dress. She, embarrassed, shrugs him off. He looks distressed, hurt. A familiar rebuff.

She moves away. She stands, looking out to sea, she's happy. Unaware of his frustration.

LEONORA (*delighted*). I want to come here every night! The air! It's beautiful. The sea! I feel alive. As if someone slapped my face. Suddenly awake. (ALFREDO's *quiet.*) Hey Alfredo. Fredo!

ALFREDO. Si, si vengo. (*He goes to her, puts his feet under hers and walks along the shore daring the waves.*) Attenzione! Attenzione! (*This is a happy sing-song voice. But the moment passes and they are left silent.*)

ALFREDO. My ears are cold.

LEONORA. I'll kiss them. (*She does so.*)

ALFREDO. Mmm. That's nice. But they're still cold.

LEONORA. I'll rub them. (*She does so.*)

ALFREDO (*distant suddenly*). Listen, what about Theresa?

LEONORA. Oh, she's fast asleep. She'll be fine in your new car. It's so warm! Anyway come on I want to play!

ALFREDO. Now what? Play what?

LEONORA. Hopscotch!

ALFREDO. Madonna! It's dark . . . Leonora . . . How can we play hopscotch?

LEONORA. Easy. Anyway. You can cheat and I won't know. Wonderful. Here's a stone. That's yours.

ALFREDO. Aiee! I don't want to.

LEONORA. Because you don't know the rules.

ALFREDO. Because I don't know the rules.

LEONORA. I'll teach you.

ALFREDO. You're crazy.

LEONORA. Yes.

ALFREDO. And your stomach?

LEONORA. My stomach's fine. We'll have a gymnast.

She marks out a hopscotch pitch.

ALFREDO. I want him to be a singer. Or a footballer.

LEONORA. Him!

ALFREDO. OK. Or her.

LEONORA. I'll start. Watch me!

She throws a pebble.

Scene Five

The present. England. The Beach. NONNA *is about to throw her hopscotch marker.*

ANASTASIA. No! Me first!

She starts to play. They laugh. She makes good progress until she hits the wrong square.

NONNA. No! Wrong square!

ANASTASIA. OK. Now you.

NONNA. I used to be terrific at this!

She can't hop.

NONNA. Oh.

ANASTASIA. Go on.

NONNA. No. I put my foot down.

ANASTASIA. Have another go.

NONNA. I can't. Hopeless. No matter. I'll watch. Where did you get to?

ANASTASIA. Here. Right.

She carries on. NONNA *watches for a while.*

NONNA (*during this,* ANASTASIA *plays, exclaiming, laughing, commenting, etc.*). Do you know something? It makes me laugh. The nicer the day the more you want to go in the water and the farther you have to walk to get to it! And when the weather's bad . . . it's just the opposite. Makes me laugh, I can't swim anyway. I just like the water. The feel of it. Up around my legs. I think I must have been a fish in another life. There are people who believe you have lots of lives to get better in. Lots of chances. I don't think that's against God. What do you think?

ANASTASIA. What? Hang on. Yes! (*She completes the circuit.*) I did it! Did you see? I did it!

NONNA. Yes, darling. Well done. Anastasia, walk out there to the water will you? I want to see how far it is.

ANASTASIA runs off.

NONNA. No don't run! I want to see how long it takes to walk there. (*Hums, then loud.*) Anastasia! Anastasia! That's enough. It's too far for me. (*Normal voice as ANASTASIA comes running back.*) I couldn't walk all that way. Not on these old legs. Much too far. In a few days the tide'll be nearer and then I'll get in properly. But not today.

ANASTASIA is back with her. She picks up her bags. NONNA touches her cheek.

NONNA. You're just like your grandfather, Alfredo. That expression. Soft. Both of you gullible. Much too gullible. Shall I tell you something? You mustn't trust everybody. That's what he did. That's what I've done. Gullible. So, don't you forget these things your old Nonna tells you. (*She sighs.*) Mmm, the water in these little pools is so warm. Look! You can see your face in it. (*ANASTASIA looks.*) Sometimes I think I can see other people's faces. Sometimes I stare and stare until they come.

Scene Six

The past. England, 1930.

ALFREDO *and* JULIA JARRETT. *Outside a concert hall.* JULIA *impatiently pacing,* ALFREDO *arrives looking sheepish and shifty.*

JULIA. Christ, Alfredo! You're impossible!

She moves towards him.

ALFREDO (*backing off, turning away, and trying hard to look as if he were waiting for someone else*). Uh, don't. I think I saw someone I know. (*Continuing to look away.*) Sorry. Hello. I love you. Don't acknowledge me please.

JULIA. Christ!

ALFREDO. Please don't, Julia.

JULIA. Don't what? I'm not doing anything.

ALFREDO. No. Use that word. I hate the way you use it.

JULIA (*sighing*). Oh.

ALFREDO. Sorry. (*Dismissing himself.*) I know.

JULIA. Can we go in please?

ALFREDO. Right.

JULIA. I mean, the overture will have started.

ALFREDO (*looking about him*). Right.

JULIA. Alfredo, I really can't manage this, you know.

ALFREDO. No, of course, just that I'm convinced I knew him. Friend of my father's.

JULIA. It's a big hall. There's bound to be someone you know. (*Pause, then archly.*) Shall we go in separately?

ALFREDO. Yes. Perhaps that's best.

JULIA. I was joking. No, OK. Right I'm going in. Enjoy the concert – you know – in case we don't get to talk.

ALFREDO (*still not looking at her*). Right. See you in there. Thanks. I love you.

JULIA. You could always wear glasses and a false nose.

ALFREDO. Sorry?

JULIA. You could always wear glasses and a false nose.

ALFREDO (*feels dim, muttering*). Non mi prendi un giro!

JULIA *works her way along a packed row in the theatre and sits down. She removes her coat and glances at a programme. It's for a Verdi or Puccini opera. A big moody duet is in full flight.*

ALFREDO *performs the same operation before sitting next to JULIA without acknowledging her in any way. After a few bars staring steadfastly to the front, he edges his hand under JULIA's skirt and between her legs.*

JULIA *stares ahead as if focussing on the music. After a few bars she sighs and her hand works its way under the overcoat folded on ALFREDO's lap.*

They stare ahead. ALFREDO hums a line of music.

JULIA *and ALFREDO leave as they arrive and stand outside the door which becomes the entrance to a lavatory.*

JULIA (*nervously, giggling*). I can't!

ALFREDO (*impatient, giggling*). Come on. Why not?

JULIA. What if somebody comes? I can't.

ALFREDO. Come on, Julia. Before the interval.

JULIA. Can't we just talk?

ALFREDO. We can't talk here. It's so difficult – you know – if we are seen together . . .

JULIA. Okay, well let's go in there and talk.

She gestures to WC.

ALFREDO. OK. (*Trying to get her in.*)

JULIA. Oh yes! I know your talk.

ALFREDO. Well, and so? I want you. Is that bad? That I want you the whole time?

JULIA (*smiling, shaking her head*). It's wonderful.

ALFREDO (*smiles*). It's fantastic.

JULIA. Come on then. We're completely mad.

ALFREDO. I know.

JULIA. I've never done this before.

ALFREDO. Right. (*Thinks.*) Is that true? (JULIA *nods.*) If you had, Julia, I couldn't. Not if you'd done it before.

JULIA (*touches his lip*). You great baby. (*Laughs.*) Come on!

They go in and close the door behind them.

Verdi. Buzz of conversation.

Man paces outside the WC with a cigarette. ALFREDO suddenly comes out, obviously trying initially to pretend he's been alone, sees the waiting man and moves into plan B.

ALFREDO (*briskly*). I'm a doctor. Excuse me. There's a woman in here who's had an asthma attack. I'm going to take her to my surgery.

Then JULIA appears as ALFREDO turns back in. She sees him and the man and moves into plan C as the man moves forward with ALFREDO, trying to help.

JULIA (*briskly*). Ah. It's uh quite all right. Thank you. My husband is going to take me to the hospital.

ALFREDO and JULIA move past the man, arm in arm. ALFREDO whispers to JULIA who begins to laugh hysterically.

JULIA (*over her shoulder to the bewildered man*). No, actually my husband is a doctor himself.

Scene Seven

The present. England. Beach.

NONNA *comes in with her bags,* ANASTASIA *behind her.*
NONNA *sits down to take off her shoes.* ANASTASIA *scampers off.*

NONNA. Do you know what I was thinking this morning? I don't
like the Holy Mass anymore. Not in English anyway. In the old
days, with the Latin, you used to get the gist. Just the gist. And
then you could fill in the rest with what you wanted. So if you'd
been telling lies or something then the Epistle or the Gospel would
be about not telling lies because God knows when you're telling
lies. That way it meant something to everybody. You see, because
one person would be feeling sorry for swearing and then perhaps
another for stealing something, and all the time I would be feeling
sorry because God had heard me telling lies. I didn't tell very
many. But you get my drift. I mean, today, if the priest starts
talking about coveting thy neighbour's wife . . . what does that
mean to me? The English spoils it. That's why I fall asleep if you
want to know. No magic. (*As she speaks, she takes off her shoes
and lights a cigarette.* ANASTASIA *scrabbles in the sand.*) What
are you doing Anastasia? Show me.

(ANASTASIA *smiles and produces three or four cockles.*) Cockles!
(*She hands them to her.*) Thank you my darling. I'll have them for
breakfast. (*Laughs, and is amused as she continues.*) With my
dandelion and garlic.

ANASTASIA *roots about in the bags and finds a deflated beach
ball. A large one. She takes it out and begins to inflate it.*

NONNA. The tide's coming in, I think. Is it? There's a story about a
man, a King . . . who tried to stop it. The tide. (*Laughs.*) He tried
to stop the tide coming in. He couldn't though. We can't now. It's
all to do with the moon. Nature. (*A couple walk along the shore
hand in hand, played by* JULIA *and* ALFREDO. LEONORA
watches them strangely.) Nature is a woman, you see Anastasia.
She makes everything happen. She makes everything happen and
men use her. And even when men abuse her she just keeps on
starting it all up, all over again. A woman with no memory and no
morals. It's not true that women are weak. It's just that they make
the same mistakes again and again. No. Men are weak. (*She
extinguishes the cigarette. Speaks sadly, watching the couple.*) Is it
getting colder, do you think? The sun's gone in.

ANASTASIA *has inflated the beach ball and throws it to her. It
passes between them until* NONNA *completely misses an*

ambitious throw from ANASTASIA *which bounces off in the direction of the couple. The man bends down to pick it up, smiles, and tosses the ball back to* ANASTASIA.

ANASTASIA. Thanks.

The couple stroll off. ANASTASIA *tries to throw the ball to* NONNA.

NONNA. No, darling. No more, I'm tired. (*Looks at her watch.*) We better go soon. You have school.

They begin to pack up.

(*Stoically.*) This is my life now. This beach. These walks. What will I do when you don't want to come anymore? Don't say it won't happen. One day you won't come anymore – that's all. I think about that time. When you're too big to want to spend time with me. That's the way of things.

Scene Eight

The past. England, 1932.

ALFREDO *and* JULIA.

JULIA *faces the audience with a saucepan which she stirs with a large wooden spoon.* ALFREDO *comes up behind her and starts kissing her neck.*

JULIA. Get off.

ALFREDO. No.

JULIA. Thought you were hungry.

ALFREDO. I am. (*Nibbles neck.*) Mmm. Delicious.

JULIA (*shivers*). You mustn't do that. (*Meaning please do that.*)

ALFREDO. I know.

JULIA. I can't concentrate on two things at once.

ALFREDO's *hands come round to cup* JULIA's *breasts.*

ALFREDO. I lay awake last night, the whole night, trying to remember the feel of your breasts in my hands.

JULIA. Well, you could have lain awake the whole night feeling them. It's your choice.

His hands disppear. JULIA *smiles thinly and concentrates on stirring.*

JULIA. Do you still love her?

ALFREDO (*moving away. Struggling*). She's my wife.

JULIA. What does that mean?

ALFREDO. She had the girls. She got old having my children. Her stomach – you know – hundreds of tiny lines, little white fish. I did that.

JULIA. I'm not talking about guilt. I'm talking about love. Because if you do, Alfredo, I don't want you to stay here. I want you to go.

ALFREDO. I love you Julia. I look at you and then I look at her.

JULIA. And?

ALFREDO. She needs me. I need you. (*Frustrated.*) Se eri Italiano mi capiresti.

JULIA (*frustrated at his Italian*). Don't do that. (*She turns to him.*) Look, I have to know if there's a marriage. If there's something that works, that's alive, then . . . (*Turns back.*) then I don't want you to come here.

ALFREDO *lays his head on her shoulder. Pauses.*

ALFREDO. How do you tell? In the bed, you know, there's nothing. For her. For me. Nothing. With you . . . Look, my hands, they're trembling.

JULIA *is weeping a little.* ALFREDO *touches her eyes.*

ALFREDO (*gently*). Hey! (*He tastes his fingers.*) What are you doing? You want to put some more salt in the sauce? Is that it?

She sobs and grins at the same time.

ALFREDO. Your taste. I can taste you for days after we've been together.

He puts his feet under hers and they begin to dance around the room. She leaning back into him, still carrying the saucepan.

JULIA. This is really hot, you know,

ALFREDO. Put it down.

JULIA *hands the saucepan to* NONNA *who remains on stage throughout.*

NONNA. I could smell her off him for days. Perfume. I couldn't afford perfume.

ALFREDO *and* JULIA *enjoy dancing together.*

ALFREDO. We only have one shadow.

JULIA. Where? We haven't got a shadow.

ALFREDO. I know, but if we did have, we'd only have one!

JULIA. You're a twit.

ALFREDO. Yes.

They kiss.

NONNA. She was a sly bitch, a bit of glamour painted on. Bait. Like a juicy worm, flesh with a hook through.

She demonstrates by making a ring with one hand and poking a finger through.

JULIA. You know, before you arrive, I promise myself it's for the last time. How long can this go on? Stolen moments. Furtive. Awful. But then I see you and I don't know why, I melt. I don't want to need you but I do, I long for you.

ALFREDO. I know. For me too. I try to stop. But I can't. You're my thrill, Julia.

JULIA. My lover.

ALFREDO. I love it when you talk like that.

JULIA. I love you. When you leave my life stops. That's the truth.

ALFREDO. When I leave my life stops.

JULIA. Then don't leave me. Leave her.

Scene Nine

The past. England, 1939. The Mare House.

The bed. LEONORA, ALFREDO, darkness. Rustling. ALFREDO lights a bedside lamp and roots about for a cigarette. He gets out of bed, appears very piqued. LEONORA lies face down into the pillows. ALFREDO clears his throat and sighs repeatedly, forcing the smoke out through his teeth. LEONORA sandwiches her head between top and bottom pillows, as if to shut off the light and his bitterness.

ALFREDO. Why do you punish me like this, Leonora, hmm? You know I can't sleep. That I don't. Night after night beside you. Nothing. I tremble. Do you know that? I shake. (*Checks his hands.*) The frustration. Is it so much to ask? Minutes. To give a few minutes of yourself to let me sleep peacefully? It's what tortures me – that for a few minutes of your bed I could sleep the whole night. It's a sin. To deny me. I hope you confess it.

LEONORA (*through the pillows*). I'll confess my sins. You confess yours.

ALFREDO. What!

LEONORA. You heard me. And don't shout, you'll wake the children.

ALFREDO. I'd like to know what you mean by that?

LEONORA. Oh please, don't bother.

ALFREDO. No. I'd like to know what you meant by that remark?

He tries to yank the pillow off her head. She clings onto it.

LEONORA. Please just leave me alone.

ALFREDO. Me! Me! Me! That's all you think about. Io! io! io!

LEONORA (*wounded, sarcastic*). Certo sicura eh! sicuro.

ALFREDO. Don't speak to me like that. (*He lifts the pillows.*) I know what you're thinking! Like you're some bloody saint. (*Thumps the pillow.*) Well you're fucking not! You try! You try selling amusement machines when there's a fucking war breaking out. And that's another thing. Those bastards. They'll lock me up, you know, they could intern me. And yet still (*Thumping the pillow.*) you do this.

GIOIA (*off*). Mamma?

LEONORA. I hope you're satisfied. (*Sits up and calls to the child.*) It's all right Gioia. It's all right. Go back to sleep, darling. (*To* ALFREDO.) You only have to look at me and I get pregnant. My insides are like broken glass from you. That poor child calling me – born with the rent man at the bottom of the stairs shouting at Theresa for his money and where were you? On business. On business! Business that costs us money.

ALFREDO. Don't start.

LEONORA. And now I manage to scrape together enough to feed us and to clothe us and you want me to confess. You talk about minutes! (*Sighs.*) You talk about minutes. Oh yes.

ALFREDO. You don't have to get pregnant. We could just – uh – cuddle.

LEONORA. Alfredo, there's money in the tin. Why don't you go and buy a cuddle?

He hits her. She puts her hand to her lip.

ALFREDO. You made me do that.

LEONORA. There are all kinds of whoring – pay with pound notes, pay in kind. No different. It's a whore.

ALFREDO. You made me do that.

LEONORA. You made me old and ugly. What's a drop of blood?

ALFREDO. Don't blame me. You let yourself go. There's no need.

LEONORA. You're right. It's easy to be beautiful. Take away the children and the work and the worry and the lies and the humiliations and it's the simplest thing in the world to be beautiful. Or love. Everyone who is loved is beautiful. Easy.

ALFREDO. I do love you. But you won't let me. How can I love you when you won't let me?

LEONORA. I refuse to cry. I'm not going to cry anymore for you. I promised myself.

ALFREDO. You'd like me to go, wouldn't you? You want me to leave you?

LEONORA. Do what you like, Alfredo. You will anyway.

GIOIA (*off*). Mamma, I can't sleep.

LEONORA (*opening the door*). Ssh now – you'll wake the others. Go to sleep.

She closes the door and slowly slides down it, the entire length, finishing crouched on the floor, her face in her hands. ALFREDO starts to scratch his head violently, helplessly. The silence is punctuated only by huge sobs from LEONORA.

ALFREDO (*crooning*). Hey Mamma, don't cry. Ssh. Don't cry. It's OK. I'm not going anywhere. Ssh. I'm not going. Don't cry, eh?

He starts to kiss her head again, whispering, until eventually she looks up and he kisses her eyes and then the blood on her lips.

ALFREDO. Mamma. Come on. Let's go to bed. Eh? Sshh.

He helps her up and half carries her to the bed.
He puts out the light. They embrace in the dark. He moves on top of her.

ALFREDO. I love you. It's OK. It's OK.

GIOIA (*off*). Mamma!

Long pause. Rustling. ALFREDO groans. Long pause.

GIOIA (*off*). Mamma.

LEONORA *goes to disentangle herself from the embrace.* ALFREDO *pulls her back. Determined.*

GIOIA (*off*). Mamma!

ALFREDO (*thwarted*). Ma Porco Dio!

Scene Ten

The past. England, 1939.

The bed. ALFREDO *packing.* LEONORA *sitting.* JULIA *pacing. The scene is played as if the two dialogues are being delivered independently.* NONNA *sits on the bed.*

JULIA. The hours and hours I have wasted. Waiting by telephones. Waiting for you to call me. Not knowing whether you were leaving or staying or what.

ALFREDO. I know.

LEONORA. Night after night. Not a whisper, could have been dead all of us for all you knew.

GIOIA (*off*). Mamma . . .

JULIA. Fredo, I don't want you to come to me, not dragging your guilt behind you. I don't want that dragging us down.

ALFREDO. I know.

LEONORA. Don't stay out of charity, Alfredo. I won't have you pitying me.

ALFREDO. I know.

LEONORA. I pity her if you want to know.

NONNA. You're a sick man.

LEONORA. Only a sick man would desert his family for a slut. I pity her. She must be simple. (*Tapping her forehead.*)

JULIA. I will not be your vice. I will not be your sin. I will not be confessed! If you're ashamed of me, give me up! No! If you're ashamed of me I'll give you up!

ALFREDO. I know.

LEONORA.
NONNA.   I know. You always say that.
JULIA.

JULIA. As if it explained everything.

NONNA. As if it was enough.

ALFREDO. What am I supposed to say?

LEONORA.
NONNA.   Don't say anything.
JULIA.

ANASTASIA (*off*). Gran?

LEONORA. Do you pity me?

JULIA. Do you really want to be with me? Well? Yes or no?

ALFREDO. No! Yes! No! Look, I do love you. I do. I do love you. Believe me.

LEONORA.
NONNA.   And what about her?
JULIA.

LEONORA. Do you tell *her* you love her?

JULIA. Do you tell her you love her?

ALFREDO. No!

ANASTASIA (*off*). Granny?

   JULIA *and* LEONORA *speak together.*

JULIA. Because if you do, Fredo, you can take your charm and your lap-dog eyes and your shrugs and your vows and your promises and your blasted operas . . . because I will not be treated as if I were a simpleton or an object . . .

LEONORA. I don't believe you, you would say no to anything to wriggle your way out of trouble . . . you would agree, to anything . . . your lies, you're a terrible liar! Am I supposed to swallow your trumped-up excuses night after night? Do you think I'm an ornament?

ALFREDO (*cutting them off*). Look! I can't hear myself think! The thing is – I look at her (*Looks at them both.*) and then I look at you.

   He looks at them both.

LEONORA.
NONNA.   And?
JULIA.

ALFREDO (*reaches inside his suitcase and starts to produce bingo balls*). On the red: number five. Kelly's Eye: number one. Clickety-click: sixty six. Me and you: number two.

ANASTASIA (*off*). Granny!

   NONNA *seems to hear* ANASTASIA *for the first time, gets up from the bed and leaves the room.*

Scene Eleven

The past. England. JULIA's *flat.*

ALFREDO *sits with* JULIA *on the bed. He takes some clothes out of the suitcase.*

JULIA. And the children? Did you say goodbye?

ALFREDO. Yes, I said goodbye. Of course I said goodbye. Everyone was crying. I walked down the stairs and out of the door and the noise was like a thousand seagulls flying above my head. It was the worst thing I ever did.

JULIA *lies back on the bed.*

JULIA. Thanks.

ALFREDO. What?

JULIA. Forget it.

She begins putting his clothes back into the suitcase.

ALFREDO. What are you doing?

JULIA. If it was the worst thing you ever did then don't do it? Everything with you is so *loud*, so . . . (*She can't find the word.*) Seagulls! It's not Verdi. You know . . . you've left your wife. You wanted to, that's all.

ALFREDO. She said she'd kill herself, that she'd kill them all.

JULIA. Well yes! I'm sure she does feel pretty badly about it. What did you expect? Flowers?

ALFREDO. No.

JULIA. I'm just trying to say it's unlikely she will actually kill anybody. I don't know, I suppose she *is* capable of killing me.

ALFREDO. Oh yes. She could kill you.

JULIA (*considering*). You could have brought the children.

ALFREDO. No.

JULIA. No. Stupid.

ALFREDO (*breaking down during this*). Theresa told me, she said I was, she said I'd ruined their lives and that I was a bad man. My own daughter. Twelve years old.

JULIA. Oh my darling . . . (*They kiss, she strokes his head.*) Poor baby. I was thinking . . . You have so many shirts. Where am I going to put them all? (*She smiles. He smiles. Pause.*) Look . . . they'll . . . Theresa is bound to be upset, all of them. Don't torture yourself. Maybe in time they'll be able to see it from your . . .

ALFREDO (*interrupting her*). Please, can we not talk about it anymore. I don't want to think about it anymore.

ALFREDO *starts to kiss up her leg. Under the cover.*

JULIA. Don't.

ALFREDO *grunts*.

JULIA. Christ.

ALFREDO (*out of desperation*). I need to remind myself why I left.

JULIA (*hurt*). Uh? And it's there, is it?

ALFREDO *continues*.

JULIA (*trying to push him away*). Don't! Christ! And what about me Alfredo, huh? Why've I . . . I mean . . . What do I get? Stories of how Leonora didn't understand you or excite you, of her stretch marks, the fat on her thighs. Hmm? What if my legs get fat? Christ! I said what if my legs? . . .

Scene Twelve

The present. England. Beach.

Seagulls. Child's sandpit. NONNA *and* ANASTASIA *are making sandcastles using little shaped buckets and spades. Neither wears shoes.*

NONNA. It's strange. When that whore took your grandfather away from me, I took to wearing black. I didn't know what to do . . . and Theresa had to do everything. She was like a father to your mother. I was stupid. I would have given him everything each time he came back. But Theresa made me give her the keys to the cash box. She was thirteen. Whenever your grandfather came home she used to leave him an allowance on the mantelpiece, and that was all she would let him have. Two pounds every week. On the mantelpiece. I couldn't bear to see that. See him humiliated like that. I used to take the money off the mantelpiece and put it in his wallet, and put a few shillings into his pocket too. Not for anything really, but just so he could pretend that it was his own money. I was wrong though. It didn't keep him with me. One day he just stopped coming. After we left the café under the railway bridge I only saw him two more times. Walking up the aisle with his daughters. One after the other . . . as if nothing had happened. He was a charming man. I always loved him. Everybody loved him. I do now. I forgave him for everything years ago . . . years ago . . . let me tell you something: I didn't know anything about anything. Not even after we got married. No one ever told me anything . . . I didn't know how to please him in that way. So you see. I blame myself for everything. Not him. I never saw him naked. In all those years I never saw him naked.

JULIA *and* ALFREDO *walk across the sandcastles, destroying them.*

ANASTASIA. Hey!

JULIA *and* ALFREDO *walk straight into the section with* EDUARDO. ANASTASIA's *'Hey' comes seconds before* EDUARDO's *'Imbecile!'*

Scene Thirteen

The past. England, 1941. Eduardo Mare's house.

Dim light of a study. EDUARDO, ALFREDO's *father, is seated in a big leather armchair.* ALFREDO *wears a raincoat, and stands, or rather paces, irritated and embarrassed by his father's tirade.* JULIA *sits, remote, on a wooden chair, smoking.*

EDUARDO. Imbecile! Vieni qui da me con questa donna a chiedermi la mia benedizione? E le tue figle? Ti credi di poter . . .? [You fool! You come to me with this woman to ask for my blessing? In this adultery? And what about your daughters? Do you think you can just . . .?]

ALFREDO (*cutting in*). Papá . . . Non e necessario dirmi quello che ho fatto. Lo so . . . [You don't have to tell me what I've done – I know]

EDUARDO. Non m'interromperre! Come osi! Ho messo al mondo due figli patetici! Uno semina bastardi a dritta e a marica, e l'altro un volgarissimo gaga! Ma che Papá e Papá! [Don't interrupt me! How dare you? Two pathetic sons I've produced. One of them siring bastards right, left and centre and the other a waster and a nothing. Don't 'Papá' me!]

ALFREDO. Talk in English, Papá.

EDUARDO. I'll talk in English all right! What do you want me to say in English different to my Italian? Fine? Marvellous? Talk in English!

ALFREDO. Look Papá. We didn't have to come here.

EDUARDO. Then why did you? Don't tell me you were being polite. You wanted me to be introduced? Is that it? Hello. Goodbye.

ALFREDO. Papá, I need money. I have debts. I owe money here and there . . . not much. I can pay it back, but I need a little to get started. Just to see me right for a few . . .

EDUARDO (*interrupting*). Don't crawl, Alfredo. It sickens me. Tell me how much you want and get out of my sight.

ALFREDO. You don't understand do you? You think luck plays no part in this? With some luck, just a little, I wouldn't be here now.

Everybody has had breaks . . . if it hadn't been for the war I might have been a rich man by now. Some of my ideas . . .

EDUARDO (*interrupting*). Ideas! Ideas! Hai la mania delle idee. [You're sick with ideas]

JULIA. Mr Mare, if you'll let Alfredo have this money, I promise you we shan't trouble you again. We're leaving for Ireland tonight. (*Turns to* ALFREDO.) Alfredo?

ALFREDO. She's right, Papá. I won't be back for more . . . Papá?

EDUARDO *takes out a cheque book and begins to write.*

EDUARDO (*emotionless*). I'm not your papá. When you take this you stop being my son. The ring on her finger, is she already married?

JULIA. My husband died.

EDUARDO (*hands the cheque to* ALFREDO). I haven't put in a number. Let your own conscience decide how much you take from me.

JULIA *gets up to go. She offers a hand to* EDUARDO.

JULIA. Goodbye.

EDUARDO *ignores her.*

ALFREDO. Papá. Please. Try and understand.

EDUARDO *deliberately turns his head away and spits on the floor.*

Scene Fourteen

The beach. The present.

NONNA. What was I doing? Uh, do you know how I knew he'd really gone? I was thinking about him – he used to sing a lot – and – he loved opera and I went to put on one of his gramophone records and he'd taken them. They'd all gone. But by the gramophone was his cigarette case and it had one cigarette in it. So I smoked it.

ACT TWO

Scene One

The past. Dublin, 1945. ALFREDO *and* JULIA's *house. The house is in Dublin. A table laid for three.*

JULIA. She's not coming.

ALFREDO. Of course she's coming.

JULIA. Will you ring the guest house and see if she's left?

ALFREDO. Darling . . .

JULIA. What?

ALFREDO. Don't . . . (*Thinks better of it.*) . . . Nothing.

JULIA (*fragile*). I've cooked lamb. You said she'd like that.

ALFREDO. Yes, she loves it. Yes! At any rate she always used to. Smells marvellous. With vegetables.

JULIA. Yes.

ALFREDO. She won't have eaten lamb for a while, I bet.

JULIA. You should have collected her.

ALFREDO. I told her to take a taxi. I arranged that with Mrs McGoldrick.

JULIA. I have to pick Peter up at ten.

ALFREDO. Oh. Why?

JULIA. Why? Well, because I thought that Gioia would have gone by then and because you know he won't sleep and anyway it's not fair just to dump him. That's why.

ALFREDO. I suppose not but I don't understand this not sleeping business . . . the girls all slept like bears. You think it's natural?

JULIA. What are you saying? That I'm not a good mother?

ALFREDO. Christ!

JULIA. Well what?

ALFREDO. I wasn't talking about you. I was talking about Peter.

JULIA. No. You were talking about babies and them sleeping and that your babies with Leonora all slept well. Maybe her milk was better than my milk. Or what?

ALFREDO. Don't be ridiculous. Anyway, Italian women – it's their vocation. It's in their blood. They feel naked without a child at the nipple or in the belly. It's a racial thing.

JULIA. Sometimes, Fredo, I think you're very dim, you know, because you can hurt so casually – like someone with great flapping feet always kicking shins or, I don't know, treading on everybody. I don't think you mean to.

ALFREDO. I don't understand you when you get like this. You're nervous, aren't you? Of Gioia?

JULIA. I expect so.

ALFREDO. Me too.

JULIA. I'm terrified she'll hate me. I wouldn't blame her. I think I'd hate me.

ALFREDO. If she's rude it's her mother talking. But anyway she won't be, I'm sure. She doesn't know about you.

JULIA. O come on! She knows. Because you all pretend I don't exist doesn't mean they don't know.

ALFREDO. Please Julia, don't do this. Don't be like this.

JULIA. Well I'm nervous, you see, of your daughter. I'd like her to like me. And she won't. But I still have to try, and I still have to smile, and I know that you don't feel you can help. And I'm nervous. That's all.

ALFREDO. I love you.

JULIA. And I love you. And the food's going to be ruined. And it's probably a racial thing with Italian women that they cook better than me too. (*Smiles ruefully.*) Oh, by the way, Peter said Mam again today. And 'burd'.

ALFREDO. What's burd?

JULIA. A thing that flies, I think.

ALFREDO. That boy's going to be a singer . . . Have you heard him laugh? Very musical.

JULIA. His yelling's not so bad either.

   Doorbell.

JULIA. Who's going to go?

ALFREDO. I should really, because officially you don't live here.

JULIA. Where *do* I live officially?

ALFREDO. I don't know.

JULIA. Fine. Well, work on that, will you?

   Doorbell.

JULIA (*to* ALFREDO *as he goes out*). In which case who's cooked?

ALFREDO. You have. That's all right.

JULIA. Oh have I? How nice. And what about the make-up in the bathroom? Is that yours?

ALFREDO (*off*). I moved it.

JULIA (*nodding*). You moved it. Good. Fine.

Greetings off. JULIA *prepares herself.* ALFREDO *returns with* GIOIA.

GIOIA *is 14.*

ALFREDO. Apparently, uh Gioia's been washing her hair . . .

JULIA. Ah, pretty.

ALFREDO. Which explains . . .

JULIA. Yes. Never mind . . .

ALFREDO. Darling, I know you've seen Mrs Jarrett before, but I don't know if you've been properly introduced.

GIOIA. Never.

JULIA. No. Silly, isn't it? I'm Julia. And you're Gioia.

GIOIA. Yes.

JULIA. Yes. Golly you've uh . . . (*Nodding, smiling.*) You've grown. I'm pleased to meet you. You were . . . (*She shows a height with her hand.*)

GIOIA *smiles politely.*

JULIA. Well, I expect you must be famished. All this sightseeing.

GIOIA. I've eaten, thank you.

JULIA. Oh? Really?

ALFREDO. I did say we'd eat together, darling.

GIOIA. I know, Papá, but.

ALFREDO. But what?

GIOIA. Well, I was hungry and I thought that perhaps you might have forgotten you'd said that . . . you know like . . . well, Christmas and things.

ALFREDO. Darling, I don't think Christmas has really got anything to do with dinner tonight. And Julia's cooked you lamb. When was the last time you ate lamb?

JULIA. It doesn't matter, really. Would you just like some tea?

ALFREDO. What about having the meat by itself?

GIOIA. Yes, if you like.

ALFREDO. In a sandwich, eh?

GIOIA. Thank you.

ALFREDO. Because Papá hasn't eaten and you wouldn't want to sit and watch us stuffing ourselves, would you?

GIOIA. No.

JULIA. Well we could perhaps eat later on, Fredo, then Gioia might have, might be more interested in food.

ALFREDO (*irritated*). Oh OK. (*To* GIOIA.) I think you would have been all right to eat a sandwich, wouldn't you?

GIOIA. Yes, of course.

JULIA (*firmly*). That's settled then. Lamb sandwiches later on.

ALFREDO *raises his eyebrows at* GIOIA *who smiles*. ALFREDO *smiles*.

JULIA (*as cheerfully as she can manage*). What? Have I said something funny?

ALFREDO. No. Nothing. (*He smiles.*)

Pause.

JULIA. Your father tells me you went to the zoo today. Was that nice?

GIOIA. Yes thank you.

ALFREDO. We had great fun, didn't we?

GIOIA. Yes.

ALFREDO. The gorilla! (*Makes a face, beats his chest.*) Ugh! Ugh!

Pause.

JULIA. What's your favourite animal?

GIOIA. The duckbilled platypus.

JULIA. Oh. I didn't know they had any.

GIOIA. They haven't.

JULIA. But, still, you like them.

GIOIA. Yes. There was one in a story Mamma used to tell us. Remember Papá?

ALFREDO (*not remembering*). Yes!

JULIA. I see. Are you fond of stories?

GIOIA. Yes.

JULIA. Yes. Me too. Very fond of them.

Silence. JULIA *produces a cardboard box.*

JULIA. By the way, uh, I came across some rather pretty frocks recently and we thought they might . . . they're terribly sweet. I just hope they're the right size. There's one each. Would you like to try yours on?

ALFREDO. Of course she would. These are beautiful dresses. For a princess. Put it on and then we can have a fashion parade, eh? You could be a mannequin, eh Julia? So slim and pretty.

JULIA. Yes. Very pretty. Young lady.

GIOIA. It seems a bit unfair.

JULIA. What's that now?

GIOIA. Doesn't matter.

ALFREDO. What's unfair?

GIOIA. Oh, I don't know!

ALFREDO. Well what did you say it for?

GIOIA. Well, that I should get a dress and a holiday and Theresa gets nothing and has to work and she could have gone to the Academy but Mamma said the uniform was too expensive.

JULIA. I bought Theresa a dress, too, actually.

GIOIA. What? School uniform? Grey?

ALFREDO (*exploding*). It had nothing to do with the cost of a uniform! Of course the money for a uniform could have been found, it goes without saying. I would have gone without personally had it just been a matter of a uniform! Yes, it's too complex to expect you to understand. You see, Daddy had to come to Dublin because of the war and then – do you know how much the fees would have been?

JULIA *tries to intervene.*

Ma lasscia stare! Eo! sto parlando! (*Returning to GIOIA.*) And what about you? Couldn't pay for both of you, could I? (*To* JULIA.) It had nothing to do with the uniform. I don't know where she's had that idea from. (*Pause.*) That's in the past anyway.

GIOIA. The war's over. We had a street party when it finished.

JULIA. Would you like to try the frock on? (*She hands* GIOIA *the box.*)

GIOIA. Is there a bathroom or . . .?

JULIA. Yes, I'll show you.

ALFREDO. No, don't you go. You're a guest. (*To* GIOIA.) I'll take you darling. And isn't that good you can take a present back for

Theresa? We'll have to find something else for her too. What do you think she'd like?

GIOIA (*exiting*). I've bought her a cigarette lighter with a picture of St Patrick on.

ALFREDO (*exiting*). Brava.

JULIA *sits, pensively. Lights a cigarette.* ALFREDO *returns.*

ALFREDO (*cheerfully*). You do fuss! She would have eaten the food. I'm starving. It's her age to be awkward.

JULIA. Is it true about Theresa?

ALFREDO. True? What? That she had a place at the Academy? Look, Julia, it's their mother talking . . . spite . . . I don't blame her. It's hard for us all. I'd love a new suit. I'm sure there are things you need. A couple of years and Theresa'll be wanting to get married, Academy or no Academy. Anyway.

JULIA. Anyway.

ALFREDO. Isn't she beautiful, eh? My girl. I can't believe how beautiful she is. Like a peach.

JULIA (*sad*). Yes, she's remarkable. And Gioia's quite right. The war's over. Will you go back to England?

ALFREDO. I'll go and carve the lamb, shall I?

JULIA. Yes, Alfredo, you go and carve.

ALFREDO. Gioia . . . It's probably . . . I mean she's lives in a different world. She's probably in a love affair. That's it. She's probably in love with some French sailor. Don't be . . . uh . . .

JULIA. Yes, I'm sure that's what's wrong with her.

GIOIA *returns.*

GIOIA (*to* JULIA). Thank you. It's very pretty.

ALFREDO. Well, why haven't you got it on?

GIOIA. It didn't fit.

JULIA (*snapping*). I'll see to the food. (*She goes out quickly.*)

GIOIA. I'll have to get Mamma to alter it a little. Then it'll be lovely, thank you.

ALFREDO (*shouting*). It's only adjustments, Julia! Then it'll be lovely! (*To* GIOIA.) Why didn't you say that? (*To* JULIA, *loudly.*) She says it's perfect.

JULIA (*off*). Lovely.

ALFREDO (*to* GIOIA. *Angry, hard*). Now you go in and say thank

you, properly, to Mrs Jarrett! Not every day somebody gives you a
new dress is it? Now you go in there, you give her a kiss and you
say thank you! Per me! Hai capito? You could help her with the
food.

GIOIA (*distressed, anxious*). OK. (*She puts down the box, hugs him.
A child exits.*)

ALFREDO (*relieved*). Good. Marvellous. (*To the women off.*) Tell
you something I could eat a whole sheep if you're not hungry.

*He pours himself a glass of wine and begins to hum and sing a
romantic Italian song. GIOIA comes through with a vegetable
tureen.*

ALFREDO. Remember this? (*He sings the chorus line. He gestures
for her to join in. GIOIA nods, joins in hesitantly, then happily.
They sing noisily. JULIA comes in. The Mares are singing at the
tops of their voices in Italian.*)

JULIA. Lovely. What is it you're singing?

They sing.

JULIA. Fredo?

They sing and clap.

JULIA (*helpless*). Fredo?

They sing and clap.
JULIA goes out.

Scene Two

The past. The Mare café. Kitchen.

The present. The beach.

JULIA, ALFREDO *and* GIOIA *leave the stage, but do not clear the
table.* THERESA *and* FATHER DAVID COGAN *replace them at
the table,* FR DAVID *bringing with him a plate of almost eaten
spaghetti with a red sauce and a red mouth and napkin with a red
stain. He finishes his spaghetti as* NONNA *comes on to the beach.
She is looking for* ANASTASIA. *The past and the beach present
are played simultaneously.*

NONNA. Anastasia! Anastasia! Ach. (*She sits wearily on the beach
and starts fishing around in her bags for a bottle of sherry.*)
Anastasia, I haven't got time to be playing around. It's late.
There'll be customers and no hot water. I can't carry all these bags
up the hill. Ach, I'm mad. I'm seventy-three. (*Puffs.*) I could retire.

I could ask for what I wanted from your dad. I started the
business. It's in my name. Oh yes, the deeds are in my name; not in
the name of Powell, in the name of Mare. You ask your papá. You
all forget that don't you? Well I don't.

FR DAVID. Ah, God bless you Theresa: that's a wonderful plate of
spaghetti and no mistake. Cheers. Now, Leonora, what's worrying
you? The little shop? You want me to help with the washing up, is
that it?

NONNA. The little café – white front, shutters . . . and a few tables:
four or five, can't remember. Not like now, eh darling? (*Looks
around.*) Anastasia! (*Puffs, irritable.*) Ah managia miseria.

FR DAVID. Gioia? Ah, it seems only yesterday she was making her
first Holy Communion. Sixteen? Is she now? Ah yes, she will be.
Little cherub . . . sixteen, you say? Time flies. Ah, dear me yes,
time flies. Marvellous drop of wine.

THERESA. Mamma?

LEONORA. What?

THERESA. Are you going to speak to Father about Gioia or what?

FR DAVID. Goodness! What's the poor child done?

NONNA (*on the beach*). I used to worry. No father to keep an eye
on them. I used to be sick with worry. And Gioia was such an
imp. Always one for the boys. Always crying over somebody. I
used to insist they always wore their knickers. Even in bed. They
always wore their knickers. Stupid.

FR DAVID. A love letter, Theresa? What does it say? Can I read it?

THERESA. She's got it. She's upstairs in her bedroom refusing to
come out.

FR DAVID. And you know this fellow, Theresa?

THERESA. Vaguely. He comes in the shop.

FR DAVID. Is he Catholic?

THERESA. Yes, but that's not the point.

FR DAVID. Well, it's a start.

THERESA. I mean, of course it's the point, Father, but he's still a
man and he's still capable of getting her into trouble, isn't he? And
Mam's not sleeping over it.

NONNA. Theresa used to get so anxious. Up half the night.

FR DAVID. Gregory Powell! Oh, I know him! He's a nice enough
lad. Harmless. He's in the Guild of St Stephen.

NONNA. The priest was a fool. Well either a fool or very wise, I could never make up my mind. He's dead now, God rest him. But he was a real priest. Not like the ones you get now. Folk guitars and free love.

FR DAVID (*to* LEONORA). I'm sorry, I didn't catch what you said.

LEONORA. I said belonging to the Guild of St Stephen doesn't stop him slobbering over Gioia.

THERESA. Mamma!

FR DAVID. No, your mother's quite right. (*To* LEONORA.) What is it you'd like me to do? I'm not the boy's father.

LEONORA. And I'm not Gioia's. That's the problem.

THERESA. Can't you speak with her, Father? Both of them? Put Mamma's mind at rest?

FR DAVID. This letter. You found it, you say?

THERESA. Yes. In her pillowslip.

FR DAVID. And it's uh provocative, or what? Does he make suggestions?

THERESA. No Father, he didn't write it. She wrote it to him.

FR DAVID. Uh – uh. So how now it was in *her* pillowslip, and not his?

THERESA. Well, I suppose, I don't know. I suppose she hadn't got round to sending it.

FR DAVID. Not urgent, then?

LEONORA. You know what men are like. And she's a child. Gullible. She'd believe anything. You know how easily impressed young girls are.

THERESA. Shall I tell Father what it said?

LEONORA. No!

FR DAVID. She's upstairs, you say. I'll go up then, shall I?

LEONORA. No. I'll get her to come down.

She exits, taking some of the crockery with her.

THERESA. I'll do that Mamma. Leave it.

FR DAVID. Your poor mother. It's a tragedy. When I see these things I wonder why the Lord is so mysterious. That he strikes the innocent. Still, life is short and heaven is long.

THERESA *opens up a tin, takes out a ten shilling note and gives it to him.*

THERESA. Father, would you say Mass, please? For the family intentions.

FR DAVID. Of course, of course. (*Refuses the money.*) There's no need for that. Monday 7.30. I know that's free. Let me just write that in my little book here. The Mare family. (*Notes the feast day.*) Our Lady of Lourdes. All right?

LEONORA *brings in a sullen* GIOIA.

GIOIA. Father.

FR DAVID. Ah Gioia, how are you? Your mother was telling me you were sixteen.

GIOIA. Yes.

FR DAVID. God bless you, you'll all be getting married soon.

LEONORA. We'll leave you two.

They exit. FR DAVID *nods and smiles weakly to them.*

We'll just have a little chinwag, eh Gioia? The two of us?

GIOIA. If you like.

FR DAVID (*to departing women*). Splendid. Good. (*Pause.*) So I gather there's some problem with a letter?

GIOIA. It's not a problem for me.

FR DAVID. Gregory Powell, what do you see in him now? He looks like a labrador.

GIOIA. I know. I don't like him anymore. He's a drip.

FR DAVID. Yes he is. God forgive me for saying it. He's not even in the parish soccer team. (*Delighted.*) What do you mean you don't like him anymore?

GIOIA. Well, I did like him but I don't anymore. He's not even in the soccer team.

FR DAVID. Exactly. So we're agreed on that, are we? He's not suitable.

GIOIA. Not in the least.

FR DAVID. Grand. Now then, this letter. Can I see?

GIOIA. No. It's stupid. It's really childish. I wrote it weeks ago.

FR DAVID. Ah, I've written one or two of those in my life.

GIOIA. Don't believe you.

FR DAVID. It's the truth. When I was at school I was class poet. Wrote anything for anybody. One penny per sonnet. Or tobacco.

The lies I wrote for a penny. You know, lot of romantic hogwash neatly written. (*Laughs*, GIOIA *too*).

GIOIA. The thing is, Father. I'm, not a child anymore and I know that if Papá were here there wouldn't be any of this fuss every time I have a friend.

FR DAVID. Yes, I know.

GIOIA (*thrown*). Oh, well, tell Theresa that, and Mamma.

FR DAVID. You think they need reminding?

GIOIA. Yes! (*Pause.*) No. (*Pause.*) No. (*Pause.*)

FR DAVID (*into preaching mode*). You see, you can be in love with a person and you can be in love with love. No matter what your age. D'you see? Now that's great fun but dangerous. And that's why there's the sacrament of marriage to protect you . . . to give you a foundation.

GIOIA. You mean like my parents?

FR DAVID. Gioia. (*Sighs.*) You light ten candles, one goes out . . . I don't know why . . . and anyway, I'm sure your father will come home. One day he'll snap to his senses. That's my feeling. I pray for it (*Pause.*) Do you hear from him ever?

GIOIA. Oh, sometimes. He sends 'sorry' postcards. Sorry I missed your birthday, sorry I forgot Christmas, sorry to hear you were sick.

FR DAVID. Try not to be bitter.

GIOIA (*meaning it*). I'm not. He's got a terrible memory. He's such a . . . you know, all over the place. And I think SHE probably doesn't remind him.

FR DAVID. Very likely. So, talking of letters. What about a little deal, eh? You give me the letter to the labrador and I'll promise I'll burn it without reading it. Then everyone will be happy. How about that?

GIOIA. Really?

FR DAVID. But listen now, that's between me and thee, though? No blabbing.

GIOIA. No blabbing.

FR DAVID. Grand.

She gives him the letter.

To the fires. (*He sets light to the letter.*)

NONNA (*back on the beach.* ANASTASIA *enters*). He gave your poor mother such a shaking. Made her read the letter out loud to him. I remember her face afterwards, all blotchy, red eyed. (*Shakes her head.*)

The letter is burnt.

GIOIA. Thank you.

FR DAVID. Not at all.

They begin to exit.

FR DAVID. Now – let's think what we can say to your poor mother.

NONNA. The letter, of course, it was to your stupid father. They were married a couple of years later. So stupid. All the fuss and tears and the . . . and then within a few years both girls were married.

Scene Three

The past. England, 1950. Pre, during and post wedding reception.

GIOIA's *wedding reception.* BRUNO, *her uncle, is setting up to take a photograph of the bride with her father.*

ALFREDO. Isn't she beautiful? Two men crying in the church for her.

BRUNO. Fantastic.

GIOIA. Oh Papá, shut up!

ALFREDO. What do you mean, shut up? It's true. No, OK, not two, three. Your father crying too. Floods. Great baby.

She kisses him. He beams.

GIOIA. I'm not beautiful and you know it. Why do you always say that I am?

BRUNO. Shut up you both and keep still.

GIOIA. I've got your nose for a start.

ALFREDO. Nothing wrong with this nose. (*He feels his.*) It's been in the family for generations, eh Bruno? (*Laughs.*) It was good enough for our mamma and her mamma and her mamma and it's good enough for you! (*He tweaks hers.*)

GIOIA. Well I hope I don't pass it on.

BRUNO. You will.

GIOIA. Greg's is much nicer.

ALFREDO. Ach Greg!

GIOIA. What's that supposed to mean?

ALFREDO. Well, if his nose is so wonderful how come he's so keen to marry yours?

BRUNO. I don't think it's her nose he's after!

GIOIA (*drily*). Ha ha.

BRUNO. Aspetta fino a stasera. Eh, Bimbo? (*He's saying 'Wait till tonight'. He thinks that's funny. He sings.*) La signora che fa cosi. Bocca bocca la notte e il di. (*Makes a sexual gesture*).

ALFREDO. Eh! Ma stai t'zit.

GIOIA. Hurry up, Uncle. I've got to go in.

BRUNO. Listen, you keep these for a lifetime. Give me a minute to make them, eh?

GIOIA. Well, at least take some with Greg and Mamma in, too! Where is she? Theresa! Theresa! Dov'é mamma?

THERESA. What?

GIOIA. We want Mamma in this.

THERESA. I'll call her. Don't be long. They want Papá to sing.

ALFREDO. Eh! Sing nothing.

GIOIA. Yes!

ALFREDO. I can't sing anymore.

GIOIA. Not even for me?

ALFREDO. Oh, for you . . . maybe . . . later maybe.

LEONORA *appears. Husband and wife briefly together. Both silent, awkward. A beat.*

LEONORA. Who wants me?

BRUNO. Me. Leonora. I want you.

GIOIA. Come here Mamma and have your photograph taken.

LEONORA. Don't be silly.

THERESA (*following up*). Don't *you* be silly. Do as you're told, and *please*, Uncle Bruno, hurry up! Greg and his family are waiting to start.

BRUNO. Hurry! Hurry! Hurry! What's the matter with everyone? OK, hurry, hurry. Smile . . . watch the blackbird.

THERESA *suddenly throws confetti all over them. Howls and shrieks.*

BRUNO. Wonderful! Fantastic!

The whole company close, elated by the event, burst into a song.

Paesano, Italian, wonderful, stamping of feet. They can be close in song without explanation but when it finishes there is a space again . . . and awkwardness.

BRUNO (*embracing* ALFREDO). My brother.

ALFREDO (*moved, sentimental*). Bruno, I would have emptied my pockets today, even if I had known it would take my last penny, just to have this moment . . . not for me, but for my wife and my children, my girls. (*Clears his throat. To the* PRIEST.) Even God cannot change the past. Not even God. For every dream goes wrong there is a new dream . . . All my life I've been in the shallows . . . (*Shrugs.*) Bogged down in the shallows, treading water . . . never enough to swim (*Laughs, gestures.*) but enough to drown. So I uh dream of oceans. I dream that my girls . . . my darlings . . . Theresa . . . Gioia . . . would each find good husbands, and now, at this moment, that dream comes true. And so (*Vacant. Lost.*) and so (*Weakly.*) Salut (*To* LEONORA.) Salut.

ALL. Salut!

VOICES OFF. Eh! Fredo! Bruno!

BRUNO. Coming! Coming!

They make their way inside.

BRUNO (*a clown*). I want to dance. Who wants to dance with me?

They all go off merrily, save ALFREDO *and* LEONORA *who stand apart and awkward. Dance music off.*

ALFREDO. A good day, eh?

LEONORA. Yes.

ALFREDO. Yes, marvellous. And the weather. This is the most beautiful Spring I can remember.

They dance.

ALFREDO. How are you?

LEONORA. Fine. And you?

ALFREDO. Yes. Fine. I'm fine. And the café? Busy?

LEONORA. Yes, yes it's getting busy now.

ALFREDO. Right.

They dance.

ALFREDO. That girl. What a beauty she is!

LEONORA. She looks like you.

ALFREDO (*proud*). No!

LEONORA. Everyone says so. They always do.

ALFREDO. She's so young to be married. It breaks my heart.

LEONORA. He's a good man. He's steady.

ALFREDO (*nods*). You know what I thought today? What I remembered? Once when I, when I was home . . . years ago . . . she must have been eleven, twelve, I barged into the bathroom and she was washing herself. The door wasn't locked – not used, I suppose, to having a man about – anyway, she was standing at the basin. Nuda. Niente adosso. The light streaming in. And it was the most lovely thing I ever saw. Like a bud, Leonora, opening.

He's stopped dancing for this last, and on 'bud opening' makes a gesture of opening between thumb and fingers. They dance.

ALFREDO. And now she's married. It breaks my heart. What am I saying? I'm happy!

LEONORA. Yes.

ALFREDO. I want them all to be happy. You know that.

They dance.

ALFREDO. And you're fine, you say?

LEONORA. Yes. I'm so happy you were able to come . . . Alfredo . . .

ALFREDO. A man is blessed from God when he has such children.

LEONORA *weeps on his shoulder momentarily.*

ALFREDO (*embarrassed*). Yes, the most beautiful Spring I can remember.

LEONORA. I expect you'll have to be going back? To Dublin?

ALFREDO (*rueful*). Yes. Tomorrow. Stupid really, but the suit. I hired it for the weekend. I'll have to uh . . .

LEONORA. Of course.

They dance.

Scene Three i

ANASTASIA *comes on.*

NONNA. Do you ever say a prayer for your poor grandfather?

ANASTASIA. Sometimes.

NONNA. Do you? Please do, darling. And for me. Pray for me, too. Prayers, you know, they're like savings. You can store them up for purgatory.

ANASTASIA. I know. I read it in my missal. You get years and years off for the rosary – and Novenas. I said a rosary for Grandfather.

NONNA. Good. Good girl, darling.

ANASTASIA. Do you know what I'd like to do?

NONNA. What's that now?

ANASTASIA. Die on the way home from confession.

NONNA. What?

Scene Three ii

Wedding.

BRUNO (*off to* ALFREDO). Eh Fredo! Bimbo! Vieni qui.

ALFREDO (*shrugging apologetically to* LEONORA). Scusa.

ANASTASIA. Yes, die on the way home from confession. Get run over or something.

ALFREDO (*exiting*). I'll come back. I'll be back.

Scene Three iii

The beach.

ANASTASIA. Why not? I mean it! I always walk in the gutter and hope somebody's fallen asleep or's drunk or you know, mad, and runs me over . . . because then I'd be in a state of grace, wouldn't I? I'd go straight to heaven.

NONNA. No!

ANASTASIA. I would! Why wouldn't I?

NONNA. No, I mean – don't think things like that.

ANASTASIA. But what's the point of purgatory if you can avoid it? If grandfather could of?

NONNA *has confetti on her.*

ANASTASIA. Hey you've got sand all over you.

She starts to pick it off.

NONNA. Have I? Oh yes.

ANASTASIA. It's everywhere.

She picks it off.

NONNA. Thank you. Thank you, darling.

Scene Four

The past. Dublin 1963.

JULIA-ALFREDO's *house. Dublin. Evening.* BRUNO *and*
    ALFREDO, BRUNO *in vest,* ALFREDO *in waistcoat and shirt
    sleeves, are playing scoba – Italian cards – on a small round table.
    A bottle of wine is half empty. It is late in the night.* BRUNO,
    *garrulous, tight, is scooping up another round's winnings – small
    change.*

BRUNO. You are the worst card player I ever met, Bimbo – but you
    don't help yourself. You always lay the wrong cards. Still –
    (*Dealing out a new hand.*) I make a few coppers – I don't
    complain. One more round? Eh?

ALFREDO (*tired*). And the next.

BRUNO. Well. What the hell? This is the best thing in life. No
    women, no babies, a game of cards and a few drinks. Fantastic!

    They play for a while. JULIA's *head appears round the door.*

JULIA (*with warmth*). I'm going to bed, Alfredo. Do you want
    anything before I go?

ALFREDO (*with warmth*). No.

JULIA. Bruno?

BRUNO. Do I want anything? Can I have something rude?

JULIA (*sharp*). Sorry?

BRUNO. Nothing. I was joking.

JULIA. I see. (*To* ALFREDO.) Don't bolt the door . . . Peter said
    he'd be late. (*Comes over, kisses his head.*) 'Night.

ALFREDO. Goodnight, I'll be up later.

BRUNO. Buona notte.

    They resume playing.

BRUNO. How old's Peter now?

ALFREDO. Nineteen . . . no twenty . . . twenty last January.

BRUNO. He's a good looking boy.

ALFREDO. Yes.

BRUNO. Not like his old man. (*Slaps* ALFREDO's *back.*) Eh, come
    on! Cheer up! You're getting serious in your old age.

ALFREDO. Ha! Come on, it's your lay.

    They play.

BRUNO. Is he still keen on this teacher nonsense?

ALFREDO. Yes – his mother wants him to carry on.

BRUNO (*sighs*). Si, si – Inglesi.

ALFRED (*nods, rueful*). Si.

BRUNO. I know what I wanted to tell you.

ALFREDO. What's that?

BRUNO. Paulo – you know, my son in Milano – he's just graduated a doctor. What do you think of that! Fantastic. I'll tell you Alfredo, this life's a funny game. Twenty-five years old and I've never seen him. (*Pours himself another drink.*) I mean . . . my own son.

ALFREDO. You don't have to tell me Bruno. I've got grandchildren. I've got two grandchildren. (*He's old, wistful.*) They send me letters. (*Nods to himself.*) I get letters from them.

BRUNO. When you think of it – that old puttana Maria producing me a doctor! – Do you remember all the fuss? . . . Papá – Whew! – I thought he was going to kill me he was so mad. And when he packed her off to Milano I never even wrote to her – not once – and then out of the blue – just like that – 'Dear Bruno, Paulo has graduated a doctor'. Fantastic. And her only a kitchen girl. I don't know . . . a funny business altogether. (*Pause.*) I remember that kitchen.

They play and they laugh.

BRUNO (*muses*). I wonder if she got fat. They all get fat, don't they? (*He begins to laugh – then* ALFREDO – *hysterically, remembering kitchen girls.*) Anita Falcinella! (*Laughs.*)

ALFREDO (*remembering kitchen girls*). Maria Bergamasco!

They laugh. Slapping each other. Coarse gestures. Then suddenly ALFREDO's *face goes white – he begins to choke and rushes from the room.*

BRUNO (*anxious*). Eh Bimbo! Hey! Bimbo!

Scene Five

The past. Dublin, 1963.

ALFREDO *is slumped in the lavatory. His face white. Blood beginning to seep from the corner of his mouth and from his nose.*

ALFREDO (*swallowing, coughing and snatches of breach punctuate all that follows*). I want a priest . . . Bruno. I want a priest . . . Quick. Madonna . . . Aiee Madonna.

BRUNO *hammers on the door.*

BRUNO. Alfredo! Let me in. Are you all right?

ALFREDO. Get a priest, quick, quick, before it's too late. ˈ

BRUNO. Come on Bimbo, open up!

More hammering.

ALFREDO (*hoarse*). Stay out! Stay out! I want to confess. Get a priest. Please. Please.

BRUNO. Christ! (*Shouts.*) Julia! Julia! . . . Look, Alfredo, hang on, can you? Just hang on. I'll be right back. (*Exits.*)

ALFREDO. Don't try and come in . . . it's disgusting.

He wipes his mouth and nose with his sleeve . . . a deep red stain on the cotton.

ALFREDO. Leonora, where are you?

NONNA (*off*). Yes?

JULIA *appears outside the lavatory with* BRUNO.

JULIA. Alfredo! What's going on? Are you all right?

ALFREDO. Julia? Is that you? Quick! Get a priest!

JULIA (*upset, worried*). What's he saying?

BRUNO. He wants a priest.

JULIA. He needs a doctor, not a priest! Can't you get him to let you in?

BRUNO. No. He said no.

JULIA (*to the door*). Darling. Open the door. Please.

BRUNO. He said no!

JULIA. Well, for Christ's sake, break it down!

BRUNO (*suddenly vehement*). No! He's my brother. Do as he says! Ring for a priest! (*To the door.*) We've sent for a priest, Bimbo. He'll be here straight away.

ALFREDO. Oi dio mamma . . . tell him to hurry . . . tell him thank you. (*Vague.*) Is he here? Is he here yet?

BRUNO (*lying*). Yes. He's arrived. He's here. Go ahead.

ALFREDO. Thank God. Bless me, Father, for I have sinned. It is (*Child's voice, tearful.*) O Father, I don't remember how long it is since I last made my confession and I accuse myself of these sins . . . I . . . (*Begins to mumble his confession.*)

Outside, JULIA *returns.*

JULIA. He was asleep. He'll be here in ten minutes. What's he doing? (*Tearful.*) What's he doing? (*To the door.*) Darling!

BRUNO (*distracted*). Sssh! He's making his confession. He's making his confession.

JULIA *slowly and methodically begins to thump on the door with her fist.*

ALFREDO (*continuing to confess*). . . . a pig's appetite . . . a pig in all things . . . forgive me . . . (*Hisses.*) weak like an animal . . . I beg absolution . . . all these years, no peace in my mind . . . forgive me . . . all of them abused . . . (*Coughs. Spasms.*) For these and for all my other sins which I cannot now remember, I beg pardon of God and penance and absolution of you, Father.

Pause.

ALFREDO. Bruno?

They stop thumping.

BRUNO. Yes. I'm here. I'm here. What? What is it?

ALFREDO. Peter. Look after him. Look after them all. Tell them all I'm sorry.

BRUNO. Yes. I'll tell them, Bimbo! Let me in, eh? Please! Bimbo! Bimbo!

They bang the door more and more violently. Finally BRUNO charges it down. ALFREDO is dead on the lavatory.

Scene Six

The present. England. Beach.

NONNA *and* ANASTASIA *are on the pier. Sitting in a shelter.* ANASTASIA *is fishing with a small handline.* NONNA, *distracted, weeping, is lost in her own thoughts. As* ANASTASIA *talks she experiments with her line.*

ANASTASIA (*very bright*). My friend caught a crab on Saturday. A big one. I bet it was under here. I don't really want to catch one though. The're horrible. That's all you catch mostly when you go fishing off the pier. Crabs and things. I'm a bit frightened of them actually . . . Uncle Anthony pulls their legs off. Mam says I can go fishing with him next week, because you're not allowed to go on the pier with a proper fishing rod until you're 14, unless you've got somebody with you. But I can if he takes me. Then I can start catching all the fish for the shop. You get sharks sometimes, you know. Great big ones. I'd quite like to catch one of *those*. I don't know what bait you'd have to use though. I don't expect they'd eat worms. Paul Charlton says that sometimes when they catch sharks there are people living inside them. Still alive. Do you think that's true? He bet me that there were sixteen pounds in a stone once, and everybody knows that's not true. His dad takes him out fishing all night sometimes, and he doesn't have to go to sleep at all. They sit in the shelter with a blanket and fish over the side. All night. I'd like to do that one day. Don't expect I'd be allowed to though because I'm a girl. Dad can't take me. He's always working. Anyway, he can't even swim!

Scene Seven

The past, Dublin, 1963. JULIA *and* ALFREDO's *house.*

JULIA *is letting in a grown-up and married* GIOIA. *Both women are strained.*

GIOIA (*off. Unsure if this old woman is the dragon of history*). Mrs Jarrett?

JULIA (*off*). Come in.

GIOIA. I'm Gioia Powell. Alfredo Mare was my father.

JULIA. Yes. I remember you. You came to this house before. Many years ago.

GIOIA. Yes, I did.

JULIA. Would you like something to drink? Some tea? Did you come straight from the airport?

GIOIA. Yes. No tea, thank you. My mother's outside in the taxi. My sister's with her.

JULIA (*nodding*). Theresa.

GIOIA *doesn't reply.*

JULIA (*sighs*). I, put, what seemed appropriate, in a suitcase.

GIOIA. Right.

JULIA. You've grown to look more like him.

GIOIA (*closed*). Uhuh.

JULIA. Most things belong to his life here, of course, but there are things, his opera records, photographs of you girls, your mother, the families, the religious uh the religious items of his I packed for you to take. He's in the next room. I don't go in. I'm afraid it's not a custom I find . . . uh, I can't think of a word.

GIOIA. My uncle said they managed to give him the Last Sacrament.

JULIA. Your uncle's in there with him now. And Peter.

GIOIA. Peter?

JULIA. Our son. He lives here.

GIOIA. We've arranged with the undertaker to take the coffin in the morning. Will 8.30 be convenient?

JULIA. Yes, that's quite convenient, thank you.

GIOIA. Anyway . . .

JULIA. Yes. Anyway. Is your mother coming in or what?

GIOIA (*embarrassed*). Would it be possible for you . . . I know that she . . .?

JULIA. There would be no need for her to see me. I can sit in the kitchen.

GIOIA *nods. Pause.*

GIOIA. I expect the solicitors will contact you about his business effects and so on.

JULIA. He had no business effects here . . . are you talking about money? Is that what you're asking?

GIOIA. Really? That's not what we were led to believe.

JULIA. Oh? And what were you led to believe?

GIOIA. Frankly, I didn't anticipate having this kind of conversation over my father's body.

JULIA. We're not having a conversation over your father's body and it was your question.

GIOIA. And obviously one best left to solicitors.

JULIA. Gioia, your father – up until Christmas last year – was a bingo caller. The hall was owned by Rank. When it closed so did his job. He retired. I work part-time in the Post Office. Those basically are the business effects.

GIOIA. I should fetch my mother. If you'll excuse me.

PETER *and* BRUNO *enter.* PETER *is about twenty years old.*

BRUNO (to GIOIA). Darling.

He embraces her miserably.

BRUNO. Your mother?

JULIA. Gioia is going to fetch her from the taxi. I wonder if you'd be good enough, Bruno, to take them in, to the, room? I'll be in the

kitchen. Where will you be, Peter? This is Peter. Peter, this is
Gioia.

PETER *nods.*

PETER (*to* JULIA). I'll come through with you. (*To* GIOIA.) We'd
appreciate it if this wake . . . (*Sighs.*) After all, you do get to take
him back with you. He lived in this house, you see, for more than
twenty years. Anyway, we'd appreciate . . . as I said.

GIOIA. My sister wouldn't come in with me. Because she said if she
saw your mother she wouldn't be responsible for her actions.

PETER. Did she! (*He could kill her.*)

JULIA (*to* PETER). Darling. Would you take my arm? (PETER *does
so.*) Excuse us, won't you?

They exit with some dignity. BRUNO *looks embarrassed and
confused.* GIOIA *is formidable.*

GIOIA. This house stinks of death.

BRUNO. It's not easy for anybody.

GIOIA. God judges us, Uncle, and He's not easy either. You can't
erase a lifetime's hurt, simply shrug it off, for the sake of
politeness. My mother's outside. She's had absolutely no life. Just
given and given and given until a phone call comes in the night to
say no more, it's gone, flushed down the lavatory. Come and
collect the husk. And if that's hard on this house I'm very sorry.

BRUNO. Gioia . . .

GIOIA. I'll go and fetch Mamma. She can't speak, probably.
Theresa's with her. We'll all cry. We start each other off. If the
noise is indiscreet, you must apologize for us. We have never had
the luxury of good manners.

BRUNO (*softly, trying to soothe her*). Hey . . .

GIOIA. Why did you never say there was a son?

GIOIA *wants him to deny it.* BRUNO *shrugs.*

GIOIA. Oh, your family! My grandfather! Closed us off. Like
turning off a tap. Not just money – though that smarts you know,
all those years to see the gold on you everywhere – in your mouths,
on your hands – and my mother scrabbling . . . no, it's the silence
that rankles, the absolute silence. Was he really a bingo caller?

BRUNO (*sighs*). Your father was never much . . . business was never
his . . . (*Trails off.*)

GIOIA. Christ!

BRUNO. You're lucky to have so little to be ashamed of.

GIOIA. Meaning?

BRUNO. Meaning? (*Sighs.*) Nothing. I'm sad. And it makes me more sad we're saying these things to each other.

He tries to embrace her. She remains rigid.

BRUNO. Really . . . mostly people live the best lives they can, darling.

GIOIA. I'm sorry, I don't believe that.

BRUNO. Yes, I know.

GIOIA. I'll go to the car. They'll be cold.

BRUNO. Gioia, why did your mother have to come here?

GIOIA. Oh, probably because her husband died, I expect.

Cries of seagulls.

Scene Eight

Dublin. The kitchen.

JULIA-PETER. JULIA *sits in the same rocking chair occupied by* LEONORA *at the beginning of play.* PETER *stands looking out, comes back as if from a window watching* LEONORA *enter the house. He comes back to his mother, stands behind her, massaging her neck and shoulders.*

JULIA (*sighs*). What did she look like?

PETER. I don't know. Old.

JULIA. When she was younger she was beautiful.

PETER. He told me once she had no passion, or something. No imagination. That none of them did.

JULIA. Did he say that? To you?

PETER. Yes. And Uncle Bruno said she'd come from a long line of sour servants.

JULIA. I don't think that's very fair. Do you?

PETER. Don't know. His daughter seemed . . .

JULIA. What did she seem?

PETER. Oh, bitter. Hard. It's quite incredible they refuse to acknowledge how much he loved you, Mother. I mean, Christ, what do they imagine? That he stayed away all this time to be miserable with you?

JULIA. Oh, Peter . . .

PETER *stops massaging.*

JULIA. No, don't stop. (*She clasps his hands.*) It's so soothing.

PETER. Why did you give them his gramophone records? I should have liked them.

JULIA. Surely not? You've never listend to them.

PETER. I did! Anyway, that's not the point. (*Helplessly.*) I am half-Italian, too, you know.

JULIA *is weeping. She nods.*

PETER. He loved that music. I've seen tears in his eyes listening to those songs.

JULIA. Oh yes.

PETER. I mean, why couldn't they just leave us alone? They're in there now, vulturing him, kissing his cold forehead. Hysterical Italian vultures. Do they know him? I mean, how do they know they've got the right corpse?

JULIA. Please, Peter . . . let's be quiet together, hmm? The two of us.

Quiet.

JULIA. Listen . . . that sound . . .

PETER. It's outside. Someone sweeping leaves.

JULIA. Yes. There are so many this year. Do you hear them in the night? Rustling?

PETER. Yes. I hear them.

JULIA. I stood at the window this morning and watched them flutter past like so many flocks of birds. Like rain. The most marvellous colours. Your father said he could not remember a more beautiful Autumn.

She takes his hands in hers and kisses them.

Scene Nine

The present. England. Beach.

NONNA *and* ANASTASIA *walking, paddling.*

NONNA. You see I always prayed that he would come back. For a few days even. Just to show him how different things could have been. And he would have. He did want to. I know that. But he died too soon. Sitting on the lavatory in November. Did you know that? He died on the lavatory. His brother was outside the door, but your grandfather wouldn't let him in. Not even the doctor. Then the priest came . . . He made his confession through the door. He died with the priest giving him absolution outside . . . Is it turning cold, do you think? The sun's gone in . . . Uncle Bruno told me that he'd died of a broken heart . . . Oh yes, all along . . . in his heart . . . he'd wanted to come back to me. I knew that. But do you know something? That Mrs Jarrett didn't even go to the funeral . . . not that I would have let her . . . she just sent me a long letter saying your grandfather had promised her a fur coat that had been his mother's and would I please send it to her? I had the coat on when the letter arrived . . . But because Grandfather had mentioned it in some way . . . in some document or other . . . or something . . . I don't know . . . anyway I would to hand it over. I wanted to suffocate her with it. She stole everything from me. She took my husband . . . then she wanted the coat off my back. I feel sorry for her now, in a way. She had no one to comfort her. Just a fur coat . . . (*Almost a laugh.*) With the moth in it.

ANASTASIA. Is she dead now?

NONNA (*continues*). We brought him back from Dublin and buried him in a double grave with my place ready beside him. That's why I feel so sorry for Mrs Jarrett . . . old puttana that she was . . . (*Triumphant.*) She had him for a few years. But I'll be with him for eternity. We'll lie there together . . . the two of us . . . for eternity.

ANASTASIA. So Grandfather didn't love her then?

NONNA. You're not listening. Looking forward to your breakfast? Yes, of course you are . . . Yes, I think I will just try and walk out there a bit. (*She leaves* ANASTASIA *behind.*) The sea looks so warm. I wanted to tell you something. Sometimes . . . shall I tell you what I think about? I want to wade in . . . just wade right up to my waist. (*Does so.*) Feel my skirts floating around me . . . These early mornings, when it's cool and fresh . . . Yes . . . In the early mornings, wade in past my waist and keep walking and walking (*Does so.*) Feel the water churning around me. Swallow me up. You know . . . they say a drowning man sees his whole life before him. Shall I tell you, Alfredo? These walks . . . these paddles . . . that's a little like drowning . . . isn't it?

She walks, determined, towards the water.

TWO PLANKS AND
A PASSION

Two Planks and A Passion was first performed at the Northcott Theatre, Exeter in 1983 in a production commissioned and directed by Stewart Trotter and designed by Tim Reed. It was subsequently revised and presented at the Greenwich Theatre, London in 1984. For the Northcott Theatre production, the cast was as follows:

EDWARD YOUNG, *Pinner's labourer*	Keith Bartlett
WILL BLUEFRONT, *Painter's labourer*	David Oakley
GEOFFREY LE KOLVE, *Master, Painters' Guild*	Ted Valentine
WALTER PAYNTER, *apprentice painter*	Sean Aita
FATHER HENRY MELTON, *Producer and Chaplain to the Painters' Guild*	Patrick Romer
THOMAS ZACHARY, *Painter's labourer*	Mike Burnside
SARAH ZACHARY, *his wife and lady-in-waiting to the Le Kolves*	Heather Williams
KATHRYN LE KOLVE, *wife of Geoffrey*	Rosalind March
RICHARD II, *King of England*	Mark Jax
ROBERT DE VERE, *Earl of Oxford*	Saul Reichlin
ANNE OF BOHEMIA, *Queen of England*	Amanda Orton
ALICE SELBY, *Mayoress of York*	Amanda Walker
WILLIAM SELBY, *Mayor of York, Merchant*	Raymond Cross
JOLYF ABSOLOM, *Herod in Merchants' play*	David Oakley
ARCHBISHOP OF YORK	Mike Burnside
GOD THE FATHER	
ADAM, *a servant boy*	
and assorted GODS, CHRISTS, SOLDIERS *and* CROWD	

The play was first broadcast in December 1986 on BBC Radio 3.

ACT ONE

Scene One

Bells for five. Late May. Early morning. York, 1392.

Outside the Pageant House. This is a sort of medieval garage and is located in York. It houses the Pageant Wagon of the Painters' Guild, shared with the Pinners and Latterners. These three crafts play the Crucifixion Play, the thirty-fifth in the Corpus Christi Cycle.

WILL BLUEFRONT *and* EDWARD YOUNG *appear, each dragging a plank of wood. During the scene they join the two planks into a cross by lashing the wood together with rope.*

EDWARD. Don't it set your heart humming?

WILL. What?

EDWARD. Doing this. Making the cross. Getting together. Saying the words.

WILL. Says my words every evening. Before I sleeps.

EDWARD. Do you? And I do!

WILL. 'Stead of prayers.

EDWARD. This is different though, eh? Every year I just have to see our wagon, have a dibble round the costumes, put on my helmet, pull out the planks and I get a little flutter going.

WILL (*grumpily*). I'm not starting before cakes and ale.

EDWARD. Well, I doubt we'll get breakfast this year, Will. Everything's cut back, innit? I heard speak of another penny wanted from us for the play.

WILL. Who says? I'm not giving another penny. Anyway, we shouldn't have to pay if we're speaking in the pageant.

EDWARD. That's all very well for our Guild, but say you were doing the *Harrowing of Hell*? Fifty odd nipper in that all told. If they never paid up there'd be no play.

WILL. That's the Merchants' do anyway. What's a penny to them? They shit pennies.

EDWARD. I shit a sixpence once. It hurt. Picked it up at a fair and swallowed it for safe keeping.

WILL. They gets ham at the Merchants' rehearsals. And best beer.

EDWARD. Well . . . we gets the better play.

WILL. Now that's true. Where's the others then?

EDWARD. Oh, be along shortly, I expect.

WILL. I half thought to find Thomas pinned up on the cross last year.

EDWARD. Not like Walter to be late, mind.

WILL. He'll be sent to search for the priest who'll no doubt be sleeping somewhere he shouldn't.

EDWARD. Shouldn't be rude about the parson, Will.

WILL. Well . . . If I puts my dick where I didn't ought it's a curse, Edward. If he do 'tis a blessing. Where's the fairness in that? So that's me and I'll not start before I'm given my breakfast.

EDWARD (*as a distraction*). Saw a dead heron this morning, me. That's bad luck. Means a famine.

WILL. Plague.

EDWARD. Aye. Or plague.

WILL. No – just plague.

EDWARD. Aye, it were a dead heron. Down by Ouse Bridge.

WILL. What do you do then? At night?

EDWARD. What do you mean?

WILL. When you're doing your words . . . who does my part?

EDWARD. Our missus. What about you?

WILL. No, I do it myself, me. I do all the parts.

EDWARD. The whole play?

WILL. Aye.

EDWARD. Oh.

WILL. I has to, Edward. I forget, see. Last year forgot my words, didn't I? Thought I'd get a fine.

EDWARD. Not forgot. Stumbled.

WILL. Forgot.

EDWARD. 'Tis easy done.

WILL. No. My brain's rusting. 'Nother year or two I'll be put out to pasture . . . I'll be off the wagon and down on the road pulling you boys round, station to station. Then you'll be first soldier.

EDWARD. Well.

WILL. No, if I give him to anyone it'll be to you. Unless your missus do him very well! How is she?

EDWARD. Oh, she's bonnie. Well, I say bonnie but you know she sold all her hair.

WILL. Never!

EDWARD. Aye. Had a new babe see. Needed the money.

WILL. I never knew. What's that? Nipper?

EDWARD. No. Little girl. Little lover, she is.

WILL (*sympathetically*). Lovely red hair she had an' all, your missus.

EDWARD. Aye.

WILL Aye. If I pass him on to anyone will be to you, Edward.

EDWARD *lifts up the cross.*

EDWARD. Well, she's done then. Shall we have a go at it?

WILL. Aye.

EDWARD. With the moves?

WILL. No, can't do the moves, can we, missing Thomas. No, just the parts.

GEOFFREY LE KOLVE *and* WALTER *approach.*

GEOFFREY. How do, lads!

EDWARD. } 'Morning Mister.
WILL.

WALTER. Will. Edward.

WILL. No Tom yet.

WALTER (*covering up*). He's here. He's with the parson.

GEOFFREY (*innocuously*). Have we had bells for five?

EDWARD. We have, sir.

WILL (*pointedly*). We've had bells for quarter past five.

GEOFFREY. Really? Well, the parson hears a confession yet but he'll be along shortly. Walter can get you going. (*Ominously.*) There are a change or two this year.

WILL. We're due breakfast, Mister.

GEOFFREY. Has that not come either?

WILL. No. Neither

GEOFFREY. I'll see to it.

WILL. Please, Mister.

GEOFFREY. Complete forgot.

WILL. Mister: we heard speak of more pageant pence wanted.

GEOFFREY (*defensively*). I know. These plays is costing the Guilds a fortune. I know, lads. A penny's a lot. *I* can't spare a penny just so. Not like some: sitting on their arses on the dry land while a ship sails making them a fortune. No, I'm opposed to more pageant pence, me. There's talk of sharing our play with the Masons.

WILL (*outraged*). Never!

EDWARD (*outraged*). What!

GEOFFREY. Oh aye! And I'm the one who's talking! Aye! These pageants is nothing but a pestilence in my opinion. An excuse for time off and clowning about.

WILL (*offended*). *Five* morning we rehearse, Mister. And that off our wage.

GEOFFREY. We has more feast days in this country than work days.

WALTER (*conciliatorily*). We should get going lads. There's new words for us all.

GEOFFREY. No use moaning to me, Will. I've got cakes and ale to dole out. I've got pullers to pay. I've got lights to buy. I've got a mask to leaf in gold. How much is that costing? (*He looks to* WALTER.)

EDWARD. We all contribute.

GEOFFREY. To me, see: I'm no reveller . . . these days is just Christ done mischief to above the wagon and more mischief done underneath. Half the watchers pissed or sleeping or feeling each other. There's more thought of whoring than of God.

WALTER (*shrewdly*). Last year it were reckoned our pageant was finest played.

GEOFFREY (*egotistically*). Oh aye. I know that. It were reckoned we were a bull among bullocks!

WILL (*bull*). We were.

GEOFFREY. I know that. I know that. But we has to save money, Walter. It is as Will says, many things come before a play.

WILL (*wounded again*). Never said that! 'Tis our play and we'll not lose it for the sake of a penny.

GEOFFREY. Then be careful not to lose it for the sake of complaining. (*Sternly.*) Now I wants reckoning of savings to take back to the Guild, Walter.

WALTER. Aye, Mister.

GEOFFREY. Else these plays is cancelled. That's my mind spoke. So. And bid the priest come see me sharpish. (*He makes to exit.*) 'Morning, lads.

ALL. 'Morning, Mister.

> GEOFFREY *exits*.

WILL (*as soon as* GEOFFREY *is out of earshot*). 'I can't spare a penny just so!' His bed cost twenty pound!

EDWARD. You shouldn't grumble so, Will. Makes matters worse.

WILL. Why? Because he threatens us? He can't cut our play. The sky would fall on his head. What would they do, eh? Miss out the crucifixion? Ach!

WALTER. No, they'd give it to the Merchants.

WILL. Every year we hear the same story; 'tis to keep our hands tied behind us.

EDWARD. One minute you moan about more money; the next about less.

WILL. Aye, I do! 'Tis a duty to play the play. And even if God would forgive us the town would not.

WALTER. An' I tell you, the Merchants would take our pageant and no one would protest, except us.

WILL. Except us. US would be sufficient! Don't give us the master's view, Mister Apprentice. We know it.

EDWARD. Leave off, Will.

WILL. Well.

EDWARD. Thing is, Walter, me and Will and the others . . . Tom . . . we done this pageant years, see. Just the thought of playing her warms cold fingers in January . . . beats the heart come Spring. It's our occasion, in' it?

WALTER (*hurt*). I love the play no less than you do.

EDWARD. Course you do.

WILL (*knowing this, but still grumpy*). What changes anyway?

WALTER. They've cut the end business with the purple cloak.

WILL. And why's that?

WALTER. Too long. Been complaints from the council about running time. It's reckoned that all forty-eight plays got to be seen within the day, including the Mass.

EDWARD. Not possible.

WALTER. I know it, Edward, but just the same we cut some. Besides, then we pay less for lights – if we're shorter . . . and if you lose the dividing-up of the cloak that's a purple cloth saved.

WILL. Ach! Saved! We know what's saved, nipper. 'Tis what's lost is the bugger. These pageant masters would be masters of no pageant at all left up to them. Yet they're never so happy while they can hoof ahead of us, all plush with our banner. Great galleybagging gang.

EDWARD. Don't yoppel on so, Will.

WALTER. They also want less of the soldiers early on.

WILL. Do they! And what about less Mary?

WALTER. No. There's less Mary already.

WILL (*caustically*). Oh aye! And not because you're groomed for pageant master. We can all clot, Mister. You clot with that lot, please yourself. We'll all clot together.

WALTER. I would do less Mary, Will. I'd do *no* Mary and something else, given the chance. I do have a beard now. (*He feels it.*) Some. And I'm betrothed. I long to act in hose and not in petticoat. But I don't choose that neither. I play the Virgin and you play less soldier. There: view the changes.

WILL. You know I don't know letters. None of us do.

EDWARD. I know some. I know E for Edward and Y for Young and P for Pinner and some others.

WILL. I'm talking about reading, Edward, and you can't. Nor can any of us saving Mr Walter here.

WALTER. I'll learn you your parts and we'll do well.

EDWARD. That's kind, Walter.

WALTER. You making blood yet, Will?

WILL. I done it a week ago.

EDWARD. Looks marvellous real. You'd think he'd bled himself. And I made new pins.

WALTER. This year our pageant's having a fresh face for Christ. I'm making him. A quarter ounce of silver in it.

EDWARD. I could eat off that whole winter. Longer.

WILL. Still. It's the Lord's face. Should be special.

WALTER. Amen.

EDWARD. Amen.

WALTER. So. We're starting. You each had five speeches before Christ had his.

WILL (*showing all his fingers*). Then ten and I call on company to lift the cross.

WALTER. No, hold up, Will. Now Thomas speaks once only for Christ and that at the end. So where he spoke first he now says nothing and you continue but lose your speech before he spoke and after. You with me?

EDWARD. So, we says five and then straight away ten and then company?

WALTER. No, you says four and then nine and then company.

WILL (*grumpily*). 'Tis irregular now though, ain't it? 'Cause I used to have one hand's worth beforehand and two hands' worth after.

EDWARD. Always were irregular, 'cause I always used to say four lines then you would say two lines and . . .

WILL. And different counts. (*Muttering.*) It's a bugger if you ask me. 'Tis buggered up for no good reason.

EDWARD. Oh, I think 'tis a nice touch to have the Christ dumb until the end.

WILL. Edward, you'd thank a bugger for bashing you!

WALTER (*delicately*). Do get more complex later, Edward, to tell you the truth.

EDWARD (*maudlin*). Oh.

WILL (*grumpily*). Aye. Bloody oh!

FATHER HENRY MELTON, The Chaplain *and* Producer, *enters with* THOMAS.

FATHER MELTON. Have I missed the breakfast?

WALTER. No Father, it comes yet.

FATHER MELTON. 'Tis a real penance the Lord sent me: hunger. I hunger through the night like no other man I know.

WILL (*close*). And what was you up to Thomas: confessing?

THOMAS. No, I . . . no, couldn't wake up.

WILL. Some of us have been here half an hour. But then we ain't got a new wife in our cots.

WALTER. We begun, Father, we're learning changes.

FATHER MELTON. Splendid. I've made alterations lads, to improve the speeches. And 'tis also shorter. If a thing is worth talking about for ten minutes 'tis better said in one. And in plain words, in English.

WALTER. I've touched on the differences, Father.

FATHER MELTON. Aye. 'Tis the picture speaks, in my view. Not the words. Oh yes. So I'm sad about losing the cloth, me, and the dice. The masters tell me 'tis an expense and not necessary. (*He shrugs.*) And Walter, do you still speak for the Virgin? You have increasingly a beard.

WALTER. I do, Father, but I'll scrape it shortly.

FATHER MELTON. Were it to me, I'd have a girl say it, no offence. A beautiful girl were chosen for the deed, a beautiful girl should say it. Still, the masters would cut the pageant and the Archbishop would stop it altogether. So, Walter, you're preferred to nothing.

WALTER. Thank you, Father.

FATHER MELTON. See, left to me I'd never show Christ wounded. No, I'd take a strapping lad and paint his whole flesh gold, not just the face alone, and have him golden, transcendent on the tree in majesty. So come the great speech, he'd slip the nails and rope and stand arms stretched in blessing, not in pain. (*Acting his fantasy.*) Oh yes . . . But the taste is for mumbling and hurt and violence and cruelty.

THOMAS *couldn't be less appropriate for this vision. He's middle-aged and fat.*

EDWARD. But surely, Pastor, if we show not Christ's suffering, how can we teach men to sorrow at it and seek forgiveness?

FATHER MELTON. Ach. The world is swollen with suffering and sorrow. I've seen enough of it. Still, let's begin and do the moves alone. All the bashing and the bother. Get yourself on the tree now, Tom. I want to show the soldiers the new moves.

EDWARD. How do, Thomas?

EDWARD *helps* THOMAS *to the cross.*

THOMAS (*cautiously*). Oh. Fair.

EDWARD (*to* WILL). Looks a bit wan, don't he, Will?

WILL (*mischievously*). I said, 'tis that new young wife of his: tiring him out. Looks older'n me now.

THOMAS. I *am* older'n you.

WILL. Aye, but you never looked it before. This year you do. I bet our young apprentice over there, him with his bumfluff, I bet he regrets giving her up for his big ideas.

WALTER *comes across to help* TOM *get on the cross.*

WALTER. What's this?

WILL. No, I'm just saying: new moves and all now, is it?

The three men rope THOMAS *to the cross which is propped up so as to keep* THOMAS *visible. During this:*

WILL. I can remember when there were four soldiers, me. Each year they takes something away. Soon they'll have the Christ crucifying hisself and no soldiers at all.

WALTER (*having had enough of* WILL). You see one bird, it's a flock, ain't it Will?

WILL. Maybe. What do one spot of rain signal to you? Signal a thousand to me. All this to-do. 'Tis bad token. 'Tis bees out of a hole.

EDWARD. Here comes our breakfast, lads.

FATHER MELTON. Thank the Lord for that.

SARAH ZACHARY, THOMAS's *wife, waiting-woman for the Le Kolves and one-time sweetheart of* WALTER, *enters. She's loaded up with cakes (bread-cakes) and beer.*

FATHER MELTON *walks towards* SARAH.

FATHER MELTON. How do, Sarah? Do you bring our beer. Bless you. Jump down then Thomas and eat.

SARAH. How do, lads. Is it hungry work crucifying?

WILL. 'Tis mistress. Particular we eat an hour after we should.

SARAH (*sweetly, to her husband*). Can I help you, husband?

THOMAS (*half-crucified but cheerful*). No. I manage. Do you, with that weight? (*Meaning the jug of beer, etc.*)

SARAH. Aye

SARAH *moves across to* WALTER *as the group settles down to breakfast and* THOMAS *disentangles himself from the cross.*

SARAH. Walter.

WALTER. Sarah.

SARAH. And how is it with you, sir?

WALTER. I'm well, mistress. An' you?

SARAH. Aye

WALTER. Fair enough.

SARAH. We heard you was betrothed then.

WALTER. Aye.

SARAH. Eleanor dell Brigg. That's a good match for you, Walter.

WALTER. Aye. They say so.

SARAH. I'm glad then. And you've got a little beard.

WALTER. Aye. A little.

WILL (*facetiously*). Going to rub off that fluff, make a paint brush, eh Walter?

SARAH (*to* WALTER). I has to measure you for your new dress.

WALTER (*uncomfortably*). Not drinking, Thomas?

THOMAS. Will do.

EDWARD. You are queer quiet, Thomas.

THOMAS (*mindful of* SARAH *and* WALTER). Ngh.

EDWARD. You sickening?

THOMAS. No.

WILL. Done hisself an injury on the planks.

WALTER. Have some cakes.

WILL. I heard say at Beverley last year, from John Lunn, that their Christ on the Pinners' pageant got hisself crucified real. Hung him up like a a hare they did. He couldn't get his breath. They thought he were pretending but he weren't. Couldn't tell, see, under his mask.

EDWARD. Poor nipper.

WILL. Oh aye, and at Coventry they didn't care much for their boy and thumped in the nails right through his hands.

THOMAS. Never!

WILL. Ah! So you *have* still got your tongue.

THOMAS. They never did!

WILL. So 'tis said.

THOMAS. Did they, Parson?

FATHER MELTON. Take no notice, Thomas.

THOMAS. I bet they never.

WALTER. Come and eat, Thomas.

SARAH. Thomas Zachary, you're an old donkey if you listen to this gang. Dip your nose in the jug, lovely, and shut up.

THOMAS *sulks across.*

KATHRYN LE KOLVE *appears.*

SARAH (*jumping up*). Mistress!

KATHRYN. How do.

The MEN *jump up.*

SARAH. No. Don't stand on ceremony, lads. I need a word apart with the priest. 'Morning Walter. How goes the rehearsal?

WALTER (*wearily*). Very punctuated, madam.

KATHRYN. How's that?

WALTER. As yet it has few starts and many stops.

KATHRYN. Aye well: proceed. Proceed. Can they proceed, Parson?

FATHER MELTON. I fear they waits on me, madam.

KATHRYN. Then come apart, quick. (*She pulls the priest aside.*)

FATHER MELTON (*as* KATHRYN *pulls him away*). Point out the changes, Walter.

There are frustrated looks from the actors at a further hiatus. They pack up their breakfast during what follows.

KATHRYN (*unburdening her news immediately*). Henry, I heard the Earl of Oxford came last night to stop at the Mayor's house.

FATHER MELTON. Oxford? Impossible. He's exiled.

KATHRYN. Not by the King. He says the King comes here. He says the King will be here this morning. And Queen. And retinue.

FATHER MELTON. Why?

KATHRYN. The King is sullen with London, is the word.

FATHER MELTON. His Majesty is a man of culture. Why should he come here? No, 'tis idle this rumour. (*Conscious of the others.*) Be with you directly, lads.

KATHRYN (*undeterred*). And what if the King came to be with the Earl? 'Tis said that when Oxford were at court he could make Richard see black as white and white as black.

FATHER MELTON (*excited*). Would it were true. Would spice the town.

KATHRYN. I'm off to spice myself.

FATHER MELTON. My God, Kathryn. I hope he stop for the pageant and like mine. I'd give my splinter from the true cross for some gold paint and good cloth and even half good players. I must plead with your husband for more money not less. Oh Christ! The King! The King! He might bring me to court and I could give up scratching here.

KATHRYN (*hurt*). Oh?

FATHER MELTON. No I didn't mean. I meant . . .

KATHRYN. What?

FATHER MELTON. I just meant good. You know: exciting.

WALTER. Should we do the moves, Parson?

FATHER MELTON. Aye, do the moves.

Bells ring severally and noisily.

THOMAS.   ⎫
EDWARD.   ⎬ Yow!

EDWARD. What's this!

All react.

WILL. Christ's blood! Them jangle! What's up, then?

EDWARD. Told you, Will. That heron! 'Tis bad luck, I bet! 'Tis a famine!

WALTER. What bells are these, Parson?

FATHER MELTON. What bells? They're all the bells!

WALTER. Aye, but what do they signify?

FATHER MELTON. I don't know, boy.

KATHRYN (*delighted*). I think it may be the King coming!

ALL. The King!

KATHRYN. Aye.

WILL (*shouting at the bells*). Why?

EDWARD. Never heard so many bells.

WILL. All right we heard!

   GEOFFREY *runs in, yelling over the tumult.*

GEOFFREY (*shouting*). The King comes! The King comes!

   The bells stop.

   (*Still shouting.*) The King comes!

KATHRYN. Aye, husband, they know.

GEOFFREY. How do they know?

KATHRYN. I told them.

GEOFFREY. How do you know, madam?

KATHRYN (*dissembling*). Oh. (*Meaning, never you mind.*)

GEOFFREY (*deflated*). Don't just gawp, nippers. There's no rehearsal now. We're out at the gates to greet the Royal Party. Get to, Walter. The Mayor's craft is half way there.

KATHRYN. They can't go dressed so.

GEOFFREY. No. You can't go dressed so. Go and change into Sunday outfit and fetch our banner.

WALTER *and* WILL *exit.*

Shift that cross, Thomas, Edward. Don't dawdle! You're all dawdling! Come on, come on! 'Tis a race not a funeral! Let's meet directly by Mickelgate.

KATHRYN. Sarah, go back to the house and pull out my maroon gown. It needs spicing.

FATHER MELTON (*excited*). I'll hurry, too. I've a sword to buckle on and 'tis a chance to wear my new cross from Venice. I'll see you both at Mickelgate.

FATHER MELTON *exits.*

GEOFFREY (*sourly*). That priest is a penance.

KATHRYN. He's nothing of the sort. He can read. And he forgives me. 'Tis two things *you* can't do. At least.

GEOFFREY. Ach! And what do this King want now? Christ! 'Tis one trial after another. And how is it, woman, you know the business of the town before I do?

KATHRYN. I listens, sir. You spend so much time talking. If you want to know, I heard the King is in sulk with London.

GEOFFREY. How in sulk?

KATHRYN. For respecting not His Majesty.

GEOFFREY. Ah! 'Tis a money thing then.

KATHRYN. Some others say the King love this Oxford more than his wife.

GEOFFREY. Woman, most men love most men more than their wife.

KATHRYN. Oh!

GEOFFREY. Not me. I kiss your fingers, madam, and if your foot came more often to my bed I would kiss that also.

KATHRYN. I hate your bed. It's straw.

GEOFFREY. Then let me come to yours.

KATHRYN. With my maid at the foot of it? 'Tis not seemly.

GEOFFREY. For my part I would throw out the maid.

KATHRYN. For my part you should throw out the bed, sir, and find a new one more suitable. That's the remedy.

GEOFFREY. Madam, I spent twenty pounds on your bed because of your horror of the straw one. Now I has the straw one.

KATHRYN. Aye, husband. That's true.

GEOFFREY. Well . . . ach, Christ's blood!

KATHRYN. Where do we greet the King, sir?

GEOFFREY. By Ouse Bridge.

KATHRYN. Oh no! Not me. That bridge stinks and I'll not sniff it.

GEOFFREY. It does not stink.

KATHRYN. You have no nose, husband, how would you know? If you would buy me parfum I could travel more. I could smell myself and not the foul air. I will not walk neither. You may be happy to greet a King with skirts beshitted. I am not. No, I'll not stand by Ouse Bridge, why should we? Where is the Mayor and his monkey meeting the Royal Party?

GEOFFREY. City Gates.

KATHRYN. Then that's where we'll go. Don't settle for second best, husband. It's a bed you make for yourself. 'Tis unattractive. Run ahead now, and arrange horses and a better view. (*Thinking.*) If a King comes, profit comes in his train. Run!

GEOFFREY *huffs.*

But not sweatily, sir!

GEOFFREY. Ach.

GEOFFREY *exits unhappily. Then* KATHRYN *exits, happily.*

Scene Two

The Mayor's house.

This is the bedroom or upper storey.

In the room RICHARD II, *his Queen,* ANNE OF BOHEMIA, *and the exiled Earl,* ROBERT DE VERE *of Oxford, are reunited.* RICHARD *is embracing* OXFORD.

RICHARD. Robert!

OXFORD. Richard! Anne! Marvellous

ANNE (*concerned*). Robert, you're grey.

OXFORD (*shrugging*). Dust. (*Concerned*). You're thin.

ANNE (*tightly*). I don't think so.

RICHARD. When did you come? Yesterday?

OXFORD. Aye. Last evening.

ANNE. Let's not go down. Let's stay up here and talk.

RICHARD. There's a feast done for us.

ANNE (*mischievously*). Say I sicken.

OXFORD. Oh do, please, Majesty. The people here will speak French and cannot. I want to speak English. I would not care if I never heard a *bonjour* or a *bonsoir* before purgatory. Tell me of London.

RICHARD. No.

ANNE. He hates London now, Robert. Without you. Without friends. Without money.

OXFORD. Is it bad?

RICHARD. Worse. The city vomits merchants and lawyers. The court conspires. Gloucester and Bolingbroke torment me. London's piss drowns me.

ANNE (*sadly*). I cannot conceive there, Robert. I lost two babies since we last spoke.

RICHARD. The Parliament would speak my words for me. They call me weak because I love not warmongering and the endless bloodying.

OXFORD. And because you once loved Oxford.

RICHARD. Still do, friend.

OXFORD. Oh, London still sounds like heaven after Calais and Bordeaux and those puddles of nowhere, Sire. Not a sun but I thought of you, not a laugh but I heard yours, not a game but I saw you play it, not a pageant but I remembered your hurrah.

RICHARD. No laughs now, Robert, nor games. London is loveless.

OXFORD. Then it is you who is London in my heart and now London is in York with Oxford.

ANNE. And Bohemia.

OXFORD. And Bohemia!

RICHARD. I kicked out the Mayor at home, Robert, and his crew, and they can linger on my pleasure.

OXFORD. Bravo.

RICHARD. It were never meant for tradesmen to govern. It is against God that a King should be worked from below.

OXFORD. But what do you hope for here?

ANNE. Rest.

RICHARD. Give them a few weeks, the fat cats will purr for me again. Meanwhile, we three can live a little out of time.

ANNE. We might move the court here if it pleases us.

OXFORD. I only fear that this place is more of the same. The Mayor here is so full of Mayor he cannot squeeze into his gown an inch of wit.

RICHARD. He bowed and scraped an hour outside the gates until I fell asleep on his speech. We waded here, Robert. Half the town oozing on us.

OXFORD. And the Mayoress is inflated. Like a pig's bladder for football. She knows nothing and insists on revealing it.

ANNE. This is a fine bed.

RICHARD. Anne judges each new place by its bed.

ANNE. I do. This bed is a better bed than ours, Richard.

OXFORD. Ask them for it. They can't refuse.

RICHARD. I might.

OXFORD. Get all their beds away from them. They'd hate you for it.

RICHARD. Is that good?

OXFORD. It will flatter them you want their beds. Each will out-peacock the other until they realize that to show off so they must lose what they most prize: the thing. 'Tis a people of thing, these guildsmen.

ANNE. What 'thing'?

OXFORD. A 'thing'. Any 'thing'. Beds, bolsters, pisspots, conduits, baubs, trinkets, hangings . . . anything. What breeding they lack inside they disguise in this weight of thing. They even die now and have these things buried with them.

RICHARD. You've not changed, Robert.

OXFORD. Demand these things. That what they own is coveted is essential to their design . . . that a King wants them is marvellous. They'll bestow them on you flushed with conceit and next flushed with anxiety. They know the worth of each thing down to the last farthing and will cost out their generosity tear by tear.

RICHARD. This polemic cost you your land, your fortune and London's favour.

OXFORD. Good riddance then, eh?

ANNE. And you have one rule for your friends and another for the world.

OXFORD. Who has not? I hate the pig with power, the donkey with degree. I hate books unread and songs unheard and glass unviewed and all beauty wasted. And I talk too much.

ANNE. You do, and I love it.

RICHARD. And I do.

ANNE. I'll have the bed. The colour suits me. I think I'll lie down on it, too. Come boys and cosset me. (*They do.*) Ah, that's nice.

RICHARD. Do you know this woman has been sick, Oxford?

OXFORD. How sick?

RICHARD. She swoons on me and fevers on me and coughs and chokes and spasms on me. No thought of my peace. (*Gently.*) Is that not so, madam?

ANNE. I'm inconsiderate.

RICHARD. January she even feigned death to grieve me. (*He clasps ANNE's hand.*)

OXFORD (*clasping ANNE's other hand.*) Hussy.

ANNE. I know.

OXFORD (*gently*). Your hands are so cold.

RICHARD. And dead babes she hands me, just so.

OXFORD. Wicked. Come on, let me warm your hands, madam.

ANNE (*sad*). The babies: 'tis too many eyes on me, Robert, none friendly.

OXFORD. Then we will make of this a season of sport to cure us all.

RICHARD. Amen.

ANNE. To mischief!

OXFORD. To mischief!

RICHARD. To mischief!

OXFORD (*only half believing what he says*). And surely come the Autumn: London, starved of majesty, will embrace you.

ANNE. And we can bring you back in our train.

OXFORD. I like this scheme.

RICHARD. Robert, what of the play here? How is it?

OXFORD. Good, I hear.

RICHARD. If it rivals Coventry 'tis the one thing the country does to out-art London.

ANNE. Richard, show him your wipe.

OXFORD. What's this?

RICHARD. My wipe!

OXFORD. I'm lost.

RICHARD produces a large handkerchief and blows his nose.

Ha!

RICHARD hands it to ANNE who blows hers.

RICHARD. Robert . . .

ROBERT blows his nose. He laughs.

It saves the sleeve, eh?

They grin hugely.

OXFORD. Whose invention is this?

ANNE. Richard's.

OXFORD. 'Tis very strange.

RICHARD. How strange! 'Tis very wondrous! I have many and use them variously: one for the nose; one for the arse; one for the brow.

ANNE. An' he mix them up.

OXFORD. True. 'Tis very wondrous.

RICHARD. Here, (*He fishes around and produces half a dozen handkerchiefs.*) try them.

ANNE. The Parliament call him woman for this hygiene.

OXFORD. I call them shit flies for theirs!

RICHARD. To women then!

OXFORD. And away with shit flies.

ANNE. Away with them!

Scene Three

The Mayor's house. A room below.

The Mayor and Mayoress wait to eat and wonder how you tell a King he's late for dinner.

ALICE. What transpires up there, husband?

WILLIAM. I don't know.

ALICE. They don't have their servants in with them. That's unnatural.

WILLIAM. How unnatural?

ALICE. Well, 'tis not done, is it?

WILLIAM. What the King do becomes what's done, madam.

ALICE *whispers confidential rumours about* OXFORD's *exploits*.

Why whisper, wife, when we're alone?

ALICE. Such things should not be shouted. (*She whispers some more.*)

WILLIAM. Well, I don't know, do I? They come from London and have different customs.

ALICE. Should we learn them, then?

WILLIAM. I don't know. What I do know is I'm hungered and my belly rumbles and churns and can sniff the table.

ALICE. We can't eat until they come down. The Queen has bathed herself. And the King. Is that the fashion too? To come in from outdoors and wash the body?

WILLIAM. I *don't* know!

ALICE. I'm certain the physic would say it risks sickness . . . but if it be the fashion we should do it, husband, and encourage the town.

WILLIAM. Woman, I am already the laughing stock with all this hygiene law you make me champion.

ALICE. 'Tis the smell of pig particular offends me.

WILLIAM. Never used to.

ALICE. And Kathryn Le Kolve told she read in a book that in Italy they have a law against *any* slops in the street.

WILLIAM. Madam . . . think for one second, pray . . . if you cannot pour out the slops onto the street, what do you do with it?

ALICE *can't think of an answer to this argument*.

ALICE. Well she said the Italians have a law against it.

WILLIAM (*sulkily*). I'll not strip my clothes every day; it's a business.

ALICE. Aye. Well. His Majesty have a cloth, too. He use it most mysteriously. Wiping. Hm. I suppose I could have some made up.

WILLIAM. Madam . . . eight shillings of mutton and venison and capon rot on our table while we prattle on about the fashion of arses – whether we should poke them or wash them or wipe them.

For me I want food in my gut so as to do with my arse what God made it for and I will continue to slop out its product until God or you show me a way of magically vanishing it.

ALICE (*placating*). William . . .

WILLIAM. What?

ALICE *strokes* WILLIAM.

Stop it.

ALICE. Willum . . . Willum . . .

WILLIAM. Whatee?

ALICE. We has a King and Queen in our house, husband.

WILLIAM. I know.

ALICE. The town be green.

WILLIAM. I know.

ALICE. So green – Kathy Le Kolve will sicken with greenness.

WILLIAM. And her husband.

ALICE. They'll be so green they dare not walk the pastures less a cow graze on them.

WILLIAM (*proudly*). Always stayed before in the Castle or the Abbey. Always.

ALICE. Get this noted in the record book then; tonight a King and Queen sleep in the bed of William and Alice Selby.

WILLIAM. Our bed?

ALICE. Where else?

WILLIAM. Where do we sleep? In the front?

ALICE. No, the Earl must sleep there.

WILLIAM. Where then?

ALICE. I'm to my mother's house and you down with your sons.

WILLIAM. With the dogs and the rabble?!

ALICE. You'll not die of it. Oh, and we must buy music, too. This King loves music.

WILLIAM. Why buy? Can't we invite someone over?

ALICE. That's no use. He must have proper minstrels. Leave it with me.

WILLIAM. Ach! It don't feel good all this cost.

ALICE. Listen, husband, you have twenty cases at law.

WILLIAM. Twenty-four.

ALICE. Well then, get the King's favour and think on it. Think, too, on *Sir* William Selby.

WILLIAM. Sir William. Sir Will.

ALICE. Lady Alice.

WILLIAM. My Lady.

ALICE. My Lord.

WILLIAM. What – my Lady?

ALICE. Oh. (*Mock sigh.*) Nothing, my Lord.

They dance gleefully. Then eventually WILLIAM *pulls up.*

WILLIAM. By Christ that flesh smells good.

ALICE. I know. It do. Let's go up, eh?

Scene Four

The Mayor's house. The bedroom.

ANNE, RICHARD and OXFORD are sprawled on the bed.

WILLIAM (*off*). Majesty? Majesties?

OXFORD. 'Tis the dog after his dinner.

WILLIAM (*off*). Majesties . . .

RICHARD. Should we stay a-bed and scandalize them?

OXFORD. Aye. Let's.

WILLIAM (*off*). Majesties.

ALICE (*off*). His Worship the Mayor and Lady Mayoress approach the Royal Salon.

OXFORD (*mock impressed*). Salon!

RICHARD. *Entrez.*

RICHARD and ALICE enter.

WILLIAM. We *entrez maintenant*, Your Most Shining Radiance.

ALICE. Forgive this *petite* intrusion.

RICHARD. *Nous sommes ici, madame. Au lit.*

ALICE tries not to look surprised.

ALICE. Pardon?

RICHARD (*very swiftly*). *Parce que vous vous dandinez en parlant le français, j'ai pensé, faussement, que vous compreniez la langue et désiriez la parler avec nous.*

ALICE (*lost*). Um . . . pardon?

WILLIAM (*hungry and very lost*). The thing is, my Lord, the feast cools and the flies visit the table before we do.

ANNE. Ugh!

RICHARD. My wife sickens, Mayor, and would eat in our 'salon'.

WILLIAM. Uh . . .

ALICE. Of course, Your Majestic . . . uh . . . Majesty.

RICHARD. What is the fare?

ALICE. Capons . . . mutton . . . venison . . . small bird, sturgeon, pike.

ANNE. 'Tis excessive, madam.

ALICE: Uh . . .

WILLIAM. 'Tis in your honour, Your Shining Beacons.

ANNE. Do you not have poor in the town?

ALICE. We do, ma'am.

ANNE. Good, then they should taste of this feast, in our honour. Say the King and his Queen wish to thank the citizens for their generous hospitality. That is our pleasure.

WILLIAM (*distraught*). Distribute it to the poor, glorious Lady?

ANNE. Aye. It should go out to the streets this minute. In truth the stench of it poisons my nostrils somewhat. (*Innocently.*) Have you ate?

WILLIAM. No, no, we waited on you, sweet Queen.

ANNE. Shame. Still, fasting's good for choler.

WILLIAM. Does our feast not please you, glorious Majesty?

ANNE. Oh yes, it do. Most sincere.

OXFORD. What pleases the Queen more, sir, is this bed.

ANNE. Marvellous bed.

OXFORD. And the King like it.

RICHARD. Very fine bed.

ANNE (*to* RICHARD). I'd like the bed, sir. Might I not have one like it?

RICHARD. 'Tis not mine to give, Lady. Though were it I'd delight in bestowing it on you.

WILLIAM (*miserably*). 'Tis mine, madam, now 'tis yours.

ANNE. No. Surely not!

ALICE. Oh yes, gracious Sovereign, 'tis our joy to gift it.

ANNE. Then I'm happy now. And like this place which hitherto I liked not much.

RICHARD (*explaining*). The Queen find too much air in here.

ANNE. Oh? Do I?

RICHARD. You do, madam.

ANNE. I do.

ALICE. One could draw the canopy, sire, and shelter from any draught. 'Tis what I do.

RICHARD. How, mistress?

ALICE. Like so. (*Struggling with the bed canopy.*) Help, William.

WILLIAM. Aye. Beg pardon.

   WILLIAM *and* ALICE *draw the curtains half round the bed.*

RICHARD. Do they not surround us, then?

WILLIAM. Can do. Can do.

RICHARD. Then do. Then do.

   WILLIAM *and* ALICE *curtain off the bed by means of the canopy. The* King, Queen *and* OXFORD *are now completely hidden.* WILLIAM *and* ALICE *exchange glances. They don't know what to do next. There's a pause. Then William coughs.*

WILLIAM. Majesty?

RICHARD. Aye? What is it?

WILLIAM. Do you want else?

RICHARD. How else?

WILLIAM. I don't know, sire. Just else.

RICHARD. No. 'Tis very snug.

WILLIAM. Should we leave you then, O Brightest Stars in the Firmament?

RICHARD. As you wish.

ALICE. We will stay Lord, if you require it.

RICHARD. Excellent.

WILLIAM. Then we'll stay. Shall we stay quiet or what?

RICHARD. Aye, quiet is best. (*Mumbles from the inside the canopy*). Oh no, best make a noise, else we shall not know if you remain.

WILLIAM. What kind of noise, Majesty?

RICHARD. Well, something pleasing, Mayor. Can you sing?

WILLIAM. No. Not uh singing as such. No.

ALICE (*hissing*). I told you he liked music.

RICHARD. Shame. Just hum then, eh?

WILLIAM. Hum?

RICHARD (*out from the giggles*). Aye, that's it, Mayor. You hum for us while your wife gets the supper out for the rabble.

WILLIAM. Oh. (*Doubtfully.*) Right-o, then.

WILLIAM *hums.*

Scene Five

A room in the house of GEOFFREY *and* KATHRYN LE KOLVE.

GEOFFREY LE KOLVE *paces about, agitated. Sitting are* KATHRYN *and* FATHER HENRY MELTON. *They're eating an elaborate meal.*

GEOFFREY. I'll tell you what's happening.

KATHRYN. Oh?

GEOFFREY. He's petitioning the King. That's what. That is what is happening at the Selby house this minute.

KATHRYN. To what end?

GEOFFREY. For my land down Hen Street. Two houses. He's had me in court twice over it and been thrown out. Now he'll petition the King.

KATHRYN. Oh, them! What do you say? Two houses? Two huts you mean, barely stood up. Where you put Thomas and Sarah.

GEOFFREY. Two labourers' houses.

KATHRYN. You don't want them huts, husband. And Thomas could go to your house in Bootham. That's bigger. And empty.

GEOFFREY. I do want 'em! An' I should be Mayor, too. It's my turn. He been Mayor three years. I should be Mayor! Then the King would sleep at our house and I could petition him about my quarrel over the five acres in Stamford Bridge. An' I promised the Bootham house to Walter. So I do want 'em!

KATHRYN. Ease up, husband. You'll be sick.

GEOFFREY. I am sick. (*To* FATHER MELTON.) I prayed over them acres, Pastor; a lot of good it done me.

FATHER MELTON. Pray? how?

GEOFFREY. How? Rosary. Um . . . Novenas. I don't know – plain prayers– 'Dear God, let me have that land' prayers. Amen.

FATHER MELTON. For prayers re: land you need a relic of some sort. Let me think . . . Uh! A piece of St Peter's keys. They'll unlock property.

GEOFFREY. Aye!

FATHER MELTON. I have a piece, but 'tis not cheap.

GEOFFREY. To buy?

FATHER MELTON. To kiss. I'll not sell relices. 'Tis corrupt.

GEOFFREY. An' 'tis bad business.

KATHRYN. To think that Alice Selby entertains a King and Queen. It makes me boil.

GEOFFREY. And me.

KATHRYN. Her kitchen's no comparison with mine. Nor her cooks. Nor her hangings. Nor her bed. *And* it's small that house.

GEOFFREY. Oh, tain't small.

KATHRYN. 'Tis small. The building is big out but 'tis not big indoors. What do you say, Henry?

FATHER MELTON. Um. I'm not worldly on the size of houses.

KATHRYN. 'Tis good you should have one thing to be not worldly on.

FATHER MELTON. I think so.

KATHRYN. Worse, the woman herself is big outside but small indoors. She buys books and talks a sort of French and understands neither.

GEOFFREY. You set too much store by books, madam. She's a good wife, that mistress. She been more Mayor than him.

KATHRYN. Oh has she? And have *I* not been *your* back legs for twenty year?

GEOFFREY. She's seen at functions.

KATHRYN (*outraged*). And I am seen, sir! And I am seen! I guarantee I am seen at functions *more* even if I attend fewer. Men have washed up at my bosom, Mister. More fellows shipwrecked on me than Alice Selby have anchored with her leaden chat at your precious functioning. Is that not the truth, Father?

FATHER MELTON. Oh. Uh. 'Tis probable.

GEOFFREY. A man cannot succeed in public when his private is wagged from tongue to tongue.

KATHRYN (*in mock outrage*). And what mean you by that, prithee?

GEOFFREY (*backing down*). I should be Mayor, that's all.

KATHRYN. Now you take heed, Mister. I'll not be scape-goat to your thin blood which has more water in it than you cheat into your paint.

GEOFFREY. Enough, woman!

FATHER MELTON: I have counsel could I get a word in edgeways.

KATHRYN: What?

FATHER MELTON. 'Tis simple. Speak to the King yourself. Gain audience. Take gifts. Kathryn will charm him. She has made walls smile; a King should not trouble her. Honeyed so, he will hear your case no less kindly than the Mayor's.

KATHRYN. Better, I should speak to the wife. She has no children. I'll cure that.

FATHER MELTON. No witchery, madam. It's a mortal sin.

KATHRYN. Herbs and good prayer, Father. Not witchery.

GEOFFREY. So you think we should present ourselves? Hmm? At the Mayor's house?

FATHER MELTON. If needs be. Course, if the King stop for the Feast day and sees the plays and like ours . . .

KATHRYN. But where would he watch from? Minster Gates?

FATHER MELTON. Oh no. Above the Common Hall, surely.

GEOFFREY. No. 'Tis uncomfortable there for so long and late in the order. (*Pessimistically.*) No, no doubt he'll stop in Selby's house to watch, and hurrah their pageant and give them my land and champion their Guild and make him Mayor for life and 'Rise, Sir William' and all is utter lost and useless.

KATHRYN. Aye, well that be positive, husband.

GEOFFREY. Well . . .

KATHRYN. First, he could watch the plays elsewhere. Second, he could like your play best. Is it best?

GEOFFREY. Well . . .

KATHRYN. Henry?

FATHER MELTON. 'Tis cheapest.

GEOFFREY. Never!

FATHER MELTON. 'Tis cheap.

KATHRYN (*Machiavellian*). Aye, and this King love a good pageant. 'Tis a sorrow.

GEOFFREY (*bristling*). You could cover our wagon with gold and Will Bluefront and them boys would still look cheap! Great galleybaggers!

FATHER MELTON (*despairing*). Aye. And a fuzz-faced Mary and a fat Christ and the best bits hacked off as saving. Let me have cloth, sir! And gold!

KATHRYN. And change the boys, Geoffrey! If you cannot catch a King on the Cross play . . . aye . . . shoo off the old crew. That's the thing. Walter'll help. Give him the Jesus. He can soft soap the whole business.

GEOFFREY (*sulkily*). I don't know.

KATHRYN. Would scare the back legs off the Mayor and his shrew . . .

FATHER MELTON. That's true.

GEOFFREY (*thawing*). I can't afford to be throwing my money away. Each shilling I make has my sweat on it.

KATHRYN. Aye but 'tis not what you have, chicken, but what you can be *seen* to have. Put your money on the planks and it will be seen!

GEOFFREY. And what if they don't stop? And go home? Then what?

KATHRYN. They'll stop. They must. Do it, husband, and let them hurrah your pageant and give you the Mayor and give you the land and 'Rise, *Sir* Geoffrey!' And all is not lost and utter useless.

FATHER MELTON. Bravo.

KATHRYN (*going to the shuttered window*). We has a stopping place outside. They can watch from upstairs. A King at our window we could charge, we could get . . . what, another twenty pound from our station. Aye: we'll win his favour and flatter his love of the play with our wagon and (*She looks out suddenly and is startled.*) husband, am I lunatic or is weird scenes going on at the Selby house?

FATHER MELTON. What's afoot?

KATHRYN. Come, both of you! Is that not the Mayor's house and is that not a feast being fed to paupers?

FATHER MELTON (*sorrowfully*). My God, look at them meats.

GEOFFREY. By Christ, there's ten shilling on them plates. Look at them trays. Mutton.

FATHER MELTON. Sturgeon. Venison. Is that venison? I love a hung venison.

GEOFFREY. The blessed Virgin Mary, Mother of God. It's a madness.

FATHER MELTON. What a terrible waste. (*Miserably.*) Quails.

KATHRYN (*a sudden epiphany*). Husband! Quick! Quick!

GEOFFREY. What?

KATHRYN. Call the servants. We must get busy.

GEOFFREY. What's this?

KATHRYN (*pacing*). We've got beef hung for the feast day and two lamb. It's a tragedy but I suppose the cidered ham must go and all.

GEOFFREY. What's this? Go where?

KATHRYN. Call John, quick! And Susan and Sarah, and get them doling out before we lose everything . . .

GEOFFREY. Woman, are you queer?

FATHER MELTON. What ails you, Kathryn?

KATHRYN. Oh, shit. I'll do it myelf. I fight a lone war without a man near me with a bean to rattle in his skull. (*Wearily, as if addressing two children.*) If the Mayor dole out food can only be because the King wills it. Therefore we must dole out food an' all, else we lag behind. Do you see? Now get to. (*Calling.*) Sarah! Sarah!

KATHRYN *runs off.*

Scene Six

The Streets.

ALICE SELBY *and her waiting woman; the* QUEEN *and hers; the two servants behind at some distance.*
ALICE *is exhausted from this unfamiliar walking.*

ALICE. If Your Majesty tires we could have the horses brought up.

ANNE. Madam, I get sore rump from riding and a joggled view of a place. I like walking.

ALICE (*mournfully*). Oh yes, I love a walk. An' you thirst not, Highness?

ANNE. I thirst for people, mistress. Do you have none in the town?

ALICE. People? Oh aye, we do, many. My husband thought you'd wish the streets clear.

ANNE. Why?

ALICE. We have the usual harvest of lepers and paupers. They affect the view. Also six sergeant run ahead, ma'am, sweeping the walk and shooing beggars. Did the Minster please you, my Lady? 'Tis said if our spire soared taller 'twould tear heaven.

ANNE. I would like it more, mistress, if you would accompany me unaccompanied by your smell. What is it?

ALICE. 'Tis an orange stuck with cloves and rosemary, Majesty, it keeps off infection.

ANNE. No doubt, but it infects me and makes my head ache.

ALICE (*throwing it high behind her*). 'Tis gone, Your Majesty. I beg pardon.

ANNE. No madam, beg not or you will be shooed off by your sergeants. I would like people, if only to measure your spires by.

ALICE. Cicely! Run ahead and tell the men to call out folk to stand against their houses. *Do* you wish any by the Minster, madam? We could return and look again with persons by it.

ANNE. Oh no, let's walk on, eh?

ALICE. 'Tis a very clean town, my Lady. Have you noticed? No pig muck. Nowt. We'll not have it. We have laws for hygiene. My husband made them.

ANNE. What think you when the people make their own laws?

ALICE (*not certain what she's supposed to think*). Um . . . how think you, Your Majesty?

ANNE. I have no quarrel with clean streets.

ALICE. Yes, my husband has achieved much as Mayor. He is out all the hours of the day and if he's not devoting his energies to the town's benefit, then he's in the court up to his girdle in litigation.

ANNE. Oh dear.

ALICE (*transparent*). By coincident we stand by two houses here which belong rightly to my husband and are contested.

ANNE. Which houses?

ALICE. Well . . . more huts, in truth . . . these madam. But for the charge of our lawyer they should be palaces. The business grieves my husband sorely.

ANNE. I'm sorry to hear it.

ALICE. Are you? Are you, Most Beneficent Majesty?

ANNE. Well yes . . . quite sorry.

ALICE. Aye. Them are the two huts of Hen Street. I expect you, like me, hold your man upright?

ANNE. I expect I do, from time to time.

ALICE (*warming to her task*). And I wager . . . just like me . . . you play Virgin to his Christ.

ANNE. How's that, mistress?

ALICE. You know, my Lady: to speak to him they must first speak to me.

ANNE. I see.

ALICE. How long may you stop with us, dear Queen?

ANNE. Oh, I know not. Past the plays, then I know not.

ALICE. Aye, but definite past the pageants then?

ANNE. Aye.

ALICE. Aye. Well, my husband's guild is most proud of its plays. 'Tis most lavish. His plans are most lavish.

ANNE. Your husband, madam, is wonderfully represented by you.

ALICE. Oh. 'Tis strange. Last night I dreamed he were Sir William. I woke with cheeks wet from tears of joy.

ANNE. If he is one quarter of the man you describe, he should be Sir at least.

ALICE (*excited*). Yes! Yes, my Queen! Were he one quarter the man! What keeps Cicely? Let me run ahead and find some folks for you to look at. Will you excuse me, dear lady?

ANNE. I will.

ALICE. *Au revoir, madame.*

ANNE. Yes.

> ALICE *runs off, leaving* ANNE *alone.*
> SARAH ZACHARY *appears.*

Hello.

SARAH. Your Majesty, I was called out to be looked at.

ANNE. Ah, thank you, and what's your name, mistress?

SARAH. Sarah, madam. Married to Thomas Zachary, labourer.

ANNE. Well, Sarah, would you mind if I leant on you, rather than looked at you?

SARAH. No madam.

ANNE. So Sarah, married to Thomas Zachary, labourer, are you the Mayoress' woman?

SARAH. Oh no, madam. I am in the service of the Master of the Painters' Guild.

ANNE. And is this your house then, there's a fuss over it? (*It is.*)

SARAH. Don't know, madam.

ANNE. I think it is.

SARAH. I think there may be some rivalry between the Masters in the town.

ANNE. I think there may be too, Sarah. Gently put. Now, do you know the route back to the Mayor's house?

SARAH. I do madam, I brought you a letter there this morning from my mistress.

ANNE. A letter?

SARAH. Aye. Inviting you to view the procession of the plays from my master's window.

ANNE. Mmm. Lead me back then Sarah.

As they exit.

SARAH. Certainly, yes madam.

ANNE. And tell me about your mistress, what's she like?

SARAH. Lovely.

ANNE. Lovely? And what else?

SARAH. She has some lovely gowns.

ANNE *and* SARAH *exit.*

Scene Seven

The Mayor's gardens. A prized lawn.

RICHARD, OXFORD *and* WILLIAM *appear armed with golf clubs and balls.*

WILLIAM (*cheerfully*). So, my Lord, what is it we aims at? (*Indicating merrily with his club offstage and up.*) The Minster glass! Ha!

OXFORD. He swing that club elegantly, eh sire?

RICHARD. 'Tis a sportsman.

WILLIAM. Well, more a Carlisle axe I'm used to.

OXFORD. Ah, a warrior!

WILLIAM. An' I like a kick at football.

OXFORD. 'Tis banished from London, football.

WILLIAM. Ay, an' here.

OXFORD. The traders say it disturb their stalls.

WILLIAM (*uncomfortably*). Aye.

OXFORD (*pointedly*). They do the same with men who disturb them.

WILLIAM. Aye?

OXFORD (*violently*). Aye, they do. They kick 'em out. Anything which disturbs their pile of coins: out!

WILLIAM. So, this golf, my Lords: a case of he who sends the ball furthest, is it?

RICHARD. Oh no, 'tis not a show of strength, Mayor, but of elegance. 'Tis one sport where brute force is not everything. No, 'tis a hole we need for a beginning.

WILLIAM. A hole? What kind of hole, Majesty?

RICHARD. Oh, a small one. Here will do nicely.

WILLIAM. This is my green, sire. 'Tis prized.

RICHARD. Aye, 'tis perfect for the game, Mayor. Congratulations. Have you seen a better green, Robert?

OXFORD. Never.

RICHARD. Nor me. Shall we start then, or must I admire your grass further?

WILLIAM (*tragically*). No. I'll just dig up a hole then. Here, you say?

RICHARD. Don't set to yourself, Mayor. You're playing. Have a boy out with a trowel. Otherwise every time we need another hole you'll be too occupied gardening to play.

WILLIAM. How many of these holes do we need?

RICHARD. As we like, Mayor. As we like.

WILLIAM. I'll get a boy, then. And a trowel. Excuse me, my lords.

WILLIAM *exits, leaving* RICHARD *and* OXFORD *alone.*

OXFORD. 'Tis almost sad were it not for his vileness.

The Queen enters.

ANNE. My lords, no golf?

RICHARD. We're due, madam. We wait on the holes.

ANNE. Ah. And how do the holes go down with the Mayor?

RICHARD. Deep, madam, deep.

OXFORD. His heart thump so, we fear it may thump out.

ANNE. No matter. His wife approaches and will have him canonized directly.

WILLIAM *returns with a servant.*

RICHARD. Ah, Mayor.

WILLIAM. Dig here, boy.

RICHARD. Aye lad: a hole the size of your fist and the length of your arm to the elbow.

The boy sets to work.

ANNE. Good day, Mayor.

WILLIAM. Oh, Majesty, forgive me! My mind wanders.

ANNE. Aye, well, how could you notice me? I am not at grass level.

WILLIAM. No. (*Wincing at the hole.*) Enough! (*Then anxiously to the King.*) Surely?

RICHARD. A finger more, I reckon. Eh, Robert?

OXFORD. Aye, a thumb.

RICHARD. That's it. Now, Mayor. Over here and tap your ball to the hole. He who sinks his ball with least strokes, wins. You begin.

WILLIAM. Oh no. You must start, sire.

RICHARD. No. You.

WILLIAM. I couldn't.

RICHARD. Start!

WILLIAM. As Your Majesty bids. (*He makes a good putt.*)

ANNE. Well done, Mayor!

RICHARD. Aye, well hit! Now me. (*He makes a bad putt.*)

WILLIAM. Good, Majesty.

RICHARD. No, sir. Bad.

WILLIAM. Aye, well: quite good.

RICHARD. Robert.

ROBERT *makes a good putt.*

RICHARD. Bravo. 'Tis your hit, Mister.

WILLIAM. Aye.

OXFORD. And you should win with it.

WILLIAM misses, quite deliberately, when it would be easier to sink his putt.

WILLIAM. No.

OXFORD. The idea of the game, Mister, is to get your ball down the hole.

WILLIAM. Aye. 'Tis Your Majesty next.

RICHARD casually and deliberately misses.

RICHARD. Missed, dammit. 'Tis your victory Oxford.

OXFORD. Aye, I'd say so.

OXFORD plays the ball behind his back and misses.

OXFORD. Oh gross *merde* of a Turkish donkey! Ah well, a formality, Mayor.

WILLIAM. Is it my hit again? Surely 'tis yours, Majesty!

RICHARD. No.

WILLIAM. I think I just had mine, sire

ANNE. You did and then the King did and then Robert did. 'Tis you again.

WILLIAM mournfully taps the ball into the hole.

RICHARD. You won, Mayor.

WILLIAM. I'm sorry, Your Majesty.

RICHARD. Hm. This hole poxes me. Let's make another.

WILLIAM. Another, Majesty?

RICHARD. Aye. A new one.

WILLIAM. Boy, dig another hole.

The servant trowels out another hole.

ANNE. How do you like golf, Mayor?

WILLIAM. Merrily.

RICHARD. You like it merrily? Good. What should I bestow on you now you've won a hole?

WILLIAM. Nothing, Majesty, other than your favour.

ANNE. Should you be hurt, husband, that the Mayor counts your favour so close to nothing?

OXFORD. More hurt he refuses a gift from you when he has a-showered you with trinkets.

RICHARD. Aye. I think I sulk somewhat.

WILLIAM. Please sire. Forgive me. I'd delight in a gift.

RICHARD. What would you like then, Mister?

WILLIAM. Um . . .

RICHARD. Name anything.

WILLIAM. I had a case at law, sir. I squabble over houses down Hen Street. I want 'em, my lord, and so do some other bugger.

There is a pause.

RICHARD. 'Tis greedy, sir.

WILLIAM. Is it?

RICHARD. What think you, madam?

ANNE. 'Tis a little greedy.

WILLIAM. Aye, you're right sire. 'Tis gross.

OXFORD. True, Mayor . . . not a little greedy: *gross* greedy.

WILLIAM. I'm sorry. I'll drop the suit.

RICHARD. Then let that be my gift: to encourage your generosity.

WILLIAM. Thank you, sire. Thank you. I love this golf. The whole town will be at golf soon. No pageants soon, for golf games.

RICHARD. Keep the pageant, sir.

WILLIAM (*quickly*). Right.

RICHARD. I like a play more than anything.

WILLIAM. And I do. And I do. Oh aye. Love a play.

RICHARD. Last year I were at Coventry.

WILLIAM. I heard, sire.

ANNE. The play there is excellent.

WILLIAM. And here, sire. Excellent.

RICHARD. What does your Guild present? (*He goes to the new hole.*) I like not this hole. Let's have another.

WILLIAM (*gloomily*). Another.

RICHARD. Aye.

WILLIAM. We could return to the first, sire, and begin again a new round.

RICHARD. No. A new one, eh Robert?

OXFORD. Oh yes. Definite.

RICHARD. You didn't speak of your pageant, sir.

WILLIAM (*gloomily*). Oh, 'tis the *'Slaughter of the Innocent'*, sir.

RICHARD. Ah, the Herod play. Wondrous Herod at Coventry. Very fine. Hair as red as a furnace.

WILLIAM. Oh, wait till you see ours, sire. 'Tis furious red.

RICHARD. Good. You to start, Mayor.

WILLIAM. Right.

They're putting only from a few yards. WILLIAM *holes in one.*

ANNE. Oh Mayor! Well hit!

WILLIAM. Oh. A fluke, Majesty. Not intended.

RICHARD. 'Tis the object, Mayor. What did you intend?

WILLIAM. Oh aye, 'tis the object, I know. I intended to be very close with my first hit. Oh.

At this ALICE *appears.*

ALICE. Majesties. My Lord. Husband. How is the golf?

ANNE. Your husband plays the game as well as he mayors, madam.

ALICE. Do he! (*Delighted, to* WILLIAM.) And have you given the King his winnings?

WILLIAM. Uh.

RICHARD. I win not, madam. In fact, I lose.

ALICE. Husband, is this true? Do you let a King lose?

WILLIAM. Uh.

OXFORD. He beats us both, madam. Skilfully.

WILLIAM. As gift for my winnings, sire, could I retreat now and count my blessings?

RICHARD. Aye, retreat.

ALICE (*furiously*). NO, Mister. You must play again. Did you need a new hole, Majesty?

RICHARD. Aye.

ALICE. Dig some more holes, Adam. Several.

ANNE. Your husband was just saying how much he liked the game.

ALICE. I bet. I mean, 'tis a Royal sport.

ANNE. Aye.

ALICE. Aye. I'd like to play myself, me. Do women, madam?

ANNE. Oh, I expect so.

ALICE. Then I'll learn.

ANNE. Splendid. In fact, mistress, as your husband has such a talent let him show you. My husband and the Earl will come with me now and I'll pass on the joys of our walk. (*She beams at* RICHARD.) Husband, give the lady your club.

OXFORD. An' here's mine!

ALICE. But Majesties!

ANNE. No buts! 'Tis our pleasure, eh my Lords?

RICHARD. Aye. We insist.

WILLIAM. Uh.

RICHARD. What's that, Mayor?

WILLIAM. Nothing, Majesty.

ANNE. So . . . adieu, mistress. Mayor.

OXFORD. Aye. Have fun.

  RICHARD, OXFORD *and* ANNE *exit, gaily.*

ALICE (*furiously*). Ach, William can I ask you a simple question? How is it you have not even the guile to manage to lose a game you cannot play!

WILLIAM (*heavily*). Boy: stop digging up my green, please, and go away.

  The servant exits.

ALICE (*with club and ball*). Alors. I just aims at the hole, do I?

WILLIAM. Madam, my patience is gouged. 'Tis a veritable sieve.

ALICE (*concentrating*). Aye? (*She hits the ball well.*) Heigh-ho.

WILLIAM (*very ill*). How many year do I breed this grass, madam?

ALICE (*sinking her putt*). There!

WILLIAM (*exploding*). OH GOD!!

  WILLIAM *whacks a ball offstage. There is a glorious smashing of glass.*

  (*Funereally.*) Oh, no.

ALICE (*looking, and nodding gravely*). 'Tis the Minster glass, William. 'Tis holed in one.

ACT TWO

Scene One

The week of the play.

WALTER's *workshop. Early morning.*
    Behind the screen WALTER *tries on the Mary costume while*
    SARAH *waits.*

SARAH. How is it, Master Walter?

WALTER. It don't fit, Sarah. I am grown at the shoulder since last year.

SARAH. Aye.

WALTER. And at the stomach. I can scarce breathe in it. (*He comes out, awkward, coy.*) I feel a right clot.

SARAH. You'll live.

WALTER. I pass for Mary?

SARAH. I think so. (*Adjusting her dress.*) Mistress Eleanor has made a man of you.

WALTER (*lightly*). Then I love her for others will only make a woman of me.

SARAH (*hurt*). That is not fair, Walter!

WALTER. I tease you.

SARAH. Well, you should not. 'Tis a raw thing.

WALTER (*taken aback*). Are you not happy wife to your Tom?

SARAH. I am.

WALTER. Well then.

SARAH. All the same, you should not tease.

WALTER. Oh Sarah. 'Tis long gone all that. Surely?

SARAH. Oh. Surely. (*Pause. Adjusting the dress. Simply.*) You look beautiful.

WALTER. What? With my beard?

SARAH. Aye, with your wee beard and your blue veil. I know you could not wed me, Walter. 'Tis one world to serve and another to be served. 'Tis not your fault.

WALTER (*awkward*). Well . . .

SARAH. I said to Mistress Eleanor I'd stitch her clothes for the church door.

WALTER. She said. 'Tis generous.

SARAH. And I'll make the christening gown, too.

WALTER. Madam you need not sew us into the sheets.

SARAH. No.

GEOFFREY (*off*). Walter?

WALTER. In here, master.

GEOFFREY (*off, nearer*). Walter?

WALTER. Here, sir.

GEOFFREY *and* FATHER MELTON *enter together.*

GEOFFREY. Ah Walter. (*To* SARAH.) 'Morning, Sarah. (*Then inquiringly, to* WALTER.) Do the merchants come for the Herod face?

WALTER. Aye. 'Tis wondrous red locks they bring for it: fresh cropped.

SARAH. Aye. 'Tis Edward's wife's hair. She sold it to pay for their bairn.

WALTER. No!

SARAH. Aye.

FATHER MELTON. See, Mister, they lavish on their pageant.

SARAH. They do, Mister. We heard they have new hose for the Jews and send for armour from Beverley.

GEOFFREY. Ach!

FATHER MELTON (*of* WALTER). See, Geoffrey. The boy grows too much boy for the Blessed Virgin.

SARAH. I do redress the dress, Father.

FATHER MELTON (*doubtfully*). But the face, too . . .

GEOFFREY. Walter, the merchants will outplay us; they plan to bring in their Herod, and the Kings, and will have a maid to play the Mother.

WALTER. Never!

FATHER MELTON. In London, Walter, the wives play the Assumption themselves. They know the King's likings and pander. So must we.

WALTER. So I am dumped, then?

GEOFFREY. Not dumped. We'll make a Jesus of you.

FATHER MELTON. 'Tis what you will.

SARAH. And Thomas?

GEOFFREY. We propose you to play the Mary, Sarah. You has a clear voice and fair face, and we hear the Queen smiled on you . . .

WALTER. And Thomas?

FATHER MELTON. Our scheme is to change all the men. Not just Thomas.

WALTER. How change?

FATHER MELTON. We search for new soldiers and may use the players from De La Poles of Hull.

WALTER. Minstrels?

GEOFFREY. No, proper players and highly spoke of. Will cost us eight pound.

WALTER. And why spend eight pound, pray, when your current men know the pageant and love it and are the pride of the Pinners and Painters?

FATHER MELTON. *Parce-que*, Walter, 'tis a play before a King.

WALTER. Does he not value these qualities?

SARAH. I think he do.

GEOFFREY. Think, Mister, of the Merchants' might. If we stick to our humble fair 'tis comparison of donkey with stallion.

WALTER. 'Tis a town, Mister, of citizens not knights, and thus have more use of donkeys. In my view.

FATHER MELTON. You wished to speak for Christ, Walter. Now you can. Your Thomas has played him too long, Sarah. 'Tis a young man's part. We all know it. And the cuts are restored. And the cloth. I have this new notion for the Christ's cloak. 'Tis so: Walter come on wrapped in the small purple. After he lay on the tree and the soldiers come to dice for it, 'tis picked up and on a sudden is lengths and lengths long.

SARAH. How?

FATHER MELTON. I have a method for substitution. The crowd will watch the *crucifying*, not the cloth.

WALTER. The business of the cloth, Parson, is similar to the business of the play. A week ago were subject to cuts, now is to be enlarged beyond belief.

FATHER MELTON. This Christ you will play, Walter, will be all gold on the planks; not simply the mask. And despite the buffeting will not be racked but will rest transcendent on the tree while the purple cloth billows out beneath him.

GEOFFREY. So . . .

WALTER. And our rehearsal?

GEOFFREY. Oh, rehearse! No harm done in that. Besides, De La Poles may not appear. No, rehearse. Don't want to upset the cart just yet, Walter.

WALTER. Then excuse me, Mister, pardon.

GEOFFREY. Aye.

FATHER MELTON. I'll follow shortly.

SARAH. May I go now an' all, sir?

GEOFFREY. Aye, do. But be bound to say nothing to the others, now.

SARAH. Aye, sir.

WALTER *and* SARAH *exit.*

GEOFFREY *and* FATHER MELTON *ruminate.*

FATHER MELTON. Hm.

GEOFFREY. The girl can be replaced. 'Tis a sop, in case the Queen do like her. Walter'll do it.

FATHER MELTON. I'm not so certain.

GEOFFREY. Oh I am, me. He'll want to get on. Aye, well if he don't, there's plenty who will. Forget this rehearsal, Chaplain, and get word to Hull. And see if you can't get them for seven pound, eh?

GEOFFREY *and* FATHER MELTON *exit.*

Scene Two

The Streets.

SARAH *and a befrocked* WALTER *are on their way to rehearsal.*

SARAH. An' will you?

WALTER. Will I what?

SARAH. Play the Christ instead of my Thomas?

WALTER. I play the fool parading the streets in this frock. I may do. I may die. I don't know. Will you play the Virgin?

SARAH. Walter, I think gold Christs and flows of purple is plays for Italians and not for farthing folk who pack the station at Corpus Christi.

WALTER. Aye. I know, Sarah. Edward, who is a saint in my mind –

Edward speak of playing the plays with such joy. He hath but a
few words in it and they gross and cruel but his cheeks ruddy as
the pageant draw out next Thursday. 'Tis our man from our guild,
as they all be, and all should be.

SARAH. Then you'll say no.

They walk towards the Pageant House.

WALTER (*uncertainly*). Aye . . . well, I may do.

*The rehearsal takes place outside the Pageant House. The wagon
is dragged out ready. The players, WILL, EDWARD, THOMAS,
sit happily on the wagon, as WALTER and SARAH approach.*

THOMAS. Wife, who is this beauty you've brought?

WILL. Has a fine rump on her . . . How do, ladies?

WALTER. How do, Edward?

EDWARD (*laughing at him a little*). Well, Walter. An' you?

WALTER. Weary.

WILL. We'll have no sulking this morning, nips. Edward's missus
sends us great cake. Thomas is happy. I knows my part backward
and the day blesses us.

WALTER. Then let's start.

SARAH. May I watch, gentlemen?

WILL. Aye. Be our audience. (*To WALTER.*) And don't tell us you
have more changes. Keep that parson out and let's get on with the
pageant.

WALTER. Let's begin then.

THOMAS. Aye.

WILL (*imitating the trumpet fanfare, then announcing proudly*). The
Play of the Pinners, Latterners and Painters. Christ Crucified.

*What follows is a version of the York play No. 35, Crux, Jesus
Extensus in ea super terram . . . In the rehearsal the play is
performed humbly, earnestly and as beautifully as possible from
beginning to end. The performance of WILL, EDWARD and
company is broad, familiar and skilful. The original play is
extraordinary. My version is faithful to its content and style and
idiom.*

The Passion Play

The two soldiers enter followed by a bloodied Christ (THOMAS),
heaving the cross.

SOLDIER ONE (*played by* WILL). This way then nipper. Up on this
                       hill lay down the tree
                       and strip to stripéd skin.

SOLDIER TWO (*played by* EDWARD). I've brought stubs to nail
                       him up and mallet to mash them in.

SOLDIER ONE.   I've brought rope to bind him
                       and crown to crown him
                       and himself cross to cross him.

SOLDIER TWO.   By Christ, he do blaspheme and calls hisself
                       many things
                       as Saviour, King and God's son.

SOLDIER ONE.   What say you sir to this event?
                       Are you King? And will you rule from this
                       tree your kingdom?

SOLDIER TWO.   He calls himself nowt now but plays the fool.
                       Let's have him up and hear him sing.
                       I'll bang the holes in with this tool
                       And stretch him out and pull and pull.
                       (*He bangs at the cross to make the bore holes*)

SOLDIER ONE.   Aye, you do that while I crown his head
                       and thorn him bloody, thorn him red.
                       Till red runs down him, joins the stream
                       into the river bed.
                       Hail King, Hail Fool, Hail Witch, Hail Pleb!
                       (*He crowns Christ, with the crown*
                       of thorns)

SOLDIER TWO (*to Christ*). Come bend you back to this tree.

  Christ obeys.

SOLDIER ONE.   An' he do, an' he do, quiet as a lamb, see!

SOLDIER TWO.   I'll do his hands.

SOLDIER ONE.   I'll do his feet.

SOLDIER TWO.   Cross them and save one nail.

SOLDIER ONE.   What? Bash it through the two?

SOLDIER TWO.   Aye, bash it through the two.

SOLDIER ONE.   Then that's what I'll do, though 'tis a to-do.

SOLDIER TWO (*having difficulty as he nails Christ to the cross.*)
                      Oh shit, that's a pain
                      I've not judged the holes right.

SOLDIER ONE.   Then stretch him again
                      and yank him to that side.

SOLDIER TWO.   Done it! by Christ! and broken the bone.

SOLDIER ONE.   To lug him down here
                      I've broken the toes
                      and smashed all the sinew.

SOLDIER TWO.   I'm knackered.

SOLDIER ONE.   I'm puffed.

SOLDIER TWO.   We'll never lift him.

SOLDIER ONE.   And he can't lift hisself now.
                      That's a sin.

SOLDIER TWO.   Well let's go for company to help do this deed.

SOLDIER ONE.   Aye, that's what we need
                      to mount King onto steed.

SOLDIER TWO.   Aye, let's not strain our souls
                      for the sake of this dolt.
                      By Christ, he's a do
                      for four, let alone two.

SOLDIER ONE *exits, then returns, bringing on two other soldiers, non-speaking.*

SOLDIER ONE.   Come on you boys
                      and help heave him high
                      he's off to the tournament
                      between land and sky.

SOLDIER TWO (*investigating*). Have they had his tongue out?
                      He were such a loud mouth.

SOLDIER ONE.   We'll soon make him sound
                      when we throw him hard down.

SOLDIER TWO.   Up boys up.

SOLDIER ONE.   Heave boys heave!

SOLDIER TWO.   By Christ, he's a bugger!

SOLDIER ONE.   Let's drop him again.

SOLDIER TWO.   See how he do shudder.

SOLDIER ONE.   That hurt him! That pained!

SOLDIER TWO.   Blast! I've done my shoulder.

SOLDIER ONE.   Shit! I've done my back.

SOLDIER TWO (*kicking the cross*). You sod!

SOLDIER ONE.   You turd.

SOLDIER TWO.   You've got a nerve.

SOLDIER ONE.   Call yourself God!

SOLDIER TWO.   Ha! Now he do whimper
                    Were he a real God he'd simper!

SOLDIER ONE.   Ha! How he do moan.
                    So much for your throne.

SOLDIER TWO.   Where is his soldiers come to rescue him?

SOLDIER ONE (*spearing Christ's side*). Here's his banner though.
                    This red flag on his bones.

SOLDIER TWO (*as they exit*).
                    Come along, boys, let's leave this scene
                    We'll raffle his cloak for a flagon.
                    He's not going to sing, is he?
                    Or jump down from our wagon.
                    This so-called King is a worm, not a dragon.
                    And we've threaded him here on the tree
                    So all he'll catch is the sun
                    All he'll catch is his breath
                    All he'll catch is his death and that slowly.

The two soldiers exit.
CHRIST is left alone on the cross, but as he speaks MARY
(WALTER) enters.

CHRIST.   Ah . . .
                    Father
                    Forgive them their cruelty
                    They know nothing of me.
                    They here have me tree'd.
                    For Adam's sin I now bleed
                    and tremble and bleed
                    and pray you will speed
                    to release me from this pain.
                    Your son swoons dear Lord
                    and I pray
                    that all that I suffer may not be in vain
                    but bring down your mercy on men
                    like an endless cleansing rain.

MARY.   Alas, my love, my life, my Liege.

> Alas, mourning now maddens me.
> Alas, my boy look down on me,
> Thy mother that did bear thee.
> You are my fruit, I fostered thee,
> and gave thee suck upon my knee.
> Upon my pain have pity.
> Alas to find my boy –

WALTER *is interrupted in mid-pieta by a suffering* THOMAS.

THOMAS. Ow! Walter I must get down!

WALTER. What?

WILL (*angry*). What's he yoppeling?

SARAH (*worried*). Tom?

THOMAS (*urgently. During this*). I must come down. I've got cramps all up my leg.

WALTER. Oh right.

WILL. You can't! He can't!

THOMAS. I has to, Will. Ow! Help me!

WILL. You can't get off the cross in the middle of the pageant!

THOMAS. I 'ave to, Will. I'm buggered. Yow!

EDWARD. Ease up, Will. 'Tis only a rehearsal. Come on, Tom, I've got you.

They begin to get TOM *down.*

WILL. Ach! It were going perfect. Come on then, Galleybag.

They lower the cross.

SARAH. You all right, lovely?

THOMAS. Ow! Ow! Ow! Don't touch my leg!

The others laugh.

EDWARD. Tom, you're dancing! In't he, eh!

THOMAS. Don't touch my leg!

Much merriment as THOMAS *dances.*

Scene Three

The Le Kolves' bedroom. Early morning.

KATHRYN LE KOLVE *and* FATHER MELTON *are in bed. They both wear shifts and take it in turn to delouse each other.*

KATHRYN. I must get myself to the Queen.

FATHER MELTON. And I to the chapel.

KATHRYN. The bugs seem to love this cloth particular. (*Meaning his shift.*)

FATHER MELTON. Is my hair busy?

KATHRYN (*exploring and finding a bug*). Here's a plump boy! (*She pops it.*) Aye. I will say I like the look of the Earl. He has a fine leg on him.

FATHER MELTON (*producing his leg*). Do I?

KATHRYN. Very fine but not so influential.

FATHER MELTON. Madam, I have access to God . . . 'tis more influence than with any King.

KATHRYN. Aye, but less rare.

FATHER MELTON. How less rare?

KATHRYN. Half the town has the Holy Orders. Only Robert has the King's.

FATHER MELTON. True.

GEOFFREY (*off*). Madam.

KATHRYN. Sir.

GEOFFREY (*off*). Are you a-bed still?

KATHRYN. Aye.

GEOFFREY (*off*). Is the priest with you?

KATHRYN. Aye, he ministers to me.

GEOFFREY (*off*). Does he?

KATHRYN. Both to my soul, sir, and to my bugs.

GEOFFREY (*off*). Can I come up?

KATHRYN (*laughing*). No. (*To* FATHER MELTON.) Not when my soul is bared so.

GEOFFREY (*off*). What's that?

KATHRYN. We shall be down by and by, sirrah. (*To* FATHER MELTON.) Cover yourself up, Henry.

GEOFFREY (*off*) We are appointed to attend the Royal Party in the hour.

KATHRYN (*as they dress*). If you are happy to bellow, Mister, we need not dress ourselves but simply stay here and converse with their Majesties so.

GEOFFREY (*off*). What, pray, madam, is a husband to do when his wife forbids him entry to the bedroom and then lives her life there?

KATHRYN. If I could learn you one thing, Mister, it is that nothing was ever solved by whining. 'Tis a dog's solution and not a man's.

GEOFFREY (*off*). Ach!

KATHRYN (*to* FATHER MELTON). I think he quiets. (*She listens.*) Yes. 'Tis the whining I can't forgive him for. That and the excessive sweat he make. Unnerve him, Parson, and the liquid dribbles from him. Or excite him, the same. 'Tis hard to clasp a man to you, so slippery.

FATHER MELTON. What wear you to the King?

KATHRYN. Oh, nothing grand, but look . . . (*She gets up from the bed and fishes around in the chest at its foot.*) How do you like this, Henry? (*It's a large silk handkerchief. She waves it above her head.*)

GEOFFREY *bursts in, clutching a bale of cloth.*

(*Glowering.*) You burst in on us, Mister. I like not to be burst in on.

GEOFFREY. This has just arrived madam. Think of me as fetcher and carrier. (*He indicates the cloth.*)

FATHER MELTON. 'Tis the cloak, Kathryn. Marvellous.

GEOFFREY. Is so much cloth necessary? 'Tis like the Red Sea.

KATHRYN. Except purple.

FATHER MELTON. Are you not stunned by it, sir?

GEOFFREY. I am stunned more by its cost.

FATHER MELTON. Will not be torn, sir. Can be re-used each year. In time 'twill be cheap. Look at it, Kathryn. Beautiful. Beautiful.

GEOFFREY. I'm just saying it won't be cheap in my time.

KATHRYN. Mister, you will bless us for the cost when the King stand by you and gasp at the spectacle.

GEOFFREY. If he comes.

KATHRYN. He will come. Don't doubt it, sir.

GEOFFREY; Aye well, I liked things as they were, when Kings were Kings and a play had less effect and more language.

KATHRYN. Yes, sir, you has the taste of a labourer!

GEOFFREY. Aye, I has!

KATHRYN. Be educated, sir!

GEOFFREY. Madam, I fork our for your niceties, there is not fat for mine.

KATHRYN. Geoffrey, you are so *pickled*!

GEOFFREY. An' you would be! My fellows blame me for the cost, my workers set a-mumbling if I enter the shop. My best apprentice will not swap words at all, I am banned from my wife's bedroom when other folk seem welcome and I am faulted for being pickled. I am pickled!

KATHRYN. Husband, we all bear crosses.

GEOFFREY. Aye, well Walter won't bear his. Have you heard that? He won't play the Christ. Makes you wonder, don't it? Makes you bloody wonder!

KATHRYN. I have Sarah sullen, and the taxing friendship of a monarch in prospect. Nor am I best well.

FATHER MELTON. Please, peace, please! The pageant will be true reward for all our efforts. 'Tis certain our play is a star will outshine all others. I have eyes and ears about the Merchants' rehearsals. They have a vulgar Herod who will say too much, too loud. By contrast we will seem an elegance.

GEOFFREY. Well, I'm not elegant, me. It would seem more elegance to me were my wife to drape this purple about herself and not the pageant. But I don't know the fashion. I'll get off and leave you to your fashion. Whatever it is.

GEOFFREY *exits sadly.*

Scene Four

The Mayor's house. The bedroom.

ANNE *delouses* RICHARD *who delouses* OXFORD. *All are sitting on the bed.*

ANNE. Husband, you're crawling.

RICHARD. 'Tis the region, madam. I was clear in London.

ANNE. Oh sir, that's false: no less than your subjects swarm to feed on you do the fleas come nibbling. You are King to too much life.

RICHARD. Well, I like not being either host to the fleas nor guest of the Mayor.

ANNE. Would you rather to the Abbey!

RICHARD. God, no.

OXFORD. Where is the Archbishop?

RICHARD. At war, somewhere. For a man ordained to save souls, he spends much time despatching them to the fires. 'Tis a hard man and a friend now of Gloucester's and Henry Bolingbroke.

OXFORD. And no friend of mine.

RICHARD. No. He would be Bishop of Westminster and Cardinal. He thinks you barred his way when you were at court.

OXFORD. I did. I would have him Bishop of the Channel and swim in his parish.

ANNE. Robert!

OXFORD. Well I would. 'Tis a lunatic church, madam, and Christ must wonder wide-eyed at us. We have two popes: the Frenchman a butcher, the Italian an oaf. And under their gaze the church is mother to a guild of tinkers and tonsured criminals for whom heaven hath arrived prematurely on earth. To call her corrupt is to call water wet and fire hot. His grace the Archbishop has more land than a Lord *and* more army. He is further from God than the flea.

ANNE (*teasing*). You like him little then?

OXFORD (*laughing*). Aye. Little. He and his like marooned me from you both and would again.

RICHARD. Your head is deserted, Robert. The bugs find little to feast on in your hair, 'tis too acid there.

OXFORD. Aye.

ANNE. Who will search me?

OXFORD. Us both. Ah, here's a lizard!

RICHARD. And here's a toad!

ANNE. Away! You're toads the pair of you and I'll not tolerate your toady hands leaping on me.

RICHARD. Toady, toady. (*He tickles* ANNE.)

OXFORD. Toady, toady. (*He, too, tickles* ANNE.)

ANNE. Get off! Anyway, the song of toads is not 'toady, toady'. So there.

RICHARD. I did not know my Queen was an expert on the toad.

ANNE. Sir, I married one (*A beat.*) and he turned into a prince.

OXFORD. Bravo.

RICHARD. Madam, you are a joy.

ANNE. Am I? Then I am a joy with a headache. So let us give audience to these painters and get us back to bed.

RICHARD. Why are we meeting painters?

ANNE. Because it suits me!

RICHARD. Oh?

ANNE. And to keep the waters agitate. A calm surface would show our Mayor the measure of his folly. This painter is his rival. Let's have them all in, let's have their beds.

RICHARD. More beds?

ANNE. The painter's wife begs me to visit hers. I have a letter from her. They would we watch the pageant from their station.

OXFORD. She writes? Perhaps *I* should visit her bed.

ANNE. 'Tis not the pen you would mingle with, Oxford.

OXFORD. One can mingle with a horse, my Lady, 'tis the conversation one misses.

RICHARD. Then let us dress ourselves and be kingly for the painter.

ANNE. I shall go with the mistress, sir. You seduce the man. We'll swap joys later.

RICHARD. Aye madam.

RICHARD *and* ANNE *kiss.*

But dally not with your sore head.

ANNE. Robert.

OXFORD. Adieu, my Lady.

ANNE *exits.*

Sometimes me thinks your Queen is wan, sir, and trembles.

RICHARD. Aye. In the night she grows hot then icy and cries out. The physician bleeds her but does not help, not quicksilver neither, nor gold. Her health is all my prayer.

OXFORD. And mine too.

RICHARD. I love her laugh more than the world and will clown all day to hear it. So long as she smiles let's sojourn here.

OXFORD. And then?

RICHARD. And then back to London and the penitent burghers. 'Tis the season of stubbornness. 'Twill pass as certain as Spring follows Winter.

OXFORD. 'Tis not long since you were drowned by this stubbornness.

RICHARD. Was I? Come friend, let's paint this painter a Royal portrait. Is there a crown for me?

OXFORD. There is, sire.

RICHARD. Then crown me and call in a page or two for the proper effect. Were we in London we could run to a few trumpets and bugger the parliament.

OXFORD *obliges*.

Scene Five

Downstairs in the Mayor's house.

ALICE *enters to find a weary, miserable* WILLIAM.

ALICE. Husband! How is it with you?

WILLIAM. Pricked, madam, sorely.

ALICE. Pricked?

WILLIAM. Aye. Like my grass.

ALICE. Why so gloomy, Mister?

WILLIAM. Ach! Half my trinkets and best relics dropped on His Majesty without effect. My thorn from Christ's crown: Pfft! Gone. And now His Majesty entertains Le Kolve and his missus by and by. 'Tis forgone between them will lard their way into his pleasure.

ALICE. I think no, sir. I think we shall outmethod them. I come via the seamstress. I have collected our wipes. And she tells me they have new costumes for the Painters' pageant and a great cloth. I worry not. We has a great Herod.

WILLIAM (*proudly*). Aye! And we have machines and devices! We have fabulous costumes!

ALICE. That's it, sir! Worry not on our standing. I'll outgrease Mistress Le Kolve. I am already confided of headaches and so forth from upstairs. 'Tis a young woman who wants a friend. I'll be it.

JOLYF ABSOLOM *enters, dressed in the Herod costume, carrying his mask.*

JOLYF. May I punctuate sir? I come for your feeling re: our rehearsal.

WILLIAM. Come in, come in, Master Absolom. Your Herod is a marvel, most monstrous roar and all.

ALICE. Aye marvellous, and with exploding arse: most devilish!

JOLYF *looks proudly at the fireworks attached to the back of his costume.*

JOLYF. So Your Worships is pleased?

WILLIAM. Oh aye. 'Twere a good rehearsal this morning.

JOLYF. Aye. 'Twas a ripe showing.

WILLIAM. Show us again.

> JOLYF *dons his mask.*

> Ha! 'Tis a marvel.

> JOLYF *roars obligingly and lengthily.*

> Aye, enough now.

JOLYF. I am particular pleased with my phrases.

WILLIAM. Oh?

JOLYF. I bring an extra speech or two with me.

WILLIAM. Oh.

ALICE. Aye, husband, like he refer to York and to our King an' all.

WILLIAM. Oh aye. Aye. Well made.

JOLYF. In truth, though I want not coin for it, I've exchanged a move here and a move there and a manner. 'Tis better for it.

ALICE. Well, Mister, my husband did say this morning of your high fee but evident you earn it.

JOLYF. I do, madam. You'd pay as much elsewhere for the voice alone. With me you get fireworks and new words. 'Tis a complete service.

WILLIAM. Tell me, sir, how compares now our pageant with Coventry?

JOLYF. Well, sir, your Herod is superior. And if he is, the pageant is. I'd say 'tis more fearsome than Coventry.

WILLIAM. Is it?

JOLYF. Should I share a secret or would you be surprised on the day?

WILLIAM. No, say sir. On the day we has ceremony to stand on and would not be surprised.

JOLYF. We plant our women in the crowd at each station.

ALICE. Ha!

JOLYF. Aye, but here's the rub. Each has in her bundle a pig's bladder loaded with gore. So when the soldiers come to slaughter the Innocents, each dip his sword to the bundle like so: in! and splash guts all over the crowd and carry off his bloodied sword aloft.

ALICE. Oh.

JOLYF. Aye, 'tis effective. I anticipate swooning.

ALICE. So do I, sir.

KATHRYN *and* GEOFFREY LE KOLVE *enter.*

KATHRYN (*briskly*). Felicitations, sir, and how do? Dear sister, a gift! (*She thrusts some flowers into* ALICE's *hand.*) Picked from our gardens in Hen Street.

ALICE. *Merci.*

KATHRYN. 'Tis a shame your garden is pock-marked so.

GEOFFREY. How do, Your Worship.

WILLIAM. How do, master. The Queen descends, madam, and will enter shortly. My garden is dug for golf.

KATHRYN. Golf! (*Anxiously not to be out-knowledged.*) Oh aye, golf. (*She pronounces it as if it were French.*) Do we intrude, madam? You seem burdened with show business.

WILLIAM. This is Master Absolom.

GEOFFREY. How do?

WILLIAM. We was just showing him the Herod mask.

ALICE. And you've been keeping the drapers busy, we hear.

KATHRYN. Oh . . . (*Shrugging.*) is your pageant prepared?

WILLIAM. We are so pecked by civic affairs we have small appetite for such luxuries. And yours?

GEOFFREY. Oh, apparently 'tis fine. How goes our play, Kathryn?

KATHRYN. Fair, I think. Humble.

ALICE. Well we was just speaking how much we look forward to viewing it.

KATHRYN. Then 'tis coincidence mistress. We was just relishing yours.

ANNE (*off*). Mistress Selby.

ALICE (*simpering*). I am called. (*Shouting.*) I come, my Queen. *Excusez-moi.*

KATHRYN (*producing a large handkerchief*). *Tout à l'heure.*

ALICE (*producing a larger handkerchief*). *Tout à l'heure.*

KATHRYN *scowls.*

JOLYF. I'll withdraw an' all.

KATHRYN. Don't mind us, we're just passing. We have royal business you see.

JOLYF. No, no, I'll retreat. I'll make an exit.

WILLIAM. Aye, sir, retreat.

JOLYF *exits.*

ANNE *enters.*

KATHRYN *prostrates herself. So does* GEOFFREY. WILLIAM *decides against it then feels at fault and prostrates himself.* ANNE *comes through.* GEOFFREY *has rehearsed his exhortation.*

GEOFFREY. Sweet Queen, gracious light of our darkness, lustre of our eye, blush of our cheek, most precious jewel in the crown, receive our humble greetings.

KATHRYN. Majesty. First woman of our realm and fairest. 'Tis our finest hour to find your favour.

ALICE (*gleefully*). 'Tis Geoffrey and Kathryn Kolve, your Royal Highness.

KATHRYN (*hissing*). Le Kolve.

ALICE (*gleefully*). Forgive me, I still think of you as plain Kolve. I forget you have added a Le. Aye, *Le* Kolve, Majesty, of the painters' trade.

ANNE. To your feet, madam. I cannot curtsy for my head confounds me somewhat. And you, sir. My husband will receive you in the upper storey. I will walk with your wife. (*To* ALICE.) Mistress Le Kolve has written inviting us to view the pageant from her room. 'Twas a bright note and I will see it.

KATHRYN. Madam, we are delirious with joy.

ANNE. I hope not; else us both will wobble on the other to your house.

KATHRYN. Should I send for a horse, Majesty?

ALICE (*smugly*). No, mistress, the Queen likes not to ride.

ANNE (*to* ALICE). Thank you, Madam Mayor. I should like to ride this once. (*To* KATHRYN.) Come madam. (*To* GEOFFREY.) Sir, get you to my husband. (*To* WILLIAM.) Mayor, you could rise, perhaps and lead your friend to the King. *Adieu.*

KATHRYN. *Adieu* husband. Sir. Madam.

ANNE *and* KATHRYN *exit.*

WILLIAM (*brusquely*). This way, sir.

GEOFFREY. Thank you, Mister. (*To* ALICE.) Madam.

ALICE (*as the men exit*). 'Tis good the Queen come to your house at this hour. She will see it gets little sun past midday.

GEOFFREY. True, madam, little glare to distract from the plays.

GEOFFREY *and* WILLIAM *exit*.

Scene Six

KATHRYN LE KOLVE's *bedroom*.

KATHRYN *enters with* ANNE. ANNE *inspects the bed*.

KATHRYN. Here is the room, my lady, quite nice glass; and a view, you know. Quite a nice view. We think so.

ANNE. 'Tis a marvellous bed, mistress.

KATHRYN. Aye, Majesty, much cherished.

ANNE. Has been my choice of gift since I have been to York. I have four.

KATHRYN. Five, my lady.

ANNE. Splendid!

The lights cross-fade to the Pageant House.

Scene Seven

Outside the Pageant House.

The original cast of the crucifixion play sit brooding on the news of their substitution.

EDWARD. And can they undo us so easy?

WILL. They can do what they will.

EDWARD. 'Tain't really a guild play if none of the guild be in it.

WILL. Never has been a guild play in that case. We're hardly guild. The masters is the guild not us, and they walks before the wagon or lords it from their window. We're doers. No more. Took me a bugger to learn them changes.

EDWARD. So you is to be Christ then, Walter?

WALTER. 'Tis broached but not agreed.

THOMAS. Aye, well good luck to you Walter. I'm not grudged. You learned us our parts each year. No need to have done that then, nor feel badly now. Besides, I know they laugh at my fat Christ.

SARAH. No, they don't.

WILL. Course they don't laugh. And no, ain't your fault Walter. The King stir up nonsense in the town. Each gentleman fears disfavour, each outwits himself so as not to be outwitted by others. So 'tis a town on a sudden of no wits, no beds and a thousand wipes. Makes me spew.

SARAH. 'Tis not the King.

WILL. Course it is! 'Tis the same Richard who pissed on our dads fifteen year ago.

SARAH. Fifteen year ago, Will Bluefront, he were a boy and others ruled in his name.

WILL. 'Tis not what I heard.

SARAH. Aye, but you heard last year the Frenchies had landed and that there were a third pope.

WILL. 'Tis known history, mistress, that the King went back on his word to the commoners.

WALTER. Aye! In that case 'twill be known history that in thirteen hundred and ninety-two we were replaced to improve the play. Is that right?

WILL. Improve? Bugger off!

WALTER. Why then?

WILL. 'Cause the masters is bloody dense is why.

EDWARD. Walter's right. Say why we've been chucked off Will.

WILL. Well, we knows why . . . 'tis a fever in the town, 'tis brain pox. (*He can't think, frustrated.*) I can't say in one go, why.

WALTER. An' I'm saying 'tis as likely what happened in the past to the King is as little to do with him being good or bad as us being good or bad now.

WILL. Not *us*, nipper. *You're* all right.

WALTER. I'll not do the play without you.

WILL. Ach!

SARAH (*delighted with* WALTER). Oh Walter! And nor I will.

WILL. Well, you should.

EDWARD. Course you should. Some of us should be up there.

WALTER. Besides . . . these players from Hull . . . They're rogues who do no honest labour but simply antic and clown for the big houses.

THOMAS. And I'll certain not have Sarah mingle with them.

SARAH. Nor will Sarah have Sarah mingle with them.

WALTER. Well, there you are. We're out.

SARAH. I will not hear the King blamed, sir, nor the Queen. They perceive the queue of flatterers no less than we do and have been gracious to me in this stay.

WILL. I still says is not *our* King any more than, now, is our play.

EDWARD. Course he ain't for us. An' why should he be? The shark is not for the sprat, Will. No, we is for him. Least I am. And proud of it.

WILL. Edward, your're proud of every cursed thing. You're proud of that Minster spire though will kill you and your kin in the making.

EDWARD. Aye, it will. And it will outlive us, just as the King's name will.

WILL. Ah but *he* won't, Edward. He'll be in the Dance of Death with the like of us and Master Le Kolve and the others. We'll all dance and none will be excused nor substituted.

EDWARD. And what's that got to do with our pageant? I've sulked sufficient, I'm to bed, me, and meet at Le Kolve's station for the *Corpus Christi*.

WILL. Oh no! I'm not viewing that play. Sod it!

THOMAS. Nor me.

EDWARD. Course you will. Come Thursday, you'll be jostling with the rabble and weeping at the two planks and a passion. And don't say you won't 'cause 'tis hollow threat. Nor you, Will.

WILL. Well I may. I may not.

EDWARD. Well I'll be there from the first and hope for your company. My missus still bakes her pasties and wish you share them with us.

WILL. Christ I'd quite forgot that! Can't miss them pasties and all. 'Tis a sore loss this business.

WALTER. Aye, I'll be there, Edward, but 'tis no two planks and a passion. 'Tis a new-fashioned cross and a golden Christ and a purple sea. 'Tis a spectacle . . . almost wordless.

WILL. So is our tree abandoned an' all? Ach!

WALTER. 'Tis all abandoned.

EDWARD. I've half a mind to say let's play it still.

WALTER. Do what?

EDWARD. No. I just thought.

THOMAS. I know what you thought, Edward. We could still play our old pageant and use the old gear and 'twould be no different than ever.

SARAH. To what end?

THOMAS. For our gang.

WILL. For half the town more like: who'll have no truck for golden Christs.

WALTER. Aye, but you can't push round the cross without licence.

WILL. More's the point you can't push round the cross with no wagon.

THOMAS. Then don't push it round. Play it stopped at a station.

WALTER. Whose?

THOMAS. Well . . .

SARAH. Hen Street! 'Tis not a station but could be.

THOMAS. Aye. Outside our house, eh love?

WALTER. And what of the masters? What of mine? Mr Le Kolve will not kiss me for betraying him.

WILL. 'Tis abandoned gear, we are abandoned players. If a man pick up what is thrown down 'tis no crime.

WALTER. Aye but we plan to compete.

WILL. And is competition a crime, then? In which case let the masters dungeon themselves for they will be first to gouge out their own eyes rather than be beaten to it by another. Does not your master undercut mine? Aye, he do, and so we shall play our play more cheaply and bid for the louder hurrah. I'm for it. What of the rest of you?

THOMAS. Aye, I'm game.

WILL. Edward?

EDWARD. I s'pose 'tis no great injury. The King will not view it, nor the Mayor nor Mr Le Kolve. 'Twill only be our gang.

WILL. Then 'tis up to you, Walter.

WALTER. Must I still speak for the Blessed Virgin?

WILL. Aye. And I'll scrape your jaw myself.

WALTER. Then I'll do it, but only for the pasties.

Scene Eight

The Mayor's house. The bedroom.

ANNE *is in bed.* RICHARD, *anxious, sleepless, presides over her.*
She wakes, coughs.

ANNE. Sir, did you sleep well?

RICHARD. Aye, love, and you?

ANNE. Mmm.

RICHARD. Madam 'tis capital to perjure a King.

ANNE. I said mmm. Mmm can mean many things.

RICHARD. As: no I did not sleep well but did fever and cry out and
tremble so this bed did shudder.

ANNE. Then you spoke not truly to me, sir. For 'tis not well slept to
catch these things.

RICHARD. Mistress. You should be attended by some physician.

ANNE. I'll have my mother and my own doctor.

RICHARD. They are not here. And they both offend you. Your
mother cannot forgive you for your quiet womb and your physic
cannot cure you of it.

ANNE. I chewed on Mrs Le Kolve's herbs for my belly, but 'twere a
penance.

RICHARD. I should return you to London.

ANNE. But will be surrender then, not triumph.

RICHARD. I am confident, sweet, that the maggots there grow
shrivelled for want of their apple and will wriggle well enough for
his return. We have sent for hint of how the mood prospers. All
being well we should return shortly.

ANNE. 'Tis all being *not* well presses us to.

RICHARD. No, madam, 'tis also true I am weary of gaming with
these people, and could not make my home here. They come too
early to fortune and choke on it.

ANNE. But if we return, what of Robert?

RICHARD. Madam, rest today, I command it. Tomorrow is the play
and a darling day for us.

ANNE. If I rest what of you, husband?

RICHARD. Oh, Robert and me may ride nearby and bathe or hawk
a little.

ANNE. Or wench a little.

RICHARD. Or wench a little. Aye, you has a stallion's image of me, I would not lose it. And you, do your lovers scale the walls as soon as I depart?

ANNE. In droves, sir. 'Tis an army. No wonder I tremble.

OXFORD (*off*). Majesties?

RICHARD. Robert?

OXFORD (*off*). Aye.

RICHARD. Then enter.

OXFORD. Sire, there is news from London.

RICHARD. They want me? See, I said. The vultures still have need of bits to peck at. Well, they must ransom me.

OXFORD. 'Tis from your uncle. He says the Archbishop returns to York for the *Corpus Christi*.

RICHARD. To what end?

OXFORD. I know not the motive, my Lord.

RICHARD. Does my uncle ask for my return?

OXFORD. He speak of the possibility.

RICHARD. The possibility! He speak of the possibility! I am King and there is possibility I return to my own court!

ANNE. My Lord.

OXFORD. He reports the Mayor and Sheriffs will welcome you back on certain conditions.

RICHARD. I will not hear of conditions. Conditions is weather and God have control of that and also makes Kings and subjects. Bear back to my uncle, the Regent, that my weather include need of changes, of gales, which will shiver the Mayor and his herd.

OXFORD. Should I not, instead, report your thanks and gratitude?

RICHARD. No sir! Report as I command.

OXFORD. 'Tis my experience, sir, that a spit from great distance is no match for a dagger on embracing.

RICHARD. Robert, why placate me when 'tis their crew who require your absence from home, and when this chaplain arrives to poison our leisure here?

OXFORD. No. Not poison. Spice.

RICHARD. How spice?

OXFORD. Majesty, the Archbishop wants crusades and war against the French pope. He wants funds for his own knights. He will not welcome this excess on the pageants. Tomorrow will be merry with bluster from both sides.

ANNE. Aye. You should join in, sweet, and make fuss of the spectacle, saying if York be so fat – then should gift more to the nation's purse.

There is a pause.

RICHARD. 'Tis two rogues I love.

ANNE. And who love you.

RICHARD. Aye, report to my uncle our thanks and gratitude. Aye. And let us tramp outdoor today and leave the Queen to her bedfellows. 'Tis, after all, a fine day, and if I am still un-Kinged I should enjoy the Summer like any citizen of the realm.

OXFORD. You will not come with us, Lady?

ANNE. I grow such a connoisseur of beds, Robert. I must savour them all day.

RICHARD. The Queen thinks we hunt for maids and not for fish.

OXFORD. Then let's promise to cook whatever we catch and supper on it.

ANNE. Best make it young girl then, Robert. Richard says my flesh is tough now.

RICHARD. Tough? 'Tis unchewable. I'll show you. (*He kisses* ANNE.) Adieu, madam, and be waited on.

ANNE. Aye, sir, and you escape from worry . . . Adieu Robert.

OXFORD. Adieu Majesty.

RICHARD. I'll send in your woman.

RICHARD *and* OXFORD *exit.*

ANNE, *alone, coughs violently and pulls the covers over her head.*

Scene Nine

Downstairs in the Mayor's house.

OXFORD *and* RICHARD *prepare for their outing.*

OXFORD. So, you'll go back?

RICHARD. Aye, we'll submit. If only to get the Queen to her physic.

OXFORD. Aye, 'tis reason enough. And I'll go back after tomorrow. I'll take a horse and ride cross country. Then a boat to Ireland.

RICHARD. I'll go to Ireland in the Autumn! We could meet.

OXFORD (*doubtfully*). Mmmm.

RICHARD. Except I may be more King then. And chaperoned.

OXFORD. Well . . .

RICHARD. More King and less Queen. She will not see September but see God first.

OXFORD. Come now . . .

RICHARD. No, 'tis fact. She has the most alive mind I know and the least alive body. The one seems to suck out the other too quick.

OXFORD. She may improve. These things are uncertain.

RICHARD. A new Queen is already arranged for me . . . not yet seven years old. I must be widowed then ringed to a baby. 'Tis a black prospect.

OXFORD. Then do not remarry.

RICHARD. Oh, Robert, we have an innocent eye of the world. 'Tis a machine and the King is but one cog and no more able to stop its workings than any other. 'Tis a great windmill and will grind us all. I am married to produce . . . to father . . . they give me a new womb to work at, once I have buried my grievance with the city — and buried the woman I love. Then, bereaved of dignity and bereaved of heart, I can stud and be put out to pasture.

OXFORD. This is bleak, my Lord. We promised to escape from worry. Where would you go?

RICHARD. To the country, sir. To the forest.

OXFORD. Aye. To forest fires, Richard, and warm, fat, forest haunches. Let's tumble off these humours — let's paddle. Let's baste ourselves.

RICHARD. Oh, sir. I want air, not smothering, not smothering.

OXFORD. Then let's have air, Majesty. Air all day.

RICHARD. Aye, but fun tomorrow, eh? There is still a little juice left in these York lemons. Let's squeeze out the last drop.

OXFORD. I never tasted a lemon.

RICHARD. I was sent six from the Roman pope.

OXFORD. What were they like?

RICHARD. Well, he also sent sugar. Sugar is better.

OXFORD. Aye, I like sugar.

RICHARD. I have some with me. Shall we taste it?

OXFORD. Aye.

RICHARD *produces a handkerchief. The sugar is wrapped inside.*

RICHARD. 'Tis milled fine.

RICHARD *licks his finger and dips it. Then he offers some to* OXFORD *who does the same.*

Scene Ten

The upstairs window of the Mayor's house looking out onto the street.

The idea is that the light on RICHARD *and* OXFORD *in their cups fades to black and this new one flashes up broad Midsummer's Day and noisy and the start of the* Corpus Christi *cycle. There are about forty-eight plays in the cycle. The Mayor's play is number nineteen, the Le Kolves', number thirty-five. What happens is that there are twelve stations . . . Le Kolves' perhaps the fourth in order and the Mayor's about eighth. Each play plays all twelve stations; the wagon being pulled from station to station. This all takes a considerable amount of time. It's unlikely that the cycle was completed within the twenty-four hours . . . It would be mid-afternoon by the time the Herod play was viewed by anyone and practically midnight for the Crucifixion. The late plays, therefore, were lit by torches: an expensive business. Great care would be taken to ensure the plays moved swiftly and efficiently: any traffic jam would have drastic consequences.*

The scene starts about seven in the morning at the latest, with the ARCHBISHOP, *the* MAYOR *and* MAYORESS *up at the window as the Creation Play, play number one, is waiting to start outside.* KATHRYN *and* GEOFFREY LE KOLVE, *with* FATHER MELTON, *are ready at the* LE KOLVES' *window. There would be a huge crowd at each station. The upstairs window above the play is, of course, reserved for the fat cats . . . it's the box at the opera. The play is held up for the arrival of* KING, QUEEN, *and* OXFORD. *This does not please the* ARCHBISHOP. *The* SELBYS *attempt to mediate.*

ALICE (*anxious*). Will you eat more, my Lord Archbishop?

ARCHBISHOP (*accepting, eating*). Hmm. 'Tis good your pie goes down well with me this morning, Mrs. For nothing else do.

ALICE. Thank you, my Lord.

ARCHBISHOP. Aye, 'tis a fat pie. But then 'tis a fat family. Indeed I come back to York and I am struck by fat. Everywhere fat.

ALICE (*mortified*). Oh.

ARCHBISHOP. I hear your play is fat, Mayor.

WILLIAM. Well . . .

ARCHBISHOP. Yes, fat everywhere. There is surely a connection between God and fat . . so much God, so much fat. More of one means less of the other. Let's have less fat, Mayor. Eh? Eh?

WILLIAM. Right.

ARCHBISHOP. Ach! The plays must begin. I think someone really should tell his Majesty that 'tis one thing to miss Holy Mass this morning, 'tis quite another to miss the Creation of the World.

WILLIAM (*acutely embarrassed and distressed*). 'Tis said he rouses, my Lord.

ARCHBISHOP. Oh marvellous! The miracle of Genesis and the miracle of his appearance all at once.

ALICE. We understand the Majesties slept not well.

ARCHBISHOP. Madam I push in thistles to my mattress to ensure I sleep not well. To sleep heavy is a venial sin, in my opinion.

ALICE (*to* WILLIAM). Should we call down to hold up the start?

ARCHBISHOP. Aye! Hold up Creation. Good idea. (*Hugely and crassly.*) Hold up down there! We wait on the King.

Dissenting murmurs are heard from below.

OXFORD *enters blearily.*

OXFORD. The King approaches. (*He sees the* ARCHBISHOP.) Good morning, my Lord.

ARCHBISHOP. Is it the Earl of Oxford?

OXFORD. Aye.

ARCHBISHOP. I am amazed, sir. The law exiled you, surely?

OXFORD. From London.

ARCHBISHOP. Oh no, sir. 'Twas from the realm.

OXFORD. The whole realm? Then I should not be here.

ARCHBISHOP. No sir, you should not.

OXFORD. 'Tis remarkable. The King and me both thought it were banished from London and the gaze of the new muscle.

ARCHBISHOP. No, I seen the papers as witness. An' 'tis not new muscle. 'Tis simply muscle long unflexed.

OXFORD. I'd best be off soon then. To somewhere deeply foreign.

ARCHBISHOP. Aye, deeply foreign were best, sir.

OXFORD. How is your hair shirt, my Lord?

ARCHBISHOP. Installed. (*He pulls at his clothes to reveal it.*)

OXFORD. Ah, there she is! I hear you wear it even when you take pleasure. That, to me, is the sign of a saintly man.

ARCHBISHOP. You missed the Mass this morning my Lord. 'Tis a mortal sin.

OXFORD. Oh I think we'll find a Mass somewhere later on. Surely?

RICHARD *and* ANNE *appear,* ANNE *fragile,* RICHARD *hungover.*

ARCHBISHOP. Majesty. (*To* ANNE.) Majesty.

RICHARD. My Lord Archbishop. This is a most pleasant surprise.

ARCHBISHOP. Ah, if you did not expect me, Majesty, then I am understood why you attended not my Mass and sermon.

RICHARD. No, Lord, we knew of your presence in the town but not of your presence at the Mayor's window. I like not to be told off before the plays and will have Mass later and without preaching.

RICHARD *walks to the window. Applause is heard. He and* ANNE *wave.*

RICHARD. That's a good crowd, eh Mayor? Not bad at all. (*Shouting down.*) Do start! (*Then back to* MAYORESS.) Any more pie? His Grace seems to have hogged all ours.

God the Father appears, if possible from a high point in the theatre corresponding to a high point in the street: say an arch of the city walls or a bell tower, to begin the first play, with dazzling light behind him, so as practically to obscure his face (which is a gold mask).

The constant murmur and humour of the crowd die away to reverence as the character speaks. There is genuine excitement.

GOD. *Ego sum alpha and O, vita, via, veritas,*
      Primus et Novissimus.
      I am gracious and great, God without a
      beginner. I am maker unmade and all might is in me.

ANNE (*clapping her hands*). Oh, I love a good God!

* * * * *

Later. The LE KOLVES' *station.*

KATHRYN, GEOFFREY, SARAH *and* FATHER MELTON *watch the explosive Herod play;* JOLYF *is doing his stuff below.*

JOLYF. No noise nippers. What!
Who dares mutter when I appear?
Herod – the mighty, marvellous, perfect.
Who dares talk
when such magnificence come to York!
I bluster and blast. I blow and blunder.
I crackle and clap and grunt and thunder.
I am most terrible, me!
Point out a man who is not on his knee
and I'll snap off his legs like twigs off a tree.

KATHRYN (*enjoying this hugely*). Gross. Ugh!

FATHER MELTON. 'Tis a reaction cheaply bought.

KATHRYN. Do Herod fart? I remember it not from the scripture.

FATHER MELTON. The mask is very fine, though, Mister.

GEOFFREY. Aye, 'tis too fine a mask for the player.

SARAH. 'Tis Walter's face, madam. He made it.

KATHRYN. Did he? Aye, 'tis well done.

GEOFFREY. Where is Walter! He were bidden aloft.

SARAH. Uh. He stays with the others of the old pageant.

GEOFFREY (*miffed*). Does he? Hmm. (*To* KATHRYN.) What time is the King due?

KATHRYN (*watching despite herself*). Sssh!

GEOFFREY. Sssh not! Beside, the rabble makes so much din the play can hardly be heard.

KATHRYN. Sssh!

FATHER MELTON. I think, Mister, he is sure to wait until this play is done outside the Mayor's station. This will not be until mid-afternoon.

KATHRYN. Later.

GEOFFREY. Should we wait on our feast, though?

KATHRYN (*not looking at him but with half an ear on the conversation*). Husband, we cannot eat before the Royalty arrives.

GEOFFREY. Madam, our play will not be here until near midnight. If the King deigns not to enter prior to then, our diet will be too much play, too little food.

KATHRYN. Oh, he will, he must. Sssh. For heaven's sake.

GEOFFREY. This King will or must do nothing.

FATHER MELTON. Aye. 'Tis true. He attended not the
   Archbishop's Mass this morning.

GEOFFREY. We heard he were discovered sleeping with the Queen,
   Oxford and a horse in his bed.

KATHRYN. Sssh, please. May not be well done, but 'tis a
   marvellous story all the same.

* * * * *

Later, outside the Selby station. JOLYF *has reached his patron's
station. He elaborates and explodes hugely.*

JOLYF.   Not just Richard come to rest
           but three more Kings from East and West arrive with word
           of some nipper born in a stable
           meant to be saviour, meant to be able to save the world.
           No bairn from a barn will compete with me.
           I am the biggest and blackest and cruellest and meanest.

Upstairs RICHARD *and* OXFORD *and* ANNE *misbehave. They
are at the cold buffet at this most inauspicious time. The Selbys are
increasingly desperate to get them to watch.*

WILLIAM (*proudly*). This be our pageant, my Lord.

RICHARD. Who's your man?

WILLIAM. He's imported sir.

RICHARD (*mischievously*). Shame.

WILLIAM. Exceptional red hair on him.

RICHARD (*mischievously*). 'Tis a wig though, surely.

WILLIAM (*defeated*). Uh.

RICHARD. The man at Coventry had most marvellous hair.
   (*Wandering off.*) Anne, are you drinking?

OXFORD. This one has most marvellous arse!

ARCHBISHOP. I cannot hear, sir.

OXFORD. The arse? Why, sir, it explodes noisily.

ARCHBISHOP. The play!

RICHARD. Who's hungry?

WILLIAM. My lord, we thought to eat *after* the play!

ARCHBISHOP. 'Tis very broad this show and foul.

WILLIAM. Uh.

ARCHBISHOP. 'Tis not meet to inflate Herod so.

OXFORD. Why's that, my Lord?

ARCHBISHOP. These pageants give too much air to evil and insufficient to good.

ALICE. Well, surely Lord, the evil parts is best fun.

ARCHBISHOP. Madam, 'tis the feast of Christ's Body, not a funfair.

WILLIAM *and* ALICE *are upset that nobody watches the play which continues during this dispute.*

OXFORD. Aye, Reverend, but a pageant of Christ and Mary and Angels would send the rabble asleep.

ARCHBISHOP. That's blasphemy, sir.

OXFORD (*enjoying himself hugely*). No, 'tis fact. A fact cannot be blasphemy, can it?

WILLIAM. Please sir, you miss the play!

RICHARD. I know. (*To* ALICE.) 'Tis your cooking, madam. 'Tis a temptation. Robert, you should taste this chicken!

ALICE (*hysterically*). No! Please! Watch the play! Please!

ARCHBISHOP. In my opinion, these plays grow annually more vulgar. 'Tis a procession of guts and violence and lewd laughter. 'Twere the subject of my message this morning.

RICHARD. And we missed it.

ALICE (*frustrated*). Sirs, he made reference to the King.

RICHARD. Who?

ALICE. The Herod.

RICHARD. The Herod? What reference?

ALICE. He mentioned Your Majesty and the town.

RICHARD. Did he? And we missed that an' all. Can he repeat it?

ALICE. Uh.

ANNE. Why?

ALICE. Why? Madam?

ANNE. Aye, why?

ALICE. Why what?

ANNE. Why did the Herod mention my husband?

ALICE. Uh . . . (*To* WiLLIAM.) Why, husband?

WILLIAM. Out of topicality.

RICHARD. Oh, topicality! Did he mention my Lord the Archbishop?

WILLIAM. Uh. I don't recall.

RICHARD (*impishly*). You're not mentioned, my Lord. Not topical
   enough.

ARCHBISHOP. I cannot follow this play for the buzz up here.

OXFORD. Buzz? Who buzzes? Do you buzz my lady?

ARCHBISHOP. The din you make, my lord!

OXFORD.
RICHARD.   Oh, the din, the din!
ANNE.

WILLIAM. My Lords, please! 'Tis the killing of the babes to come.

   Below, JOLYF *continues.*

JOLYF. I am the biggest and blackest and cruellest and meanest.
   I've sent out soldiers to scour the town
   and butcher all brats to bits and pieces. Tomorrow I'll
   breakfast on babby bacon and childy chops and smoked
      nipper
   and infant pie and guarantee that come tonight there'll be
      no
   tiny Messiah. There'll be no star in the sky.
   There'll only be me, horrible Herod,
   There'll only be myself, there'll only be I!

   Herod's soldiers splash the guts of the butchered babies. The
   ARCHBISHOP *is flecked.*

ARCHBISHOP. By Christ! I am all a-bloodied.

OXFORD. You are, my Lord. Your ermine looks freshly killed.

ARCHBISHOP. Ach!

ALICE. I sicken sir.

WILLIAM (*in despair*). Oh, madam!

ANNE. Oh dear!

WILLIAM. Oh God. Don't swoon, please.

ANNE. I think she do, Mister.

   ALICE *faints.*

OXFORD. Aye. There she goes.

ARCHBISHOP. Is there mess on my face?

OXFORD. Um. (*He inspects gravely.*) 'Tis hard to say, Lord.

ARCHBISHOP. I must go in and clean myself. Ach!

WILLIAN (*abjectly*). My Lord, you'll miss the play.

ARCHBISHOP. Would it had missed me, sir!

The ARCHBISHOP *exits, flicking imaginary blood from his clothes.*

* * * * *

Minutes to midnight, back at the impatient LE KOLVES'.

GEOFFREY (*funereally*). 'Tis our play next madam.

KATHRYN. Some minutes off.

GEOFFREY. Some minutes! The day is finished and no King. How much later can he be and not miss it?

KATHRYN. Some minutes. Sarah has fetched them. Calm yourself.

GEOFFREY. Do you know the bill of the play?

KATHRYN. Aye, you said.

GEOFFREY. God's teeth. And I starve madam!

KATHRYN. You had food earlier.

GEOFFREY. 'Twould not fill a rabbit.

KATHRYN. Sir, more will spoil your feast. Shut up now.

FATHER MELTON. Sir, we are in good stead. Each pageant processes, none to rival ours. 'Tis a triumph. Our crowd is vast and high spirited and will hurrah us.

This signals a cheer from below.

GEOFFREY (*in a voice of doom, looking out and down the street*). See! 'Tis our pageant.

KATHRYN. Is it?

GEOFFREY. Aye, madam. It comes.

KATHRYN. Bother.

GEOFFREY. *It* comes but the King comes not. 'Tis wasted. (*He sits down.*) Ach! (*Muttering.*) Blessed Virgin Mary, Mother of God. 'Tis complete wasted. 'Tis money melted. 'Tis harvest rotted. 'Tis feast unfeasted. I said this would happen. God, God, God.

KATHRYN. I bet 'tis the Mayor. I see his hand in this, or his shrew. They sulk so miserable after their flat affair they cannot bear the King to see ours. Witch!

FATHER MELTON. Can we not send horses?

GEOFFREY. We can send nothing with the wagons cramming the roads.

KATHRYN. Then we'll wait.

GEOFFREY. Can't.

KATHRYN. We can. We says 'Wait' and they wait.

GEOFFREY. 'Tis an offence and will be fined: six shillings and eight pence.

KATHRYN. Then we will be fined but the King will see the play.

GEOFFREY. The additional torches?

KATHRYN. Sir, we are in danger of losing everything and you carp at torches!

GEOFFREY. Do you know the price of a torch, madam?

KATHRYN. Please don't tell me.

GEOFFREY. We paid Margaret Chandler fourteen shillings for six.

KATHRYN. Will you cry wait to them?

GEOFFREY. Ach.

KATHRYN. Then *I* will, and I'll barge through the throng also to fetch this King. Since no one else offer. If you want something doing, Kathryn, do it yourself.

KATHRYN *stomps off.*

Scene Eleven

The Streets.

The Royal party walk with SARAH *to the* LE KOLVES' *house. It is dark and in the distance light and noise come from the various stations.*

SARAH. Sir, we must hurry.

RICHARD. Must we?

SARAH. Aye. That were the pageant before the Cross play we passed.

ANNE. Aye, Richard, let's be swift. 'Tis my favourite and has Sarah's husband in it. He do the Christ.

SARAH. No, he don't madam. They've changed the crew.

ANNE. Oh?

SARAH. Aye. To flatter you. They have foreign players. They have a maid to play the Mary.

OXFORD. A woman?

SARAH. Aye. They wanted me.

OXFORD. Well, that's novel. Is she pretty?

SARAH. She comes from Hull.

OXFORD. Aye, but do she come prettily from Hull?

ANNE. Sir, hold up a second. (*She coughs and holds her side.*)

RICHARD. Madam?

ANNE *coughs violently.*

ANNE. God. (*She sinks down to the ground.*)

OXFORD. Majesty, do you sicken?

ANNE. Aye. (*She coughs into her handkerchief. It comes away from her mouth bloodied.*)

SARAH. Oh ma'am, you bleed!

ANNE. Aye, it seem so.

SARAH. My Lord. There is my house nearby. 'Tis poor but you are welcome to rest up there awhile. And . . . you could watch the old Cross play . . . if you wished to. My husband's boys play it there for their own gang.

ANNE. I'd like that. Richard.

RICHARD. Let's to it. We'll carry you, darling.

ANNE. Aye and get me to a bed, sir.

RICHARD (*worried*). Madam you are a devil for a bed.

SARAH. This way, my Lord.

They struggle off.

Scene Twelve

The LE KOLVES' *house.*

The position of the house has changed so that now we see less front on and therefore beyond the house catch a glimpse of the new wagon complete, in the flickering torchlight, with all-gold Christ. Acres of purple and some soldiers hanging around waiting to begin. There are restless sounds from the unseen crowd.

GEOFFREY *is suicidal at the window. There is a noise below.*

WILLIAM *and the* ARCHBISHOP *enter angrily.*

WILLIAM. Mister, what is the meaning of this delay? The wagons jam up behind.

GEOFFREY. We wait on the King, sir.

WILLIAM. The King? The King left my house an hour ago to join you.

GEOFFREY. He come not.

ARCHBISHOP. This King needs no fool to entertain him. He do the job for himself. 'Tis an outrage.

WILLIAM. By Christ, our day is poxed by his manners and we are the laughing stock, sir. He yapped, him and his two dogs, throughout our pageant and now will dodge yours altogether.

ARCHBISHOP. Aye, Mister.

WILLIAM. No more. Go ahead, sir.

GEOFFREY (*adamant*). I'll not. The King must view the play.

WILLIAM. The King, Mister, may be in Coventry for all we know.

GEOFFREY. Sir, has broken us, the brunt of this pageant and the King *must* view it. There's a gold Christ and a purple sea.

ARCHBISHOP. A gold Christ. 'Tis inappropriate. 'Tis pagan.

FATHER MELTON. Oh no, my Lord, 'tis majestic.

ARCHBISHOP. 'Tis unchristian, Parson. We'll have sacrifices next.

WILLIAM. We'll have the play next and now. Or I'll call in the sergeants . . . The rabble boil and are all end-o-day shirty and hackled. There'll be a Carlisle axe swung before long unless they gets their pageant.

KATHRYN *and* ALICE *enter*.

KATHRYN. Husband, order the play started.

GEOFFREY. Do the King appear?

KATHRYN. He does not, sir, but our old pageant starts up outside a private station.

GEOFFREY. What's that?

KATHRYN. The men from the play, your apprentice and gang, make the old pageant. Now our play play not, the crowd wander down to view it. Soon will be deserted below.

ALICE. 'Tis a devil, this business, and I sorrow for you, mistress.

KATHRYN. Thank you, my Lady. I love your wipe. Is it silk?

ALICE. Aye, a little silk. Our day is spoiled an' all. And I've swooned.

KATHRYN. Dear madam, friend Mayor, my Lord, let's view the pageant severally. King or no King.

ALICE. Thank you madam.

WILLIAM. My Lord, the Archbishop, tells us this is the colour of his Majesty. Unworthy of the crown. Our brothers in London know it and work on it.

GEOFFREY. Do they? (*To* KATHRYN.) I smelled that from the off.

WILLIAM. Aye and we should learn, eh, Archbishop?

ARCHBISHOP. You should.

WILLIAM. So sit eh? And be peaceful.

ARCHBISHOP. Is there blood in this pageant?

FATHER MELTON. None, my Lord. 'Tis a serene cross.

ARCHBISHOP. Well that's something.

KATHRYN. Do we start then husband?

GEOFFREY. Aye, we start. Go to, down there, and begin.

The crowd roar their approval. Trumpets sound. The burghers, ominously united, hold their handkerchiefs aloft, waving them like banners.

Scene Thirteen

Hen Street. A hut.

ANNE *is in* SARAH's *bed.* RICHARD *sits by her.* SARAH *and* OXFORD *stand facing front half-watching the play: the old Cross play. In the background throughout the new Pageant proceeds, illuminated from time to time by a torch which shows the golden Christ crucified, then later the ubiquitous purple sea.*

ANNE. I am feeble, sir.

RICHARD. You're drained, sweet, 'tis too long a day and too much sport.

ANNE. Aye.

RICHARD. How's the bed!

ANNE. Oh. Fine.

RICHARD. Best bed?

ANNE. Most welcome, sir.

RICHARD. Then sleep, eh love?

ANNE (*regretfully*). I miss the passion play.

RICHARD. Aye. 'Tis a rough and ready one proceed outside.

ANNE. Can I not view it?

RICHARD. Madam, you can sleep.

ANNE. I can sleep later.

RICHARD. Robert?

OXFORD. Aye, my Lord?

RICHARD. How is the play?

OXFORD. Humble, sir. Very special.

RICHARD. Then help me drag the Queen's bed to the doorway.

OXFORD. Aye, most willingly.

   RICHARD *and* OXFORD *drag the bed down to the doorway.*

RICHARD. Can you see, my Lady?

ANNE. Almost.

RICHARD (*helping* ANNE, *gently*). Let's plump up more cushions. There.

ANNE. Aye! I can see now: oh, the Christ have a fine leg on him.

OXFORD. Aye, he do.

SARAH. 'Tis my husband, madam.

ANNE (*smiling weakly*). Is it, Sarah? I like a nice Christ.

RICHARD. Madam, this is the most dilute apology to spend your life in bed.

ANNE. Shut up, Richard.

RICHARD. Must I take you back to London still in it?

ANNE. Aye. Come you both, sit by me, 'tis a fine view.

   They watch. And with them we hear the climax of the Crucifixion.

CHRIST (THOMAS).   . . . your son swoons dear Lord
                And I pray
                That all that I suffer may not be in vain
                But bring down your mercy on men
                Like an endless cleansing rain.

MARY (WALTER).   Alas, my love, my life, my Liege.
                Alas, mourning now maddens me.
                Alas, my boy look down on me.
                Thy mother that did bear thee.
                You are my fruit. I fostered thee,
                And gave thee suck upon my knee.
                Upon my pain have pity.

Alas to find my boy above me
Tugged! Lugged! Broken! Tree'd!
Nails thrust in and crowned of thorns.
To see my birth that I have born, bleed:
Tears my heart to tatters.
And though you hang above me, racked on
   high
I, at the tree's foot, am also crucified.

OXFORD (*after a moment*). You're weeping, madam.

ANNE. I do, Robert. I always forget, 'tis such a cruel play.

The End

Appendix

Expanded Herod play.

Depending on the production it might prove expedient to have
additional text for the Herod and his gang to cover proceedings at
the two households.

HEROD.
No noise, nippers. What!
Who dares mutter when I appear?
Herod, the mighty, marvellous, perfect.
Who dares talk when such magnificence come to York!
I bluster and blast, I blow and thunder.
I am most terrible, me.
Point out a man who is not on his knee and I'll snap off his legs
like twigs off a tree.
Point out a man who carps of a King:
I'll pull off his skin
roast his carcass, you'll see.
I'll not have noise of some brat in a cradle
I'll not have nonsense of stars and fables
I'll not tolerate talk of a Messiah . . .
Did anyone say Messiah?
Was the word Messiah whispered?
Or Emmanuel? Or Son of God? I hope not.
And kings. Everywhere kings.
A man cannot walk Mickelgate without bumping
Kings. Are you a King? Bash his bonce.
Not just Richard come to rest,
but three more kings from East and West
arrive with word of some nipper, born in a stable
Meant to be able to save the world.
No bairn from a barn can compete with me!
I am the biggest and blackest and cruellest
and meanest.
I am fattest and foulest and filthy uncleanest!
I am dazzlingly bad! I am evil. I'm mad!
I make grown men weep, I make babies screech.
I make mothers tremble. I am gurt bad!
And I hate hearing of Messiahs.
I hate the word Messiah.
I hate it, it hurts, I'll clap the next bugger
who mumbles Messiah. I don't like the word.

SERVANT.
Sir, there's noise of a nipper just born.
Full of light, yet unadorned.
Born with nothing, under a star
followed by kings from off as far as Egypt
and France and Belgium and Wakefield and
Norway. All these kings will bow down, it's said.
To this bairn in a stable
Born with the moon and stars on his head.
'Tis a marvellous thing and the joy spreads like fire.
From every house all over York:
Messiah! Messiah! Messiah! Messiah!

HEROD.
I've sent out soldiers to scour the town.
And butcher all brats to bits and pieces.
Tomorrow I'll breakfast on babby bacon and
childy chips and smoked nipper and infant pie.
And guarantee that come tomorrow, there'll be no
Tiny Messiah. There'll be no star in the sky.
There'll only be me, horrible Herod.
There'll only be myself. There'll only be I!

Screams and chaos as HEROD's SOLDIERS *butcher the babies and splash the guts.*

CHORUS OF WOMEN.
They've killed our boys. They've butchered them.
They've broke our hearts, our babbies slain.
Our babbies slain: they'll never cry or laugh again
or learn their names or live to learn that they must die
to save the boy who'll never die:
Messiah! Messiah! Messiah!

The CHORUS *sing the 'Sanctus'.*

MADE IN BANGKOK

Made in Bangkok was first presented in London at the Aldwych Theatre, London on 18 March 1986 by Michael Codron. It had the following cast:

ADRIAN WEST	Benjamin Whitrow
GARY ALEXANDER	Christopher Fulford
STEPHEN BRITTER	Paul Shelley
FRANCES BRITTER	Felicity Kendal
EDWARD GOVER	Peter McEnery
NET	David Yip
COURIER/MRS LWIN	Diana Choy
THAI GIRL	Leanne Hong
THAI GIRL	Tia Lee
THAI GIRL/AMPHA	Susan Tan
FACTORY OWNER/MR LWIN	Vincent Wong
ARMY OFFICER/MASSAGE PARLOUR PROPRIETOR	Eddie Yeoh

Directed by Michael Blakemore
Designed by John Gunter
Lighting designed by David Hersey
Costumes designed by Diane Holmes
Scene: Bangkok, Thailand
Time: Now

The play was first presented in the USA, with a different cast, at the Mark Taper Forum, Los Angeles on 13 March 1988 in a production directed by Robert Egan.

ACT ONE

Scene One

Scene: *Don Muang airport, Bangkok, Thailand. 5 a.m. Baggage reclaiming area. A carousel with a single suitcase revolving. Somewhere, perhaps a flight number indicating this is the location for passenger baggage arriving on a Thai international flight from London, Heathrow.*

At Rise: *A small group of travellers remain at the carousel. They are all part of the same tour, "Eastern Promise" Tours. They have evidently been waiting for some time. Each couple, and EDWARD, have luggage trolleys to the ready. Their hand luggage is labelled with "Eastern Promise" tags. FRANCES is reading avidly, sitting on her trolley, STEPHEN is temporarily absent.*

GARY. This is a joke, isn't it? (*He pulls off his shirt and drapes it over the trolley, then loudly and drawing attention to himself.*) Excuse me, but we are rather struggling over here on the luggage front.

EDWARD. I think you'll find – we're all with the same tour – that our bags are held up for some reason.

GARY. Give the man a medal.

EDWARD. No, I'm just pointing out . . .

GARY. We had deduced that ourselves, that we are all standing by this conveyor belt because out luggage hasn't turned up.

ADRIAN. Shut up Gary.

GARY (*to ADRIAN*). Apart from anything else, I've had a hard-on since Heathrow.

STEPHEN *enters.*

STEPHEN. Outside apparently, it's 103 degrees. And raining.

FRANCES. What did they say?

STEPHEN. I don't know. Nothing. Everything's closed. The chap over there pointed back over here and I said we knew that.

FRANCES. We should ring the hotel.

STEPHEN. I haven't got coins.

FRANCES. Well surely the . . .

STEPHEN. Yes, all right. I have been on a plane for practically a year.

FRANCES. I just thought . . .

STEPHEN. Inevitably, as soon as I get through the baggage will arrive or the courier, the tour operator, the rep, whatever, and . . .

(*In a hugely irritated gesture he pulls the suitcase off the carousel.*)
I'm sorry but I can't just watch this thing lurch about. Is it
anybody's?

GARY (*of* EDWARD). Ask Mastermind.

EDWARD. (*To* GARY *who's smoking.*) It does say no smoking. It's
bad enough as it is without the fug to contend with.

GARY. Oh, the fug!

EDWARD (*intimidated!*). I'm going to find out . . . (*Picks up the
suitcase.*) Is this anybody's? (*It's heavy. He puts it down and exits
weakly.*)

GARY. Wanker.

ADRIAN. Go away, Gary, will you.

GARY's *attention is caught by some signs in Thai, a flowing secret
script, all dashes and undulations.*

GARY. Have you seen this writing, joke eh? Do you reckon it
actually means anything?

ADRIAN. Oh, I doubt it.

GARY. Is it advertising women? This is the question.
*He settles down with his walkman, which is playing loud rock
music. He jigs occasionally to its hidden beat.*

FRANCES (*reading from her* 'Insight Guide to Thailand'). I'm glad
Katie recommended this. It is good. Quite vivid.

STEPHEN. (*Of the wait.*) This is a farce.

GARY *sings noisily and tunelessly along with the song on his
headphones.*

STEPHEN (*to* ADRIAN). Are you going on to Hong Kong?

ADRIAN. Yes.

STEPHEN. Yes. And what, Eastern Promise Tours?

ADRIAN. Yes.

STEPHEN. Us, too. (*Of the wait.*) Not the best of starts.

ADRIAN. No.

STEPHEN. We'd understood the courier, the rep would be here.

ADRIAN. Right.

STEPHEN. It's typical.

ADRIAN. Why? Do you know Bangkok?

STEPHEN. No. I suppose I meant . . .

FRANCES. This is good. It describes Thailand as an arm with Burma as its epaulette and Malaysia as its glove. Very military. (*She looks up*.)

STEPHEN. This is my wife, Frances.

ADRIAN. Hello.

STEPHEN. I'm Stephen.

GARY. (*Slipping his headphones and addressing* ADRIAN.) Talking to me?

ADRIAN. No.

FRANCES. Is Cambodia the same as Kampuchea? I'm embarrassed to ask.

STEPHEN (*doesn't know*). What?

ADRIAN. Yes.

Then EDWARD *returns followed by a Thai* ARMY OFFICER.

OFFICER (*to the assembled*). I am sorry for this problem.

EDWARD (*confidently*). Apparently the Royal Family is driving out of Bangkok this morning and the roads have been cleared, which explains the . . .

STEPHEN. What about our luggage?

OFFICER. A slight delay. (*Smiles*.)

ADRIAN. A long delay.

OFFICER. We are cursed in our country with the problem of drugs. We have to be most scrupulous.

STEPHEN. What, and you think we're bringing in drugs?

ADRIAN. I thought the problem was drugs going out.

OFFICER. As I say: There is no problem and your luggage will be with you in a few moments.

EDWARD (*pointedly, in* GARY's *direction*). Clearly some of us look like drug pushers.

GARY (*slipping his headphones*). What's going on? Coup, is it?

ADRIAN. Apparently some of us look like we're on drugs.

GARY. Oh, yeah? Terrific. (*Back to walkman*.)

STEPHEN (*irritated, to the* ARMY OFFICER). It's just we have actually been flying all night.

Two Thai GIRLS *appear, very respectable and conservatively dressed. They have a baggage trolley. They aim for the stranded suitcase. It's very heavy.* GARY *springs to his feet.*

GARY (*helping them*). There you go. All right?

The GIRLS smile their thanks and make to leave.

GARY (*to them*). Speak English? Eh? Thoughts of Chairman Mao? (*Then mischievously, at a safe distance.*) I suppose a fuck's out of the question?

The GIRLS steer the trolley away.

EDWARD (*to the ARMY OFFICER et al*). We were wondering whose that was. The suitcase.

OFFICER. Very pretty girls, eh?

GARY. Brilliant.

OFFICER. Patpong I! Good!

STEPHEN. Patpong? So they say.

FRANCES. What's that?

OFFICER (*to EDWARD*). You like nice Thai girls?

EDWARD. What? Yes. I mean I like the Thai people. I speak some Thai actually.

OFFICER. Oh yes?

EDWARD. Mai pen rai. Obviously. And Kawpkun. Sabmidi Kawpkun.

OFFICER (*correcting pronunciation*). Kawpkun. Very good.

EDWARD. I mean obviously I'm not fluent. My Cantonese is quite good. And I can manage a few words in Vietnamese. I'm not a linguist. I'm a dentist.

OFFICER. Ah.

EDWARD. Yes, as a matter of fact I work in the Vietnamese Refugee Camps in Hong Kong. Do you know who I mean? The Boat People?

OFFICER. For the Thai . . . Vietnam . . . (*Shrugs.*) We argue like brother and sister. Very close, very big arguments.

FRANCES (*now reading again*). The South sounds amazing. And the North. Unspoiled.

EDWARD. That's right, because many of these people speak of having run the gauntlet of Thai pirates before reaching Hong Kong.

FRANCES (*reading*). Bangkok, though, is sinking. Apparently.

OFFICER. What do you mean, Thai pirates?

EDWARD. Obviously not ordinary, and now they have to live like prisoners in these camps in HK, like rats . . . the hygiene is . . . ach! No, of course, most Thai people are terribly friendly.

OFFICER. We smile all the time.

EDWARD. Yes. Marvellous teeth.

OFFICER. So you came to Bangkok to meet nice Thai girl?

EDWARD. Well . . .

FRANCES. (*Reading.*) God! Stephen . . . Listen to this . . . 'A less well-known shrine in Bangkok, but highly regarded by its followers, consists entirely of erect phalluses, from the small to the gargantuan, sculpted from wood, wax, stone, cement, with scrupulous fidelity to life.' Talk about self-worship.

STEPHEN. I don't particularly want to talk about anything. I'd like our luggage to arrive and a car to the hotel and then a sleep.

FRANCES. We can't sleep now. It's morning.

STEPHEN. Nevertheless.
  The carousel suddenly lurches to a halt.

GARY (*sarcastic*). Brilliant.

STEPHEN. Now what?

OFFICER. If you would excuse me. I will investigate.
  He exits, talking sharply into a crackling walkie-talkie.

GARY (*to* EDWARD). Nice chat?

EDWARD. I hope you're not carrying drugs.

GARY. Don't worry, they're up my arse.

ADRIAN. It's not drugs . . . I expect it's just military paranoia. They go in for it these days. It's like landing at an army base, not an airport.

STEPHEN. That's right. Probably think we've got a bomb or something.

EDWARD. Could be my fault. I'm politically quite, you know: I get various journals.

GARY. Eh up, its Mikhail Gorborchev.

FRANCES. They wouldn't think of building a shrine of vaginas.

STEPHEN. It would be a bit odd, wouldn't it?

FRANCES. Why?

STEPHEN. There's no need to shout.

FRANCES. I'm not shouting. Why would vaginas be odd?

STEPHEN. What do they look like for God's sake? It's what they're not rather than what they are, isn't it?

FRANCES. Is it? Oh, I see.

STEPHEN. You might at least have the good grace to concede that the one is an accepted symbol and the other is not. There are not to my knowledge any leaning Holes of Pisa . . . the Eiffel Hole . . .

FRANCES. I think that was my point.

STEPHEN. Well then, Frances: you win.

NET *and the female* REPRESENTATIVE *from Eastern Promise Tours arrive.* NET *works for the hotel. The* EP REPRESENTATIVE *wears a sash with the company logo.*

EDWARD. Ah, finally.

REP. So sorry. Good morning. Welcome to Bangkok. No baggage yet? (*Quite cool and collected. She consults her clipboard.*) Mr, Mrs Britter?

STEPHEN. That's right. No baggage yet.

REP (*to them*). Room 202. (*Then to* ADRIAN *and* GARY.) Mr West. Mr Alexander.

ADRIAN. Yes.

GARY (*from inside the walkman*). Ah, is this action on the action front?

REP. Room 203. (*Looks to* EDWARD, *mispronounces his surname.*) Mr Gover?

EDWARD (*correcting her*). Gover.

REP. Room 205 –

GARY (*interrupting*). Excuse me, there are two of us. (*The* REPRESENTATIVE *shrugs.*) And we're not going out with each other.

REP (*consulting list*). This was our booking detail. You must check at hotel.

ADRIAN. Don't worry. We'll sort it out.

GARY (*of sharing a room*). Fuck that for a game of soldiers.

EDWARD. We're all rather aggravated about this luggage business.

REP. I will ask about the delay.

EDWARD. It's not as if we're a party or anything, so why we should all have to wait simply because we booked through the same company –

EDWARD *is interrupted by the renaissance of the luggage carousel.*

STEPHEN (*arch*). Hurray.
  The first luggage belongs to ADRIAN *and* GARY.

GARY (*at the carousel*). OK, let's go.

NET. No problem. (*Helping* GARY *load the trolley.*) Net help.

FRANCES. These are ours, Stephen.

STEPHEN (*weary*). Yes OK.

REP (*of* NET). This man will drive us to the hotel.

EDWARD. Where are mine? (*A case appears.*) Well, that's one . . .
  but there's a large package, a . . . now what's happened?

GARY (*ready*). Where do we go?

NET. This way.

REP. Just wait for Mr Gover.

GARY. Why? (*Mimicking.*) Just because we're in the same party?
  Come on.

EDWARD (*watches the carousel with increasing impatience*). This
  really is . . . (*Snorts.*) . . . Ach! How can one bag just . . .

REP. Expect just coming.

EDWARD (*arch*). Do you?

STEPHEN. Well . . . There's clearly some sort of problem with your
  bag which is probably why we've had to . . .

EDWARD. I don't see why you . . .

STEPHEN (*to* ADRIAN). I mean, it must be.

FRANCES. It doesn't matter. We can wait. Stephen?

STEPHEN. We don't seem to have much . . .

GARY. Why do we have to hang around waiting for Gorby? It's not
  a school outing.

ADRIAN. Then grow up. No actually just shut up.

EDWARD. Thank you.
  Along comes EDWARD's *parcel . . . bustling down the chute on
  to the carousel. It's a brown paper sack, like a potato sack, which
  has been taped and strung, but clearly opened. As it makes its
  entry, to* EDWARD's *relief and other weary grunts, it spills its
  contents all over the floor. Hundreds of toothbrushes.*
  Sod it! Buggeration! Sod it!

GARY (*picking one up*). Aye-aye! He's smuggling in toothbrushes.

EDWARD. Yes, well I'm a dentist. (*Scrabbling to pick them up.*)

GARY. A likely story, Arthur.

EDWARD. This parcel has been deliberately . . . sod it! (*As he picks it up the remainder of the brushes scatter.*)

NET (*helping*). No problem.

REP. Best thing, Net help you pack bag. I take other guests to minibus. This way please.

FRANCES. Well, I'm sure we can . . .

STEPHEN (*as he exits*). Fran . . . Fran.

FRANCES (*sympathetically to* EDWARD). Well, good luck. (*She leaves, leaving* NET *and* EDWARD *alone, retrieving toothbrushes.*)

EDWARD. Thanks for . . .

NET. No problem.

EDWARD. I didn't, did you say your name?

NET. Net.

EDWARD. I'm Edward.

NET (*of the toothbrushes and the events*). Army. Very suspicious. Very powerful.

EDWARD. Right.

NET. Mr Edward dentist?

EDWARD. That's right.

NET. I have very bad mouth all night. (*Opens mouth.*) Big pain.

EDWARD. I can't look at your teeth at the minute.

NET. How much you want?

EDWARD. No, it's not, it's just . . .

NET. No problem. Finish here. Net take Mr Edward to hotel room. Come up later for teeth.

EDWARD. I don't . . . really, I'm on . . .

NET. Net understand. No problem. You Bangkok business or fun?

EDWARD. Uh . . .

NET. Half-half?

EDWARD. Tourist.

NET. You have wife? Girlfriend?

EDWARD. No. Not at the minute.

NET. Net find Mr Edward nice girl.

EDWARD. I don't think so.

NET. Boyfriend?

EDWARD. No.

NET. She-boy? Drug? Cokey Cokey?

EDWARD. No! Nothing. No girl. No boy. No drug.

NET. Funny. Everybody come to Bangkok say no girl, no boy. No nothing. Later they ask Net find something nice.

EDWARD. Right. I'll remember.

NET. Everybody say no at first. If Mr Edward embarrassed I can have girl come to room. Very private. Talking 1,000 Baht.

EDWARD (*saying no*). Really.

NET. Eight hundred. Special price. Eight hundred. Yes or no?

EDWARD. No thank you. I don't want a girlfriend.

NET (*hot on colloquialism*). There you go. (*As they complete the collection of toothbrushes.*)

EDWARD. Ta. Good. I'll have to just try and . . . (*As he struggles to repair the sack in some way.*) Bloody thing. (*A brush slips out again. EDWARD gives it to NET.*) Have it, go on.

NET. For me?

EDWARD. Well don't worry. I've got plenty. Hundreds.

NET. Thank you. Mr Edward kind man.

EDWARD. No. Anyway they're for the refugees. In Hong Kong. I look after their teeth. So they're not for sale or anything. (*Wearily but thawing.*) Anyway, come on. Let me see. Open your mouth. (*NET obliges instantly. His mouth wide open.*) Which one is causing the problem? Here? (*NET groans in acknowledgement.*) Yes. Well can't say I'm surprised. Do you brush your teeth after you've eaten? Hm? You see, you've still got your wisdom tooth there haven't you? Up top? You haven't been getting around it. I think you're going to need that looked at. Do you use floss? Floss?

NET (*now able to talk for the first time as EDWARD cleans his hands on a handerchief*). Up here hurts. Sometimes blood in mouth.

EDWARD. Well, yes, you're infected, your gums are sore, you've got great build-up of plaque, and you smoke too much, your teeth are all stained, and you need some filling work. Go to the dentist. When I'm unpacked I'll give you some oil of cloves . . . Remind me. It's nothing fancy, but it'll ease the pain if you rub it into your gum.

NET. Rub in . . . (NET *copies* EDWARD.) No kid?

EDWARD. No kid. And I've probably got a mouthwash: Chloroseptic or something. If it hasn't been . . . (*Referring sulkily to his luggage.*) Anyway, we'll sort you out.

NET (*as he stacks the parcel on to the trolley*). Hundreds of toothbrush. (*Impressed.*) Fa!

EDWARD. So.

NET. We go now.

EDWARD. Right.

NET. OK, before my friend leave Bangkok, Net make sure he has good time.

EDWARD. OK. Listen, have a toothbrush for your wife.

NET. No. No problem. We share, thank you. OK, let's go.
   They exit, pushing off the trolley.

Scene Two

GARY *and* ADRIAN's *room in the hotel.* GARY *is disgruntled with the sleeping arrangements.*

GARY. At least they're double beds.

ADRIAN. You'll live. It's only for a few days.

GARY. A very important few days.

ADRIAN. If you're so anxious you can book into another hotel.

GARY. I might. I told you the geezer on Reception said he could fix us up, no bother?

ADRIAN. I'm sure he did.

GARY. Well.

ADRIAN. Look. Let me tell you something about this place . . . if you want to piss all over a woman in Bangkok you can, if you can pay for it, and you don't have to pay much.

GARY. Who wants to piss all over a woman?

ADRIAN. You'd be surprised.

GARY. He said these girls are really fresh, from the country, young and – you know – not . . .

ADRIAN. Listen Gary, you do whatever you want. OK, just turn up to our appointments and don't fornicate in my bed.

GARY. Fair dos.

ADRIAN. In fact, don't fornicate in your own bed when I'm in my bed. I might get embarrassed.

GARY. I'll get you lots of brochures for guided tours. Fancy a long walk this afternoon?

ADRIAN. I fancy a long sleep.

GARY. What are you doing?

ADRIAN. Checking the sheets. I don't want to lie in somebody else's sweat.

GARY. My shirt's gone dry now. (*Taking it off.*)

ADRIAN. You think this sheet is clean? Probably not. It's probably like your shirt.

GARY. 'Cause you look out the window, it looks like nothing, the weather looks like London practically, but outside it's a real bastard.

ADRIAN. You haven't been outside. I'm going to have these sheets changed.

GARY. At the airport.

ADRIAN. Don't behave like a prat while we're here, Gary. I brought you along to learn some things, learn some business. Be grateful. Don't be a prat, eh? (*To the phone.*) Hello. Hello. Room service?

GARY. What do you mean?

ADRIAN. You were a prat on the plane. And at the airport.

GARY. I was bored.

ADRIAN. You were boring. And pissed . . . (*To the phone.*) Yes, I'm in room, yes is this room service? Yes I am in Room 203, yes, 203. I'd like the linen changed on the beds please. The sheets. (*Pause.*) Because they're not clean. (*Pause.*) That's what I said. No, I just want them changed. Thank you. (*To* GARY.) Because I haven't got the patience.

GARY. What do I do before the night life?

ADRIAN. There was a lizard in the bathroom. You could warm up on that.

GARY. There's a coffee shop with a juke box. What time do you think that gets going?

ADRIAN. You're serious, aren't you?

GARY. I didn't come for the food poisoning.

ADRIAN. What did you come for?

GARY. Now you're being serious.

ADRIAN. Well?

GARY. To help you find a factory.

ADRIAN. Go on.

GARY. I've got a good eye. I know what will sell. You know this.
   I know what people are wearing. I can tell the difference
   between . . .

ADRIAN. No, why else did you come?

GARY. To fuck. You can't embarrass me.

ADRIAN. Terrific. Why?

GARY. I like it.

ADRIAN. But why here in particular?

GARY. No, I always like it. Here it's cheap. Why did we come here
   for clothes. Good stuff: good price. No one asks too many
   questions. I told you you can't faze me.

ADRIAN. And what are you looking for? What turns you on?

GARY. Fuck off.

ADRIAN. No, I'm interested. (*Knock on the door. To the knocker.*)
   Just a minute.

   It's the MAIDS, *two of them, come to deal with the sheets. They
   walk straight in. They begin to change the linen on* GARY's *bed.*

GARY. (*To the maids.*) Don't mind us.

ADRIAN. It's the other bed that wants changing.

GARY. We could have been doing anything. Just walking straight in!

ADRIAN. You think they haven't seen it before?

GARY. Not mine, love.

ADRIAN. Where were we? Oh yes. What about these two? Any use?

GARY. Don't fancy yours.

ADRIAN. I'm still serious.

GARY. Don't fancy yours.

ADRIAN. Shall I ask? Save you the bother of going downstairs.

GARY. I know you're just winding me up.

ADRIAN. Excuse me, my friend seems to have a problem with his
   willy.

GARY. Just leave it out.

ADRIAN. Now I'm confused. You come here for some women. Here are some women. What's the problem? I'll have a bath.

GARY. Just leave it out.

ADRIAN. You've lost me, Gary. They look clean I'd say. Have 'em both. Ideal. Room service. Get a glass of beer thrown in and the sheets changed after. You'd better hurry. They'll be going.

GARY. Apart from anything else, they're not tarts, are they?

ADRIAN. What? What's this? They're not tarts? Are you saying they've got to be prostitutes? Oh, I see. No, that's right because in these parts they don't make the distinction. I said: Pay them enough and you can piss on them.

GARY. Shut up!

ADRIAN. I would like you to explain to me the difference between you going out and finding a girl and offering her money to come back here, and asking a girl who's already in the room, in fact already half in your bed?

GARY. You think you're being so clever, don't you?

The girls are ready to go out.

ADRIAN. Missed your chance. (*Fishes out a tip.*) Thank you. Thank you very much.

They exit.

ADRIAN. Anyway. I'm going to have that bath. There was a time when I could have slept anywhere. Now I must have clean sheets.

Scene Three

A boat. We're at the destination of a boat trip to Ayuthya, the old capital city of Thailand. The boat is a small launch belonging to the Oriental Hotel. STEPHEN would prefer to stay on it rather than set out on another expedition. It's hot and grey, and has briefly stopped raining.

FRANCES. I don't want to walk around by myself.

STEPHEN. Nobody's going to jump on you.

FRANCES. I don't enjoy looking at things by myself. It's no fun. (*Pause.*) The rain's stopped.

STEPHEN. I'm quite happy to sit here.

FRANCES. There's no way of measuring anything unless you're with me. It's not the same. You look at something alone, it's different. It's not the same.

STEPHEN. Well I want to stay here and you want me to come and look at more Buddhas. It's a quandary. What do we do?

FRANCES. Oh, Stephen.

STEPHEN. Oh Stephen what?

FRANCES. You think banter is conversation, Stephen. Banter is instead of conversation.

STEPHEN. Well, as they say it takes two to banter.

FRANCES. I want this to be a real holiday. Something special. It doesn't happen anymore. Us alone. Us alone properly, without Christopher, to spend time, to talk.

STEPHEN. It won't happen anyway. Once we get to Hong Kong I won't see you and Katie for dust.

FRANCES. We're not in Hong Kong.

STEPHEN. Hong Kong is my holiday, in case you'd forgotten . . . I'm working here.

FRANCES. Stephen, you have to, it's a gesture, you have to show your face at the factory, that's all. You know it.

EDWARD *comes rounding up stragglers.*

EDWARD. I think the guide's waiting for us.

FRANCES. Oh, right.

EDWARD. Seems like the rain's given up, anyway.

FRANCES. Yes.

STEPHEN. My wife and I are at loggerheads. She wants me to troop round this temple and I'm knackered.

FRANCES. Well.

STEPHEN. Not so much knackered as a bit fed up with all these bloody temples.

EDWARD. It's the Buddha's birthday.

FRANCES. I thought it was.

EDWARD. The guide's explaining. He's very good, actually.

STEPHEN. I can't follow a word he's saying

EDWARD. Yes, he's Dutch.

STEPHEN. Typical, isn't it? Get a Dutchman to be a guide for English tourists.

EDWARD. I expect he has to speak many languages besides English.

STEPHEN. That's his problem.

FRANCES. My husband thinks the whole world should speak English.

STEPHEN. No.

EDWARD. You're welcome to walk around with me if that would help.

FRANCES (*saying no*). Really . . .

EDWARD. I'm not an expert but I'm . . .

STEPHEN. You don't need to be. I could describe the inside of this temple without looking at it.

FRANCES. You have to exaggerate.

EDWARD. This one is the biggest. You can't see it all in one go. It's extraordinary. There's no point inside the building where you can get far enough away to see the whole thing.

STEPHEN. Ironic, isn't it, they spend all this money on worship – these temples . . . they'll do that and half the country's starving. You can tell the temple, it's the clean building made of stone not the corrugated rat huts, those warrens that look like miles of scrapyard. That's where the people live . . . the temples are white.

EDWARD. You can be angry about the poverty and still appreciate the culture. I am. I do.

STEPHEN. I'm not the slightest bit angry with it. You'll miss your guided tour.

FRANCES. Why have you never said that before? (*The polemic.*)

EDWARD. I'll . . . (*Exiting.*)

FRANCES. I will come with you if I may.

EDWARD. Right, but can we . . .? (*Anxious to catch up.*)

STEPHEN. Wish Buddha happy birthday for me.

GARY *appears, looking for a suitable surface to force off beer cap. He surveys the boat, river, the party exiting.*

GARY. Can't stand this weather.

STEPHEN. No.

GARY. I could do without living in my own sweat.

STEPHEN. Yes.

GARY. Why are they giving us a guided tour of the graveyards? My interest is strictly in the living bits.

STEPHEN. Have you had a walk around Patpong?

GARY. Oh yeah, done a recce in one of those motorbike things, but

I've got a few addresses from a friend at home. A few special places.

STEPHEN. Right. What? Sort of . . . (*Prompting.*)

GARY. Like the man said, why go for something with a lot of miles on the clock?

STEPHEN. You mean in the sense of . . . (*Prompting.*)

GARY. You still can't be too careful. I'm a real boy scout me. I've got enough antibiotics to paralyze a fucking elephant.

STEPHEN. Right. Otherwise . . . (*Prompting.*)

GARY. Otherwise, a touch of the early-morning stingeroonies.

STEPHEN. Yes, I've noticed there's a lot of information about clinics.

GARY. Listen, if you were a germ in this country! Imagine, imagine being a germ in Bangkok.

STEPHEN. And what about the other thing, the AIDS thing? Doesn't that bother you?

GARY. Why? Are you a turd burglar? Do you pack fudge?

STEPHEN. Do I pack what?

GARY. I'm saying are you a poofter?

STEPHEN. No! Me? Am I? No! No! Absolutely not!

GARY. So what's your problem? Look: you double bag it and keep off the bum-hole. Safe sex, love.

STEPHEN (*relieved*). Because they say you can just do anything, get anything you want.

GARY. Oh yes.

STEPHEN. Some of the things you hear people want, people will pay for, makes you laugh, ridiculous things. I've heard people will pay a lot of money to lie under glass tables while women squat on the tables . . . as if they were on the loo.

GARY. Mental. No, I'm normal, me. Up against the wall I'm happy as a sand boy. (*A short laugh.*) Look at the state of that river. Swim in that!

STEPHEN. They do though, don't they?

GARY. It's like when you've washed up after cooking curry, the big pots; and it won't go down the plug 'cause it's too thick and greasy. Do you like curry?

STEPHEN. Yes. Oh yes. I like . . . not too . . .

GARY. I wouldn't eat them here though. Bugger that. We were eating last night and there was a lizard by my foot staring at me so I started looking and they're everywhere. They'll be straight in the pot, a bit of sauce over the top and it's Jumbo Prawn Masala. I can't stand the way they move, lizards. That's one thing I've learned. Don't let them cover anything with sauce.

STEPHEN. And these special, these addresses, you'll go and, you'll check them out?

GARY. Oh yes.

STEPHEN. With your, is he a, what is he? Your colleague?

GARY. Well, we don't kiss.

STEPHEN. No.

GARY. Yeah, he'll come I expect. He makes out he's not interested. That's his view on it, but he'll come. He's my boss.

STEPHEN. What's the business?

GARY. Fashion.

STEPHEN. Right.

GARY. You probably bought your shirt from one of our shops.

STEPHEN. My wife kits me out.

GARY. I have to say you should tell her how old you are. Did you bring her with you or is that your secretary?

STEPHEN. My secretary's twenty-two, no, yes, it's my wife, she's my wife. My secretary, as it happens, is exactly the kind of woman you'd want to bring with you. Not that she'd come. She does tai chi. She'd break my fingers if I . . . the fact of the matter is she got attacked, well practically. She was followed, chased, by a group of, a gang, and they, I don't think they actually but they frightened her. Quite badly. She has this way of not looking at you.

GARY. They can go frigid, can't they?

STEPHEN (*agreeing*). She's very nice. I'll tell you she's one of those women . . . I'll give you an example. Last week, before we left, she had a top on and it was slashed down one side, so depending on how she sat, if she was leaning a particular way you could see all her (*Demonstrated.*) just . . . and so all afternoon I kept, it was really distracting, and I'm just supposed to, and then she's just as likely to turn around and tell me to . . . (*Short sigh.*)

GARY. What's her name?

STEPHEN. Uh . . . Maggie.

GARY. Well, if Maggie comes on like that but is not prepared to take the consequences, what I'm saying is if she won't go down on you she's a cunt. Half of London has got this attitude about behaviour. It's a disgrace.

STEPHEN. Anyway, it's my wife who's here.

GARY. Who's buggered off with our dentist friend.

STEPHEN. I can't face another temple.

GARY. Questions have to be asked about old fluoride features. You don't mind her going off with him?

STEPHEN. I doubt if they'll get into heavy petting in the temple.

GARY. A fuck begins with a look in my experience.

STEPHEN. You can't stop people looking at each other. I can't stop her looking at people.

GARY. He's got bad breath. That's a joke, isn't it. Unforgivable in his profession. Extremely lacking in class.

STEPHEN. These addresses? Are they clubs or what?

GARY. What? Yes. Clubs. Clubs and private addresses. So you want to come along then, is that it?

STEPHEN. No, I . . .

GARY. I suppose the problem is giving your wife the slip?

STEPHEN. Well I wouldn't go as far . . .

GARY. Or does she get off on . . .?

STEPHEN. No. No. I suppose if I were by myself . . . no but my wife's not . . .

EDWARD *returns*.

GARY. Here! What have you done with his Mrs?

EDWARD. She's making her way back.

GARY. Chivalrous.

EDWARD. Your friend is walking with her.

GARY. Is he? (*Gives* STEPHEN *a conspiratorial look.*)

EDWARD (*to* STEPHEN). It's your loss, you know, sitting here. It's a marvellous temple.

GARY. We'll take your word for it.

EDWARD (*slyly*). There were dancing girls.

GARY. What? A disco?

EDWARD. I went to dental school with a chap just like you.

GARY. Terrific.

EDWARD. He liked to inject himself with valium.

GARY. Terrific.

EDWARD. Your wife says I can buy special computers for dentists.

STEPHEN. Yes, software packages – records and accounts packages. Yes.

EDWARD. I don't know anything about computers.

GARY. I thought he was going to say he didn't know anything about teeth.

EDWARD. I do know they make a lot of computer components in Asia.

STEPHEN. That's right. We've got a factory here.

EDWARD. Your company?

STEPHEN. Yes.

EDWARD. I read somewhere companies farm out work to places like Bangkok which workers in Europe and America won't do.

STEPHEN. What do you mean?

EDWARD. Work that wouldn't pass the scrutiny of Health and Safety at Work legislation.

STEPHEN. I have to say that's actually a fiction.

EDWARD. Possibly. I read that the eye gets damaged doing repetitive . . . is it welding work? . . . on the circuit boards. No, they're not called circuit boards, the . . .

STEPHEN. I know what you mean.

EDWARD. And I'm wrong.

STEPHEN. We do ship work out. It's a multinational. There's a global labour force. Different skills in different places.

EDWARD. I thought it was just that in the East the labour was cheap and uncomplaining.

GARY (*stirring*). Heavy!

STEPHEN. I'm not responsible for the policy of . . .

EDWARD. I wasn't suggesting you were.

GARY (*stirring*). I think he was.

EDWARD. It was an article I read.

STEPHEN. As it happens, Asian women are particularly good at bonding chips. They use gold wire. The chips are minute. It's a very delicate operation. The women have tiny hands and they're patient.

EDWARD. That's all right then.

STEPHEN. As I said it's not my policy.

EDWARD. I'll have to find out more about these dentist packs.

STEPHEN (*irritable*). Did you say Fran was coming back or what?

GARY (*to* STEPHEN). He's winding you up.

EDWARD (*heated*). I'm not talking about Stephen, I'm talking about multinationals. (*Checks.*) Stephen?

STEPHEN. I happen to have a certain loyalty.

EDWARD. No, but I'm saying you're not responsible for that, that's what you said yourself.

STEPHEN. You see, people want the most up-to-date technology at the most competitive prices but they don't want to know how it's achieved.

EDWARD. What?

STEPHEN. Your Dental Records Program would use semi-conductors bonded in Bangkok is what I'm saying.

EDWARD. Well then I don't suppose . . .

STEPHEN. Everyone is so pious.

EDWARD. You think it's all right, then do you, that we abuse – we abuse, OK? – so many people, peoples, countries, so that we can . . .

STEPHEN. You're distorting, you're absolutely distorting.

EDWARD. . . . . enjoy certain creature comforts because I don't . . .

GARY. Aye-aye! (*Glee.*)

STEPHEN. And there is no reliable evidence about eye deterioration.

EDWARD. This was a medical journal!

STEPHEN. If you want to talk about boredom then I'd agree with you it's a pretty boring job.

EDWARD. I bet it is!

STEPHEN. That's what I'm saying, it's bloody boring!

EDWARD. And menial and appallingly paid!

STEPHEN. Yes! OK!

EDWARD. – You know – and I've been to these hostels, actually, where they accommodate these women and you wouldn't live in them!

STEPHEN. OK, so let's hear the solution!

EDWARD. Ach!

STEPHEN. Because they're starving in the North, they're starving in the South. They kiss us, they literally kiss us for the work, they burn incense, they dance because we give them a job so don't!

EDWARD. What did your company, what were your company profits – ?

STEPHEN. Christ!

GARY. (*To* STEPHEN.) Ask him what he makes.

EDWARD. I'll tell you how much I make.

STEPHEN. OK.

EDWARD. I don't believe this.

    FRANCES *and* ADRIAN *return*.

FRANCES. Stephen, you missed a wonderful show, wonderful dancers, has Edward told you? And an exquisite temple, honestly, the most beautiful: sod's law.

GARY. Edward's been winding your husband up something rotten.

FRANCES. What?

GARY. We've been highly political on the old water front.

FRANCES. What's going on?

STEPHEN. Nothing.

EDWARD. Nothing.

FRANCES. Stephen?

STEPHEN. Nothing.

EDWARD (*to* STEPHEN). I'm sorry. It's a hobby-horse.

STEPHEN. Yes. (*To* FRANCES.) You forgot your camera.

FRANCES. Did I?

STEPHEN. Obviously engrossed.

FRANCES (*to* ADRIAN). We were, weren't we? (*To* STEPHEN.) I was. Adrian was telling me – you've met Adrian, haven't you?

ADRIAN. We talked at the airport and in the lobby.

STEPHEN. Right.

FRANCES. Adrian was telling me that – have you seen that next to houses, in the gardens, there are like elaborate birds' houses, like little temples . . .?

EDWARD. Spirit houses – they're spirit houses.

FRANCES. Yes, that's right.

EDWARD. Yes, the thing is, Thai people, Buddhists, believe there's a spirit living on every plot of ground.

FRANCES. And every time they . . .

EDWARD. . . . so obviously if they build on it, they're building on top of a spirit's house, so what they do is to build another little house, tiny, in which the spirit can live and they even put food . . . and (*He trails off as he realizes he's stolen* FRAN'*s thunder.*) I'm sorry, was that what you were going to . . .?

FRANCES. I think I'll see if I can get a drink or something on the boat.

EDWARD. It was, wasn't it?

ADRIAN. I'll have a look.

STEPHEN. No I'll, what do you want?

EDWARD. I'll do it.

STEPHEN. No.

FRANCES. Really, it's –

EDWARD. I'd like to. Please. I would like to . . .

FRANCES. All right.

EDWARD. What would everyone like?

A WAITER *appears. Permanent smile. Polite. Frosty.*

WAITER. I'm to tell you that we are serving buffet dinner on boat.

EDWARD. I can go along, ahead. Save places in the queue.

WAITER. No queue.

EDWARD. Good. Can we order wine?

WAITER. Anything you like.

EDWARD. Chilled wine?

WAITER. Anything you like.

EDWARD. I'll get a bottle of chilled wine, shall I?

They're exiting: STEPHEN, FRANCES *and* EDWARD.

GARY. Questions have to be asked about old dental floss.

ADRIAN *doesn't respond. He's settling down for a gaze at the water.*

GARY. Nice walk?

ADRIAN. What?

GARY. He's desperate, the husband, Stephen . . .

ADRIAN. Is he?

GARY. It's so funny, because he adopts this kind of pose, of curiosity: what do you think about the weather? About Bangkok? About Buddhas? And he's really asking you if you've managed it yet, and if so, how, where, how much and is there any way he could join you.

ADRIAN (*weary of* GARY). Do you know where we are?

GARY. On a boat? By a river?

ADRIAN. How old are you?

GARY. What?

ADRIAN. Have you got any idea of the name of this place? Do you think we're to the North of Bangkok? The South? Could you point to Bangkok on the map?

GARY. No, we had a choice at school between geography and sex. But listen, I hear it was a really interesting temple?

ADRIAN. Just for the record, because it's a pity, and because I'm not going to allow you the pleasure, it used to be – this place – it was supposed to be the most beautiful city in the East at one time, and now it's just rubble and these broken bits of stone, but it's a wonder, it's something to see and you sit on your arse and . . . there are people who have walked for miles, who are sodden, carrying little baskets of, I didn't know, bits of food and flowers and gifts to give to these stones, and they're throwing counters and burning incense and . . . whole families and dancers, and you sit here nursing your hard-on.

GARY. Everyone's keen on these dancers.

ADRIAN. That's right.

GARY (*goading*). And how was Mrs Stephen? Was she interesting?

ADRIAN. Go away, Gary.

GARY. I tell you what impressed me: those fish, the carp this morning, completely brilliant. In the pond, wherever it was, this morning, eating rolls, bigger than their mouths, bigger than their stomachs, huge fuckers eating everything, like submarines, and you watch the people with their, with these rolls, 'cause they're not throwing for the little sprats, nice colours, lovely. No. They're chucking for the big bastards, cruising along with their jaws open, ugly, perfect. That impressed me.

ADRIAN. And what do you deduce from this observation, Gary?

GARY. Oh, bastards win.

> FRANCES *appears.*

FRANCES. I wasn't sure whether you'd realized they've started serving, looks very good, good fish . . .

GARY. I'm coming.

FRANCES. Adrian was telling me that you are his best salesman.

GARY. He's a sweetie, that Adrian. I had a nice chat with your hubbie. I'll see you chaps on the boat.

FRANCES. Yes, I'm following on.

> *Exit* GARY.

FRANCES. Are you coming, Adrian?

ADRIAN. It's too hot to eat.

FRANCES. Yes.

> *A pause. They stare out at the river. All this brief exchange is charged with mutual attraction.*

ADRIAN. What are those kids selling?

FRANCES. Salt, I think. I enjoyed our walk. Thank you.

ADRIAN. So did I.

FRANCES. What next, do you know?

ADRIAN. I think we go back.

FRANCES. Stephen hates these things, tours, organized things. I rather enjoy them. I like guides and . . .

ADRIAN. Right . . .

FRANCES. I didn't actually mean that, anyway. I meant what next in the sense of us sightseeing together, or, you know, when you said . . . on the walk . . .

ADRIAN. Yes, I'd like that.

FRANCES. Yes.

> STEPHEN *appears.*

FRANCES. I was just coming.

STEPHEN. If I'd known you were coming back out here I would have sent your fish back.

FRANCES. It's OK.

STEPHEN (*to* ADRIAN). Not hungry?

ADRIAN. No.

> *They exit.* ADRIAN *sits.*

Scene Four

A clothing factory. A lobby. A sort of reception area where reception space is at a premium, like a parish priest's vestibule. A small room with a table and two or three chairs and some bizarre furnishings.

OWNER. Can I offer you gentlemen a refreshment?

GARY. You can offer me one. I'd like a beer.

OWNER. Singha? Carlsberg Special?

GARY. The coldest.

OWNER. And for you, Mister West?

ADRIAN. Can I drink with you?

OWNER. I drink tea, I'm afraid.

ADRIAN. Tea would be good.

OWNER. Excuse me for a moment or two. (*Exits. A beat.*)

GARY. He speaks English better than me.

ADRIAN. And he's got better manners.

GARY. That's easy. What is this place? His garage?

ADRIAN. This is it. He probably makes everything here.

GARY. Himself?

ADRIAN. I wouldn't like to guess how many girls he's got working here.

GARY. Will he show us?

ADRIAN. No. They won't show you anything other than the garments. It's the same in Hong Kong. No questions about how, just about how much, how many.

GARY. Are you seriously thinking you might buy from him?

ADRIAN. Depends how much, how many.

GARY. There's no point in buying denim.

ADRIAN. He'll make anything.

GARY. I'm just saying, we can't give denim away. Frank rang up, offering me a lorry load, any name, two pounds a pair.

ADRIAN. Just remember it's not barrow boy tactics out here. We look and we stay quiet. Everything is done quietly. If you're good I might take you out tonight.

GARY. Mum, I'm on a promise.

ADRIAN. Three days' celibacy I thought would be too much for you.

GARY. But on the third day it rose again. (GARY *is distracted by his stomach*.) I knew I'd get the runs.

ADRIAN. You should be more careful.

GARY. There's a jacuzzi going on in here. (*His stomach*.) Bastard. That was the buffet yesterday. That's why you're all right.

OWNER (*returning*). One very cold beer.

GARY. Ta.

OWNER. And for us, Mr West. (*The tea*.)

GARY. Ta.

ADRIAN. Thank you.

OWNER. How do you like Bangkok?

GARY. Yeah. OK.

ADRIAN. We were on the river yesterday.

OWNER. To Ayuthya.

ADRIAN. That's right.

OWNER. A good day to go, the Buddha's birthday.

ADRIAN. Yeah.

OWNER. But the weather.

ADRIAN. Not great.

OWNER. My wife and I call this weather American weather.

ADRIAN. Oh?

OWNER. I don't know why. The Americans are not – in this part of the world – some people say they have had a bad influence on us . . . too much Coca Cola, other things we copy . . . For myself, I have many American friends but we still call this bad weather American weather. Just an expression.

ADRIAN. Well it's very American weather.

OWNER. Will you stay and eat with me?

ADRIAN. Thank you, no.

GARY. Anyway, I've got gut rot.

OWNER. I'm so sorry. I am afraid this is very common. Same for me when I visited London. I have upset stomach for many days. If you want the lavatory . . .

GARY. I'll let you know.

OWNER. So, the weather American, the stomach unhappy, anything good?

GARY. Cold beer.

OWNER. Good. (*A gear change.*) So.

ADRIAN. So.

OWNER. How can I be of service?

ADRIAN. I don't know.

OWNER. I understand you may be interested in buying from my factory.

ADRIAN. Then you misunderstand. I have a very good relationship with my supplier in Hong Kong.

OWNER. Quite so. But perhaps, for interest's sake, you would like to see some examples of our work. I think you will agree it is of the highest quality.

ADRIAN. Unfortunately, in London certain people speak badly of Bangkok. They say expect poor delivery, perhaps not top quality finishing.

GARY. Crap fabrics . . .

ADRIAN. Uneven dye, I don't know . . .

OWNER. And yet: here you are. More tea?

ADRIAN. Thank you. There are big changes in Hong Kong.

OWNER. Oh yes. 1997.

ADRIAN. Yes, 1997 but also more and more legislation, union difficulties . . .

OWNER. I understand. Too much light. Times change. Big light on Hong Kong. In Bangkok, still many shadows, lots of shadows.

ADRIAN. That's right.

OWNER. I understand. (*He claps his hands.*) I have arranged a small entertainment. This is Minna and Malee.

Two attractive girls appear, one wearing a skirt and a blouse, the other wearing a dress . . . both smart. MINNA carries a large cassette recorder and MALEE some clothes – another dress, a pair of jeans and a tee shirt.

GARY. Hello.

The GIRLS smile.

OWNER. This is a small demonstration. A few minutes.

He nods at MINNA who turns on the cassette which plays middle of the road, slightly dated, disco music. She starts to dance, then MALEE dances too, just jogging around.

OWNER. Everything the girls wear was made by us, all 100 percent cotton, machine washable.

The GIRLS turn around.

GARY. Very nice.

OWNER. Thank you. Would you like to look at the jeans? Very good.

GARY. Yeah.

ADRIAN. We're not interested in denim.

OWNER. See! No harm in seeing. These are Italian designs.

He nods to the GIRL in jeans. She removes them. The GIRLS undress, still attempting to move gracefully. Not a striptease. They wear bikinis.

OWNER. The bikinis also made by us.

The GIRLS give GARY and ADRIAN their clothes. The GIRLS redress in second outfits: jeans and blouse, and a dress.

OWNER. The finish on these jeans is especially well done.

GARY (*disappointed*). I had a feeling they were going to do that.

The GIRLS dance.

OWNER. This is single needle stitching. These designs are our own. We will also make up to any pattern.

GARY. I think we might have to examine the finish on these as well.

He laughs. He's quite nervous, excited; the GIRLS smile.

ADRIAN. Shall we talk about money?

OWNER. I don't want to talk about money.

GARY. Well, we talked about the weather, it's lousy.

OWNER (*to ADRIAN*). I think perhaps your friend would prefer to be entertained a little more . . .

GARY. Do they work for you?

OWNER. Yes. They have been with me a long time. See how happy they are. They don't sew anymore, of course.

GARY. Oh?

OWNER. Three or four years: time to do new job, the hands become . . . the fingers are tired, not so good.

ADRIAN. So then what?

OWNER. These girls are very pretty, lovely dancers. I like to show my clothes being worn . . . on a body.

ADRIAN. Until the bodies get tired.

OWNER. Oh, sometimes my wife says she thinks I run a hotel, not a workshop.

ADRIAN. Are you leaving these girls with us?

OWNER. I had thought you might like their company.

ADRIAN. Well, that's enough then, isn't it? So as we don't confuse business with pleasure.

OWNER. Absolutely.

ADRIAN. We're very happy about the girls, thank you.

OWNER. Just so.

ADRIAN. Gary? Are you happy with the girls?

GARY. Yeah. Thanks. Very happy.

ADRIAN. The clothes, of course, are a different matter.

OWNER. Quite.

ADRIAN. So let's keep the clothes. Perhaps the best thing would be to send the girls away, then, until we've finished our business together.

The GIRLS remove all the clothes.

ADRIAN. Thank you.

GARY. See you later.

One GIRL picks up the tape recorder, smiling, goes to hand it to ADRIAN.

OWNER. From my company with our compliments.

The girl turns off the cassette machine and in the process drops it. It stops playing. Nobody speaks.

OWNER. Butter fingers.

Scene Five

Scene: *The bedroom. STEPHEN, FRANCES. FRANCES is in the room STEPHEN in the bathroom.*

At Rise: *As the scene begins, we listen, with FRANCES, to the unmistakable noises of lovemaking coming through the wall from the adjacent bedroom. FRANCES turns up the air-conditioning. Then STEPHEN enters, sporting a new Lacoste tee shirt.*

FRANCES. Not bad for two pounds fifty.

STEPHEN. It's all right, isn't it?

FRANCES. It's marvellous.

STEPHEN. I think it actually is a Lacoste.

FRANCES. I think so.

STEPHEN. No – really.

FRANCES. We should ask Adrian or Gary. They'll know, of course.

STEPHEN. Not necessarily. It's not stuck on, it's sewn. (*Pulling at the label.*) How much was it?

FRANCES. Before we beat her down? Well, 180 baht, so that's four, practically five . . .

STEPHEN. Even that's a fraction of what, I've seen them for over twenty-five at home.

FRANCES. Well, I'm very pleased with myself.

STEPHEN. I must say I was impressed, a new side of you, pretty ferocious.

FRANCES (*prodding him*). Stomach.

STEPHEN. Ach.

FRANCES. You can't wear a Lacoste tee shirt and bulge over the top of your belt.

STEPHEN. Stodgy food.

FRANCES. Hmm. What shall I wear?

STEPHEN. I must go to the gym. There's no time. It's impossible. I paid all the bloody money and I never go. I save a couple of quid on a tee shirt and (*Sighs.*) drives me . . . I don't even get a lunch break these days.

FRANCES. Let's go somewhere nice tonight, eh? There's that list Katie gave us.

STEPHEN. We can't go mad.

FRANCES. They're not all expensive, I don't think. They're not, I'm sure. (*Scrabbling around.*) We could take a tuk-tuk and hold hands.

STEPHEN. OK.

FRANCES (*happy*). Can we?

STEPHEN. Yeah.

FRANCES. It's all right, isn't it? Being together . . .

STEPHEN. We could even go on to a club or something after.

FRANCES (*finding this ominous*). Right. (*She takes off her kimono*

and hunts around for something to wear. She's in her underwear.)
I'd love to buy a silk dress while we're here. Or Hong Kong. But
you're supposed to buy silk here. And sapphires. Am I allowed
sapphires? (*She touches him.*) Darling? (*No response.*) Stephen?

STEPHEN. Can you hear anything?

FRANCES. Hear what?

STEPHEN. Hang on. (*He turns off the air-conditioning.*) Listen . . .
(*They listen together.*) That's from thing's room, your friend,
Adrian.

FRANCES. Is it? It's a twin room. They're sharing.

STEPHEN. No, listen . . . (*She starts pulling on clothes. Frisson.*)
Bloody hell.

FRANCES. Bloody hell, what?

STEPHEN. Well there's obviously something going on.

FRANCES. Stephen.

STEPHEN. What?

FRANCES. Are you just going to sit there and listen?

STEPHEN. Do you think they're both, I mean, how many people can
you hear? Bloody hell.

FRANCES. Well, are you?

STEPHEN. I tell you one thing which is very interesting – for all the
bragging this is the first time, because these walls are pretty thin,
evidently, and this is the first time I've heard anything. Do you
think they'd both, with the other in the room, I can't imagine.

FRANCES. Clearly you can imagine.

STEPHEN. It's early evening.

FRANCES. And?

STEPHEN. Well it's just early.

FRANCES. You mean it's not dark.

STEPHEN. You know exactly what I mean.

FRANCES. Funny, isn't it? Because – it's exciting you, isn't it?
You're with me in a bedroom and I'm half naked and we could
make love, we don't have our son barging in, or your work, we
could just make love here, now, in the early evening . . . and you're
getting turned on by the sounds in the next room.

STEPHEN. Do you want to make love? (*There's a long pause.*
STEPHEN *can't help listening.*)

FRANCES. I don't miss Christopher, you know.

STEPHEN. What do you mean?

FRANCES. I don't miss him. I hope he's all right . . . but I don't miss him.

STEPHEN. OK.

FRANCES. I just want you to know that.

STEPHEN. Well OK you've told me.

FRANCES. Sometimes I don't like him very much, Stephen.

STEPHEN. He can be naughty, he's a boy, he's seven, he's not . . .

FRANCES. No, I mean, I'm saying I don't like his personality, not that he's a child or a responsibility . . . I don't like him.

STEPHEN. That's not the point, the responsibility, you don't actually mean you don't like your own son. It's just the, obviously every single day to have to, obviously it's going to, it's not Christopher and it's not you, I'd probably . . .

FRANCES. Right.

STEPHEN. Well, isn't that right?

FRANCES. That's probably it then.

STEPHEN. We should send him a postcard.

FRANCES. I did.

STEPHEN. (*Can't help listening.*) Remind me later to buy one.

FRANCES. Stephen, are you listening to me?

STEPHEN. You said that it, you agreed with me about what I said about Christopher. Christ.

FRANCES. Do you wish you were in there with them?

STEPHEN. No. (*Pause.*) No.

FRANCES. I'm not criticizing you.

STEPHEN. Aren't you?

FRANCES. I think, in other circumstances, I could find it erotic, listening.

STEPHEN (*not believing*). Sure.

FRANCES. Well, I could. (*Pause.*) Why do you hit me sometimes when we're in bed?

STEPHEN. What do you mean, hit you?

FRANCES. When we make love. You've hit me.

STEPHEN (*appalled*). Don't be, I haven't, don't be ridiculous.

FRANCES. You have, Stephen.

STEPHEN. I've slapped, this is ridiculous, not even slapped, that's the wrong word, I've in the most playful sense, I would never hit you, and you should say if you didn't like, I obviously, I assumed you quite, otherwise you would have said, we're talking about years, Frances, Christ. I would never hit you.

FRANCES. Now I've said it then.

STEPHEN. That makes me fell terrible. Terrible.

FRANCES. You're right. I should have said.

STEPHEN. You should have done. Bloody hell. Fucking hell.

FRANCES. I don't want to stay in this room any longer now. Let's go out.

STEPHEN. Sometimes when I think about you it's like a bathroom and it's white and tiles and locked.

FRANCES. What is?

STEPHEN. What is what?

FRANCES. What is like a bathroom and locked and white?

STEPHEN. You. I just said. Just sometimes when I think I suppose I don't know what you're thinking. Because you can be very cold.

FRANCES. What are you going to do Stephen? Because you can lie there and eavesdrop all evening, that's all right with me, if that's what you want, but I would like to eat something.

STEPHEN. I'm waiting for you. I'm ready.

Scene Six

The Hotel Coffee Shop. Much later that evening. A foursome in progress. ADRIAN and GARY are drunkish. MINNA and MALEE are worse for wear, but not drunk, not animated. Weary hostesses who have been fed at last.

On the table, full ashtray, empty Singha bottles, liqueur glasses, cans of Coke: the evening's debris.

GARY. What's the score about later then?

ADRIAN. I don't know.

GARY. Same bedroom?

ADRIAN. I'm not intending to sleep with anybody. Are you?

GARY. Well . . .

ADRIAN. What for?

GARY. What do you mean what for?

ADRIAN. How many ways are there?

GARY. You haven't even had yours yet. She's fallen asleep. Look at that!

ADRIAN shakes MINNA, *his companion, who's dropped off.*

ADRIAN. Eh!

She wakes up, startled. Eats a bit.

GARY. She got bored waiting. Don't you fancy her?

ADRIAN. Not a lot.

GARY. I wouldn't mind it. Look, she's gorgeous. What about a swap?

ADRIAN. No.

GARY. Why not?

ADRIAN. Because I've formed a relationship with Minna, haven't I? (*He shakes her.*) Eh? You can't just throw that out of the window.

GARY. You're a bastard. You're winding me up.

ADRIAN. Besides, I want to get some sleep and if you swap you'll be . . . I don't want to have to listen to you.

GARY. You might learn something.

ADRIAN (*somewhere else*). You reckon?

GARY. Well, what about giving me another half hour . . . If I go up ahead now . . . I'll go up with her for half an hour, eh?

ADRIAN. It'll drop off.

GARY. Oh no, it's very solid. Look she's gone again, she's completely, she's in a trance.

ADRIAN. She's knackered.

GARY. Malee's all right though, isn't she? Look: first division.

He prods her affectionately. She smiles. He looks over to MINNA.

GARY. Go on, let's swap and I'll just have half an hour's worth.

Smiles at MINNA, *who smiles, tired, back.*

ADRIAN. They're both ready to go home.

GARY. I don't think so. I bet they're having a bloody good evening in comparison.

ADRIAN. In comparison to what?

GARY. Come on: we haven't hurt them, and we've fed them. I bet this is a great evening for them. I'm not joking. Look in her bag.

ADRIAN. What?

GARY. Look in her bag – Oy, wake up! Oy, gorgeous! Wake up! (*He shakes her.*) She's really struggling, isn't she? Just open your bag, let us see. We won't take anything. (*To* MALEE.) Tell her we won't take anything. I just want to see inside. (*Puts out his hand.*) Your bag. (*He takes it, opens it up . . . folded inside a serviette is a piece of chicken and there's a small plastic bag filled with rice.*) Look at this; half the meal in this bag. Poor cow is probably starving. That's why she's nodding off: not used to eating so much.

ADRIAN. Give her the bag back.

GARY. I'm positive about this. Look at that club tonight. Having to fondle those guys – they were German – with shorts on and those turkey legs. This is Christmas in comparison. Malee here agrees.

GARY *smiles*, MALEE *smiles. They hug, quite friendly.*

ADRIAN. It's all one, I expect. If you have to do it. I expect it's all one. It's like a car park this place, isn't it?

GARY. Oh Christ, don't go bleak.

ADRIAN. I think they sent over their architects to train in London or Switzerland or somewhere and they went to the wrong place. They went to Car Park and Garage Design classes and they all came home and designed Bangkok and they think they've built a city but in fact they've built a car park.

GARY (*exploring* MALEE). Have you seen their fingers? They're all twisted, supposed to have pretty hands but they're ugly. It's like arthritis, like old people's hands.

MALEE *attempts to hide her fingers.*

ADRIAN. It probably is arthritis. You heard what their boss was saying: a few years sewing nonstop and their fingers are ruined.

GARY. Adrian, no, I tell you what got me, about earlier, the first show, the sex show, no, was how afterwards, they were all bashful – did you see? With him covering himself. I thought that was really funny. After all that. I thought that was a real crease up.

ADRIAN. The thing is (*Of* MINNA.) I expect she's hoping she won't have to. If she just keeps her eyes closed then she'll fall asleep and wake up and she's won't have had to.

GARY. You do fancy her don't you?

ADRIAN. Yeah, I expect so.

GARY. You do!

ADRIAN. Yeah, I do.

GARY. Well, you go on up, Adrian, go on, and we'll wait. Go on, and we'll have another drink. Yeah!

ADRIAN. I don't know. Maybe.

We join EDWARD *and* NET *who have just arrived after a happy tour and meal and chat.*

EDWARD. This time you must let me buy the drinks.

NET. No. My pleasure.

EDWARD. No, really, let me, you've spoiled me all evening.

NET. I am a man with a happy mouth; must celebrate. (*His teeth are OK.*)

EDWARD (*dismissive*). Oh . . .

NET. Half lager?

EDWARD. Half lager, chai. (*Yes.*)

NET. Chai! Chai!

EDWARD. Chai kawpkun. (*Yes, thank you.*)

NET. Kawpkun! (*He slaps* EDWARD's *back, then goes to get lagers.*) Chai krap kawpkun krap.

EDWARD *alone, has to acknowledge the foursome. He nods.*

GARY. All right?

EDWARD. Now then.

GARY. Good night?

EDWARD. Yes, thank you.

GARY. What'd you get up to?

EDWARD. Oh, had a drive round.

GARY. I bet you did. (*To* ADRIAN.) He had a drive round. (*To* EDWARD.) So did we. Took a few snaps and all, eh?

EDWARD (*has his camera with him*). I did as it happens.

GARY. They'll never see the photomat, eh? Eh? (*To* ADRIAN.) He'll be developing them at home. (*To* EDWARD.) Oy, come on, come and join us.

EDWARD. I'm being bought a drink.

GARY. That's all right, bring your friend (*Loaded.*) and pull up a chair. Come on.

EDWARD. Really . . .

NET *returns with the lagers.* GARY *addresses him.*

GARY. Oy . . . You're being invited to come and join us.

NET. Oh. Thank you.

GARY. That's all right. Come on then. Come and join me. Adrian's just off upstairs. He's got to have a chat with Minna, his friend.

EDWARD. We don't want to disturb . . .

GARY. No, a private chat upstairs. (*To* NET, *who's come across.*) I'm Gary, this is Minna and Malee and here's Adrian.

NET. I am Net.

EDWARD *reluctantly comes over. To* ADRIAN.

EDWARD. Don't let us keep you.

NET. You meet nice Thai girls?

GARY. Yeah.

NET. Have a good evening?

GARY..Oh yeah, brilliant.

NET. Us too. Very good evening, much laughing.

GARY. Oh yeah, we laughed and all. Lots of chatting, lots of laughing.

NET. Mr Edward make Net's teeth very happy. Great friends.

GARY. Oh yeah?

EDWARD. Net's insisted on taking me out to show his gratitude. I didn't even do anything. Gave him some oil of cloves and a toothbrush. I didn't catch your friends' names . . .

GARY. Minna and Malee.

EDWARD. Hello.

MALEE *smiles.* MINNA's *too tired.*

GARY. They're presents.

EDWARD. What's that?

GARY. The women. They're presents.

EDWARD. It wouldn't surprise me.

NET. Now Net tell Mr Edward his special present.

EDWARD. Yes?

NET. Same present as your friend. Tonight Net arrange pretty girl come to your room.

GARY. Whooo!

EDWARD (*nervous laugh*). What?

NET. No charge. Net arrange. Nicer girl than these. Really. Very nice, very young, very clean, honest to God. All arranged. Surprise.

GARY. Who's a jammy bastard?

NET. Mr Edward, Net's special friend.

STEPHEN *and* FRANCES *enter arm in arm. They've also had a good evening. They've come for a nightcap.* FRANCES *tries to steer* STEPHEN *straight out again.*

STEPHEN (*to* FRANCES, *nonplussed*). What?

ADRIAN. Hello.

STEPHEN. Evening.

FRANCES. Hello.

ADRIAN. You should join us. We're having an impromptu party. Come on, I'll get the chairs . . .

GARY (*to* ADRIAN). You've woken up.

FRANCES. I'm tired actually.

STEPHEN. Well . . .

GARY. We're all going to bed in a minute.

STEPHEN. Fine. Darling?

FRANCES. I said: I'm tired.

ADRIAN *returns with a chair and a* WAITRESS *who carries the second chair and then hovers for the drink order.*

ADRIAN. What are you drinking?

FRANCES. I think we're going to bed.

ADRIAN. Oh.

STEPHEN *is fascinated by the women.*

STEPHEN. Come on, let's have a quick one. Yes? (FRANCES *impassive. To* ADRIAN.) Whisky, please.

FRANCES. Lemon tea.

STEPHEN. Have a drink.

ADRIAN. One whisky, one lemon tea. Anyone else? (*To the* WOMEN.) Cokes? (*No takers.*) No? (*To* GARY.) You?

GARY. Southern Comfort. Ta. (WAITRESS *exits*, ADRIAN *gets up again.*) Now where are you going?

ADRIAN (*exiting*). Guess.

GARY. So, this is Minna, Malee.

EDWARD. And this is Net. And this is Frances and Stephen.

NET. We met already. Net have to fix air-conditioning in your room.

STEPHEN. That's right. Yes. It's fine now, thanks.

NET. No problem.

STEPHEN. Sorry I didn't recognize you at first.

FRANCES. Hello.

There's a pause.

GARY. Nice evening?

STEPHEN. Yes.

FRANCES. Yes.

GARY. Have a meal?

STEPHEN. Yes. We had a place recommended to us. And it was wonderful. Wasn't it?

FRANCES. Yes. Wonderful.

GARY. We went to one of those clubs you were asking about.

FRANCES *looks at* STEPHEN.

STEPHEN (*not wanting to pursue this*). Right. Drinks. (*As the* WAITRESS *approaches. Then to* EDWARD.) How about you? What have you been up to?

EDWARD. I had a meal. (*Of* NET.) We had a meal. Quite local, I think. Quite genuine food, I think.

GARY. Nothing like genuine food is what I say, eh Minna? Minna's falling asleep on us. (ADRIAN *returns.*) Adrian, I think Minna's desperate for you to take her to bed.

ADRIAN (*settles with his drink*). Cheers.

FRANCES. Gary was telling us you went to a club. How was that?

ADRIAN. OK.

GARY. It was very naughty.

ADRIAN. It wasn't naughty, it was a garage.

GARY. Adrian's decided all Bangkok is actually a garage.

NET. Maybe garage. Many clubs in Bangkok garage once upon a time.

FRANCES. But entertaining nevertheless.

GARY. That's right.

FRANCES. Did your friends enjoy it or did they come with the club?

GARY. We all had a good time, eh chaps?

FRANCES. And have you been to a club as well, Edward?

EDWARD. No.

GARY. But he's got a nice surprise coming later, eh Edward?

EDWARD. There's been a misunderstanding.

FRANCES. Oh?

GARY. That's not what I would have called it. (*To* NET.) You tell them. (*Embarrassed a little in front of* FRANCES, NET *is silent.*) Tell them! He's fixed Edward up for later.

EDWARD. He hasn't. It's a mistake. He, Net's kindly . . . but, I think what it is, is that women here are not counted for as much. It's not a political attitude, as such, but religious as far as – which is political, of course – is that women are seen as an earlier incarnation, I think that's at the root of it, in Buddhist terms. I don't think Net, I think it was intended as a kindness.

FRANCES. You're saying it wouldn't happen in England?

EDWARD. I don't think it's so likely women would be given as presents. (*Pointed.*) These ladies are presents, apparently.

GARY. Absolutely. They came with bows and everything.

NET. I'm sorry, Mr Edward, if I make bad idea.

EDWARD. Don't worry. No harm done.

FRANCES. Fine. (*To* ADRIAN.) Your present's fallen asleep.

NET (*to* EDWARD). Net thought nice idea for his friend.

EDWARD. Don't worry.

FRANCES. Have you spoken to her?

ADRIAN. She doesn't really speak English.

FRANCES. That figures.

STEPHEN. Anyway.

FRANCES. If there's anything worse than the taste of tea, it's the taste in my mouth.

EDWARD. Anyway, I think I will . . .

FRANCES. I'll walk up with you.

STEPHEN. Do you want me to come up?

FRANCES. So what was it then? A sex show?

ADRIAN. Yeah.

FRANCES. What sort? Animals?

ADRIAN. No.

FRANCES. No. Just women treated like animals.

ADRIAN. There were men as well.

STEPHEN. This is Fran's hobby-horse, I'm afraid.

FRANCES. What do you mean afraid?

STEPHEN. I'm just warning them.

FRANCES. And so: you sat and watched couples having sex.

ADRIAN. Yes.

FRANCES. Was that erotic?

ADRIAN. No, it was a bit like watching a swimming lesson.

GARY. That's exactly what it was like.

FRANCES. But you watched anyway.

STEPHEN. Fran . . .

GARY. What's your point here, love?

FRANCES. Just curious.

GARY. So were we.

FRANCES. And you took your lady friends?

GARY. Yeah, they came.

FRANCES. Wasn't that odd?

GARY. Lot of couples there. All ages. Americans, Aussies, Germans, all sorts.

FRANCES. A big garage.

GARY. It wasn't a garage.

STEPHEN. I think we should go to bed . . . Fran . . .

EDWARD. Yes, if you'll excuse me as well, I think I'll . . .

FRANCES. So let me get this straight: you went to a club, with these women, and you watched couples having sex? Is that right?

GARY. Yeah, we did. It wasn't just fucking. There were novelty acts, weren't there? (*To* ADRIAN.)

ADRIAN. That's right. A woman expelled ping pong balls into a glass of water.

GARY. Except she couldn't do it!

FRANCES (*genuinely lost*). Sorry, what?

GARY. She had ping pong balls up her and she aimed them at a glass of water.

FRANCES (*a beat*). Why?

GARY. I don't know. It was a laugh. She kept missing. It was a laugh.

FRANCES. What was?

GARY. What she was doing. She laughed. We all laughed. Minna laughed. Malee laughed. It wasn't very clever, but she had a go, and you could reload her . . . yeah? . . . so that was fun.

FRANCES (*disgusted*). Oh, right.

GARY. It was actually pretty harmless. You know: no one died . . . No one complained.

FRANCES. I bet.

GARY. That's all right, then.

FRANCES. Was this free entertainment? The ping pong show?

GARY. No, actually, they're doing very well out of it: ten quid a throw.

FRANCES. You paid ten pounds to watch a woman insert ping pong balls into her vagina?

GARY. And aim them at a glass of water. Yeah. Or maybe that was free and we paid to watch the humping. Or maybe the humping was free and we paid to watch the ping pong balls, or five quid each. Who knows? It's a mystery. You're very quiet.

STEPHEN (*thinks GARY is speaking to him*). What? No, I just . . . (*Shrugs.*) What can . . . ?

GARY. Not you. Adrian.

ADRIAN. Yeah.

GARY. You laughed.

ADRIAN. Yeah, I laughed.

NET. You see, I think pretty girls very important for Thailand. Not rich country – like London – many people have empty stomach . . . so tourist very good. These girls come Bangkok make lot of baht no problem: tourist happy, girl happy, family happy, Thailand happy.

FRANCES. I see. Are you married?

NET. Net married, yes.

FRANCES. Would you let your wife sell herself?

NET. My wife? Not so pretty. Too many babies. (*He beams.*) I think nobody buy.

Small chuckles. FRANCES *weary.*

FRANCES. Yeah.

STEPHEN. Come on, Frances, you've made your point.

FRANCES. No I haven't actually! Christ! You men, seem to arrive here and reveal this, because it's available, this great underbelly of . . . it's as if suddenly you kick off your shoes and there are hooves and these great phalluses.

GARY. Don't keep mine in my shoes.

FRANCES. Oh fuck off.

GARY. Whoo!

FRANCES. Yes, whoo! It's so ugly and its nothing to do with Bangkok, with Thailand, that's the point . . . what's happening here, it's to do with us.

GARY. Does anybody understand this because I don't?

ADRIAN. I think she's asking you to go outside and tie a ribbon around your prick and charge people to look at it.

GARY. What?

FRANCES. No. I'm not saying that.

EDWARD. It's the Americans, they make this place into one big Rest and Recreation Zone. They spread Thailand's legs and the rest of the West has – you know – ever since. That's what Frances is talking about.

FRANCES. Don't tell me, please, what I'm trying to say.

EDWARD. Oh, I thought that was your . . . sorry, what were you . . . anyway it's true about, you don't get two million prostitutes from nowhere . . . What was your point? I'm sorry: I wasn't . . .

There's a pause. FRANCES *doesn't respond.* NET *has been whispering in* MALEE's *ear for some seconds. She nods.*

NET. My friends, I think girls want to get home before too late. I can take them in minibus.

GARY. That's all right, we can arrange a taxi.

NET. No problem.

ADRIAN. Great, do that.

GARY. What: him run them home?

ADRIAN. Yeah.

GARY. I think a few questions have to be asked here.

ADRIAN. Yeah?

GARY. I do. (*Doesn't ask them.*)

FRANCES. It is the power of the erection, a man with an erection
loses the capacity to think or hear. He loses the capacity to speak
coherently, or act with any sense of others, of morality, everything
gives way to the demands of the penis . . . take me there, put me
here, fly me six thousand miles, get me out, get me up . . .

STEPHEN (*over this*). Frances, that's enough.

FRANCES (*dogged*). Talk about a sanctuary of pricks . . . you know
that don't you, that Bangkok has a shrine dedicated to your
genitals!

GARY (*over this*). I'm going to laugh, what a crease up. Beats the
ping pong balls.

ADRIAN. Shut up, Gary.

GARY. Not until she does. It's not my fault she hasn't got a willy.

NET. We go now.

EDWARD. Yes. And me.

STEPHEN. Come on, Frances.

FRANCES. Please. Stop doing that. Stop being embarrassed for me.

GARY (*to MALEE*). See you around then. Here, take this. (*He
presses some money into her hands.*) Give us a kiss then. (*They
kiss.*) So. All right? See you then.

ADRIAN (*simultaneous with GARY's valedictions*). OK? (*To
MINNA.*) Sleep tight.

*He, too, gives her money. She raises her hands in a prayer of
thanks. Then* FRANCES *comes across to the two girls.*

FRANCES. I'd like you have this and this. (*She hands them both
more cash and then pulls her bracelet off. To ADRIAN.*) Which
one was crying out in your bedroom all afternoon? Or was it both
of them?

ADRIAN. I wasn't in my room this afternoon.

A beat in which ADRIAN *and* FRANCES *look at each other.*

GARY. It was Malee.

FRANCES. Malee?

MALEE *looks up.* FRANCES *gives her the bracelet.*

FRANCES. I want you to be given something without having to go
on your back for it. (*To MALEE.*) Take it.

MALEE *very grateful.*

FRANCES. No, it's my pleasure.

STEPHEN. I gave you that bracelet.

FRANCES. Well now I've given it to Malee. She entertained you this afternoon as well. Now you've paid for it.

STEPHEN *is fantastically embarrassed.*

FRANCES. I'm going to get some air. There's no air in here. I'll see you upstairs. (*She exits.*)

EDWARD. Goodnight. Net, goodnight. I'll see you I expect.

NET. I ring tomorrow, Mr Edward. Sorry about . . .

EDWARD (*dismissing*). Finish.

NET (*smiles*). OK. Finish.

EDWARD. OK. 'Night. (*To* MINNA *and* MALEE.) 'Night.

NET *and* MINNA *and* MALEE *go out.*

EDWARD. 'Night. (*To* STEPHEN, GARY *and* ADRIAN. *Mumbled goodnights from the trio who remain in the litter of the evening. Then a long pause.*)

STEPHEN. Sorry about that. She's very sensitive. I don't know, we saw a lot of prostitutes tonight and I think . . . it's understandable in a way. Some of them are just children. Our son's nearly seven. Some of them didn't look much older although I'm sure they are, it's the features, all so delicate. She gets very angry about things for some reason. She's not even a feminist.

GARY. What did she mean about this afternoon?

STEPHEN. Oh she was, it was because we could hear. The walls aren't exactly . . . we could hear something through the walls. She was just making a point. (*A beat.*) You know.

GARY. Quite the detectives, aren't we?

STEPHEN. They are very thin walls. Doesn't leave much to the imagination.

ADRIAN. And you thought we were all in there, did you? A foursome?

STEPHEN. We didn't spend a lot of time speculating.

GARY. I'd say your Mrs has a few problems.

STEPHEN. Oh, I think I don't think . . .

ADRIAN. Nor does Gary: think.

GARY. Bought a tee shirt then, eh?

STEPHEN. Yes, it was really cheap. But still: supposed to be a good label, isn't it?

GARY *manages to make his silence a disapproving one.*

STEPHEN. Anyway, I quite like it, quite cool. (*Pause.*) I'd like to buy Fran a silk dress or something. I think a lot of it's attention, asking for attention. (*Laughs.*) I thought a silk dress or something like that would, I've already had tee shirts and things.

ADRIAN. Yeah, you should buy her a dress.

STEPHEN. I think it would be a good idea. I'll have to guess the size. Or I could have a look inside one of her dresses. (*Prompt mode.*) Sounded like a pretty, uh, explicit show this evening.

ADRIAN. Well it wasn't subtle.

STEPHEN. Were they actually doing it?

ADRIAN. Oh yes.

STEPHEN (*impressed*). Christ! And this was the place you had recommended?

GARY. One of the places, yeah. Listen: go! Go to one. You're so deperate I can smell it.

STEPHEN. I'm not desperate. I must confess I am curious. And I'd feel as if I'd missed something if I had come all this way and not just had a look. But it's impossible – Christ! Even you must see that. Well . . .

GARY. You could arrange it.

STEPHEN. It's impossible. You're joking.

GARY. Say you've got an evening meeting or something.

STEPHEN. No. It's a nice thought. What would you pay, do you know?

GARY. Dunno. Not much.

STEPHEN. It's academic, anyway.

GARY. Sort it out! Come out with us! You'd have a field day.

STEPHEN. Bedtime! (*Pause.*) If by some fluke I did work something out, I'd be able to tag along with you guys?

GARY. Go for it.

STEPHEN *exits.*

GARY. There are some fucked-up people.

ADRIAN. Go to bed, Gary.

GARY. Is this going to happen every time I want to bring somebody back to the room?

ADRIAN. I expect so.

GARY. I think I'll get another room.

ADRIAN. Fine.

GARY. Loads of people checked out today. I'm going to ask.

ADRIAN. I said OK.

GARY. Don't worry, I'll pay the difference.

ADRIAN. Right.

GARY. Anyway: don't fancy not being able to fart without somebody cataloguing it through the wall, so . . . (*Takes a swig of beer, pulls a face.*) Flat. Shall I tell you the nicest person in the room tonight. This is the truth: Malee. She wasn't dim, you know. She was actually very nice. She was perfectly happy, staying. (*He gets up.*) I'm definitely going to see about another room, first thing tomorrow. Definitely. And I tell you something else for nothing, the difference between us, I thank fuck every day I'm not in the middle classes. (GARY *exits.*)

ADRIAN *sits with his scotch.* FRANCES *appears.*

ADRIAN. He's gone upstairs.

FRANCES (*she comes towards him, sits down*). You know I thought it was you, this afternoon.

ADRIAN. It could have been.

FRANCES. But it wasn't. Yes it could have been. I'd made this decision based on nothing at all, an impression, that you wouldn't be casual and then I thought, there he is being casual and I was so disappointed. And anyway. Because somehow over the past few days, at Ayuthya, I'd just thought to every rule there is an exception.

ADRIAN. Where did you go just then?

FRANCES. I'd meant to walk but the streets frighten me. Then I went to the pool, I wanted to dip my feet, but there's a dog . . . it must be a guard dog, I expect . . . so: all a bit abortive.

ADRIAN. We could walk together.

FRANCES. How could you accept a girl as a present?

ADRIAN. So many questions.

FRANCES. I know why anyway. Would you have slept with her?

ADRIAN. I don't know.

FRANCES. It made me so uncomfortable this afternoon. Stephen lying on the bed, enthralled by the performance.

ADRIAN. Yes.

FRANCES. No, not because of Stephen. I used to listen to this couple above me, at night – I'm talking about in London, years ago – and they used to have sex all the time. Great long loud sessions, really long and really loud and I used to lie in the dark and strain to listen, to hear them, screw up my eyes to catch the whole performance and imagine it: and my face used to go hot . . . I remember that sensation: the sense of my face going hot, and straining to hear and these great groans and gasps and cries. You'd see them in the day – this girl was perfectly ordinary, honestly, you wouldn't have given her a second look . . . a quiet hello, she'd be gone, and I'd know she has these fantastic orgasms. And I remember waking up one night and – being woken by this familiar noise – and straining to hear and my face going hot and then realizing it wasn't them, it was a baby, it was a baby crying and it was Christopher, my son, and we weren't even in the same flat any more by this time and I'd woken, hardly woken, and made myself come to the sound of my son crying, waiting for me to feed him. I've been staring at the pool and it's black and I've been trying to remember that room, what it looked like: the room underneath the couple. And I can't. Where does it belong, out fantasy world? Do you know?

ADRIAN. No.

FRANCES. I don't want to despise it but I don't know where it belongs. Because here, it's here isn't it? Out in the open. And it's terrible. And it's terrible bottled up. (*She's at the table. A beat.*) I want you to know there's no possibility of anything happening between us. I just want that to be clear.

ADRIAN. OK.

FRANCES. You don't say enough. I don't know who I'm talking to.

ADRIAN. Then I'll talk non-stop from now on. OK?

FRANCES. OK. So take me for this walk. (*They exit.*)

ACT TWO

Scene One

A massage parlour. NET has brought GARY and STEPHEN to a massage parlour. NET clearly has some arrangement with the proprietor.

NET. My friends, this is Mr Harry. He is boss of Massage Parlour. Best Massage Parlour Bangkok.

HARRY (*shrugs, but immodest*). Maybe.

NET (*to HARRY*). These are my friends. Mr Gary and Mr Stephen.

EVERYONE shakes hands, STEPHEN distracted by the women. NET then begins to speak in Thai, but GARY quickly interrupts.

GARY. Hey, talk in English!

NET (*easily*). Sure. No problem. Just explaining to Harry this first time in Bangkok and massage parlour.

HARRY (*nodding*). First time!

GARY. That's right. So let's get on with it, eh?

This parlour, typically, has a viewing area from which a number of girls can be inspected, behind glass, and apparently oblivious to the attentions of their prospective clients. They wear bikinis and a tag with a number sewn on.

NET. Sure. No problem. (*He shepherds STEPHEN to where he can view the girls.*) Don't worry, they can't see you. This is a one-way mirror. Choose! You choose and you tell Harry the number.

HARRY. You can ask me about girls.

NET. Yes, ask him about each one, he can tell you anything.

HARRY. Just ask! Number 35: number 6, any number: I tell you everything.

NET. They can't see you. Look carefully: choose. You tell Harry: Harry call their number.

HARRY. Number 45: come on down!

NET. Girls meet you in the cubicle. Each cubicle has a tub –

HARRY. New tile by the way.

NET. All clean – a tub, lots of suds, girls make lots of suds, and then you bathe.

HARRY. Rub-a-dub-dub!

NET. They bathe you. No one wears any clothes.

HARRY. Very nice. Have a drink, all air-conditioned. – Whole God damn place air-conditioned by the way.

NET. – Then you come through to the place where you have your massage. And also here is a bed to relax afterwards. The massage . . . lots of suds . . . not done with the hands only, but with the whole body –

HARRY (*beams*). Called B Course!

NET. Yes . . . this is called B Course. Hard if you are doing the massage.

HARRY. Not so hard if you are the lucky one underneath.

NET. You pay for the massage now. Choose first, then pay, of course!

HARRY. All my girls show card stamped every week at clinic, no AIDS, no VD. This rule for me, no stamp: no work. (*Checks with NET, who nods authoritatively.*) Very strict.

NET. OK? So now: choose. Take your time. We leave you. Girls can't see you. One-way mirror. Like window shopping.

GARY. And we get special price, yeah? Coming with you?

NET. Sure. No problem. Net get friends special price. Choose first. Talk money after. Don't worry. But Net must go now. Back to hotel. Work-work. (*He and HARRY make to exit.*)

STEPHEN. Hang on, Net. Hang on a minute. (*He fishes out a bank note and gives it to NET.*)

NET (*accepting it*). Very kind. (*He exits.*)

STEPHEN. (*Excited, incredulous.*) They really do have numbers! It's staggering. How much do you think they'll charge us, you know, for the massage? And then if – I have to know how much in toto – because otherwise I may have to cash another travellers' cheque which is fine but will take explaining away. (*Looks.*) It is actually staggering.

GARY. Pay with plastic.

STEPHEN. What? Credit card?

GARY. It said they took it.

STEPHEN. What would they charge you for? What would they call it?

GARY. You wouldn't be the first. There's probably some code, something dead diplomatic: get your Visa bill: Fuck – forty quid.

STEPHEN. You think forty, do you?

STEPHEN. Why do they call it B Course?

GARY. I dunno.

STEPHEN. I've got to be back by 5:30 and pick up Fran's dress. I really have. 3 looks quite Western.

GARY. I'm bagging 3.

STEPHEN. One of them's knitting! 12!

GARY. 12? Oh yeah.

STEPHEN. White bikini.

GARY. Yeah.

STEPHEN. Do you really think they can't see us? 27 is nice, isn't she? Looks quite intelligent.

GARY. Well she's reading. What has intelligence got to do with anything? Are you going to play scrabble?

STEPHEN. I will probably just have the massage, I expect.

GARY. Reckon!

STEPHEN. I'm glad we're doing it this way round.

GARY. What way?

STEPHEN. Well, here first and then to the clothes place, because otherwise all I mean is obviously we're going to be quite clean, aren't we, with the bath and what have you, which might seem a bit off, given the weather, but if we –

GARY. Thank you Sherlock Holmes.

STEPHEN. Listen: my wife is no fool.

GARY. So you had a massage. What's your wife doing?

STEPHEN. She's gone to the Grand Palace, to look at some Buddha or other, an emerald Buddha. (*Distracted.*) Actually she's nice, too.

GARY. Where?

STEPHEN. Next to 27. With the gold chain. 30 something.

GARY. Oh yeah. (*Looks.*) Yeah, well, have two together.

STEPHEN (*dismissive*). Oh . . .

GARY. Rub different bits. You look so excited!

STEPHEN. I suppose I am. It's an experience, isn't it? I love massages anyway.

HARRY (*reappearing*). Well, my friends, very difficult to choose, eh?

STEPHEN. Very.

HARRY. Want my advice? 27 very good.

GARY. What about 3?

HARRY. 3 also excellent. Tell the truth: all special girls. 3 half not Thai. Maybe American. Very young.

STEPHEN. I like 18.

HARRY. 18 also special. Good for round the world.

STEPHEN. Round the world? What's that?

HARRY (*laughs*). Round the world? Just ask. Say round the world, 18 understand. Then enjoy.

STEPHEN. Well OK, I think 18, then.

HARRY. For you, 18, and for you, sir?

GARY. 3.

HARRY. 3? I could tell. OK. (*Goes to microphone, or off, and bawls out the numbers.*) 18, 3, Beht! Sam! (*Then turns to* STEPHEN *and* GARY.) You pay me nine hundred baht each now . . .

GARY. Is that our special price?

HARRY. All special price for friends.

Two GIRLS *appear in bikinis. They carry towels. Number 18 and Number 3.*

HARRY. Who was Number 18?

STEPHEN. Me.

HARRY *jerks his head at 18 . . . who comes to* STEPHEN. GARY *walks towards 3.*

GARY. Hello 3.

HARRY (*smiles*). American Express?

Scene Two

ADRIAN's *bedroom.* ADRIAN *and* FRANCES *alone, early afternoon.*

FRANCES. I don't just want to make love. What present would you get from Thailand for a seven-year-old?

ADRIAN. Is this your son?

FRANCES. He likes hitting things. And guns. No, actually he can be very sensitive. He has a real problem with the loo. He doesn't go. For days at a time. I think I must have done something wrong at one time. Do you have guilt? It goes round me like blood. It's a family characteristic. And I've passed it on. Anyway, what should I get him? Someone tried to sell me a knife at the market. He would have loved that.

ADRIAN. We don't have to make love at all. We can go and look at the Emerald Buddha. We can buy your son a present.

FRANCES. Do you know what happens in Dante to the lustful? They wander around for ever. That's their fate. The roving eye can never stop roving. Pretty good, eh? The lustful wander and the seducers are scourged.

ADRIAN. What would we be? Lust or seducers?

FRANCES. Oh, lust. That's mutual.

ADRIAN. Good: I've always travelled. I'm not so keen on getting whipped.

FRANCES. Do you go in for holiday romance? Don't answer that. This morning there was a condom in the bathroom. It must have come up through the plumbing or something. I hate those things. A friend of mine had a problem with their drains a couple of years ago. They live in the country and it's all fairly primitive. I know I'm talking too much, but I'm, and this is my first rove, as they say, scrub that, it's a lie, nevertheless relatively unroved, so . . . they live in the country, problem with drains, and they call in the thing, the person, whatever board it would be, the Water Board, whoever, no the drain cleaners, and this chap arrives with all the equipment and Jan took him to the cover outside and he lifted it up, they were chatting all the while, and inside the cover, underneath, blocking the drain, was about a year's worth of their waste in all its glory, this jamboree bag of Durex and Tampax mixed up with everything else. And Jan said they both stared at this, (*Shrugs.*) and then she went back indoors and, well she did nothing, that's not the point, the point is that the effort to appear civilized is so thin, is such a sham.

ADRIAN. To answer your question, no I don't.

FRANCES is confused.

ADRIAN. Holiday romances. Go in for them.

FRANCES. Do you think Stephen has flings? (*She asks in a way that encourages the negative.*)

ADRIAN. I expect so.

FRANCES. Actually, I don't think so. I think there's bravado. I really don't think he does.

ADRIAN. If you were painting a room, lots of rooms in a house, what colour would you paint them?

FRANCES. This is a game, isn't it? What's it called? Where you say: if I were a room what room would I be? What flower?

ADRIAN. No, I'm serious. I've bought a house and I need to paint it. It needs decorating. And I want it to be . . . I don't know . . .

FRANCES. What?

ADRIAN. Somewhere nice. I've bought all the magazines. My daughter has ideas, of course.

FRANCES. I didn't know you had a daughter. Have you got a wife?

ADRIAN. No wife.

FRANCES. How old's your daughter? What's her name?

ADRIAN. Jeannie. She's twenty.

FRANCES. Jeannie.

ADRIAN. I think she thinks she's in love with Gary.

FRANCES. Gary as in Gary here?

ADRIAN. That's right.

FRANCES. Oh.

ADRIAN. That's one of the reasons I brought him with me.

FRANCES. I see.

ADRIAN. Not only that reason.

FRANCES. And does Gary think he's in love with your daughter?

ADRIAN. I haven't asked him. Judging from his performace to date I'd say if he is he's keeping it a closely guarded secret.

FRANCES. Can I assume you're not delighted about this love affair? It is a love affair?

ADRIAN. I'm not delighted, no.

FRANCES. You're being quite calculating bringing him with you, aren't you?

ADRIAN. Maybe.

FRANCES. Oh yes, and does he know you know about this?

ADRIAN. No. (*Pause.*) Look, first of all I don't even know what it means for him, but Jeannie it's . . . and he works for me. They both know how I feel about that. That's not on.

FRANCES. This explains a lot.

ADRIAN. Does it?

FRANCES. Yes, because when I first met you, I suppose I tarred you with the same brush, except I didn't of course, but I couldn't quite work out the double act, now I see it was just a protective dad, perfectly clear.

ADRIAN. You see what you like.

FRANCES. I'm not sure if I like it much.

ADRIAN. I'm not asking you to. I love my daughter. I'm not going to let someone like Gary mess up her life. And I know all about Garys. (*Tapping his chest.*) I know. I've been there.

FRANCES. What does Jeannie's mother have to say about all this?

ADRIAN. I have no idea. We don't see her.

FRANCES. This is going wrong. (*A beat.*) I've been fantasizing, yes, anyway, about falling in love with you. Now, I'm not sure whether this is because in my mind, because of this guilt business, I have to convince myself I'm in love with you before I can get into the bed with you, or whether it's because I'm in Bangkok and you are the only good thing to have emerged, along with the Reclining Buddha, or because you seem to listen to me, or what . . . I don't know . . . (*She touches him.*) Is there a woman at home?

ADRIAN. Yes.

FRANCES. Right.

ADRIAN. Well, there's a husband in your luggage.

FRANCES. Declared.

ADRIAN. I've declared a woman at home and a daughter.

FRANCES. It's just I want to think there's one relationship I can have in my life which is honest. I want to think I can say everything without fear.

ADRIAN. Well you can.

FRANCES. And so can you.

ADRIAN. Right.

They can't think of anything to say. They chuckle.

ADRIAN. Who's G?

FRANCES. G?

ADRIAN. You had a handerchief on the boat, on the walk, the other day, it was initialled . . . G . . .

FRANCES *produces the handerchief.*

ADRIAN. That's it.

FRANCES. I don't know. (*Pause.*) Honestly. (*Pause.*) Do you really want to know?

ADRIAN. Yes.

FRANCES. It was given to me by a lover.

ADRIAN. So you do know.

FRANCES. His name didn't begin with a G either. Really. He said it was given to him, too. And the person, woman, who gave it to him wasn't a G either, so . . .

ADRIAN. Glad I asked.

FRANCES. You don't believe me, do you?

ADRIAN. I do! I do.

FRANCES. He gave it to me when I was crying about something, to do with him or us or, it was hopeless and I was crying and he gave me his hankie and off we went identifying it or failing to just like now and I've always treasured it because I think of it as being handed on from lover to lover for tears, etc.

ADRIAN. Etc.

FRANCES. I should give it to you.

ADRIAN. Oh, are you anticipating I'll cry?

FRANCES. I'm anticipating etc.

ADRIAN. OK. Thank you.

And they embrace for the first time.

Scene Three

The Coffee Shop. NET *brings* EDWARD *cheese on toast.*

NET. Cheese on toast.

EDWARD. Thank you Net.

NET (*stays*). OK?

EDWARD (*eating*). Ngh. (*Yes.*)

NET. Want ketchup?

EDWARD. Ngh. (*No.*)

NET. Today weather not so good.

EDWARD. No.

NET. Some days Buddha sunbathe the whole day, some days he take big bath.

EDWARD. That's right.

NET. Today Buddha have big bath. Net get very wet. Mr Edward get very wet?

EDWARD. No.

NET. No kid?

EDWARD. Mr Edward stay in hotel.

NET. All day?

EDWARD. All day.

NET. (*Impressed*.) No kid.

EDWARD. Net, does no one mind you talking to me?

NET. Mr Edward my customer. No problem. (EDWARD *eats*.) So: what my friend do today? Read books! (*He seems to find this quite funny*.)

EDWARD. Yes, I did, that's right. Why's that funny?

NET. Just funny.

EDWARD. Why?

NET. No, just Net wonder maybe Mr Edward have girlfriend in room but you don't tell Net maybe, maybe not like other men who go up and down in elevator with Thai girl, slap bottom, make big joke, big noise. Edward quiet, go up and down elevator by yourself but still Thai girl in room. I just wonder.

EDWARD. Are there only two types of men? Those who admit to having girls in their rooms and those who don't?

NET. Sorry. Don't follow.

EDWARD. Well, no matter. I was actually reading a book about Thai politics.

NET (*unimpressed*). Ach.

EDWARD. Your army is very powerful.

NET. Very powerful.

EDWARD. Too powerful, my book says.

NET (*unimpressed*). Ach.

EDWARD. What does Net think?

NET. Not so interested in politics, to tell truth.

EDWARD. You should be. You can change things.

NET. Net change things? Ha! Not possible. Always say: Buddha can change world; Net change tyre.

EDWARD. Not true. Really. Not true.

NET. Net think true. No problem. What you do tonight: more reading!

EDWARD. A walk perhaps. I don't know. Depends on the weather. Maybe a walk.

NET. Tomorrow night, Net not work, is Mr Edward's last night or not?

EDWARD. Yes, that's right.

NET. OK. Maybe tomorrow night Net show Mr Edward Thai boxing?

EDWARD. Maybe.

NET. Special evening for my friend. Maybe go Thai boxing then cousin's house watch special film.

EDWARD. Net, really . . .

NET. Understand, Edward not like to do anything except maybe look.

EDWARD. That's right.

NET. Still, maybe look at film, same thing. Very sexy film.

EDWARD *points at* NET, *and pulls imaginary trigger.* NET *laughs.*

FRANCES *enters, from the elevator. She sits at another table. Smiles politely at* EDWARD *and* NET. *They nod greetings.*

NET. OK. Net bring Edward more food?

EDWARD. No thank you.

NET. Net find just sweet for friend. Come straight back. One you like.

EDWARD. Thank you. Kawpkun.

NET. Mai penrai. (*Goes to* FRANCES.) And for madam?

FRANCES. Tea please.

NET. Lemon tea.

ADRIAN *enters, again from the elevator.*

NET. Want something sir?

ADRIAN. No thanks.

FRANCES. Hello.

ADRIAN. Hello.

FRANCES. Are you going to join me?

ADRIAN. No.

FRANCES. I'm just waiting for Stephen.

ADRIAN. What are you doing tomorrow?

FRANCES. I'm not sure.

ADRIAN. I'd like to take you to dinner tomorrow evening.

EDWARD *can hear all this. He looks at his tablecloth.*

FRANCES. I don't know what we're doing.

ADRIAN (*levelly*). Just you, Frances.

FRANCES (*levelly*). Well I'd like to but obviously I can't if Stephen
has already made other arrangements.

ADRIAN. Frances there is only tomorrow.

FRANCES. There's Hong Kong.

ADRIAN. Let me know about tomorrow.

FRANCES. I will.

He exits. There's a pause. Eventually FRANCES *addresses*
EDWARD.

FRANCES. Horrible weather.

EDWARD. Afraid so.

FRANCES. I'd hoped to get out, go to the market, but I couldn't face
it. My husband's still out. He's got business today. He'll be
drenched. I don't suppose you've seen him?

EDWARD. Sorry, no.

FRANCES. I get a headache in this kind of weather. I had a sleep.

EDWARD. I've been reading a very interesting book. About Thai
politics.

FRANCES. Really? And is that, what, is that interesting?

EDWARD. Just makes me so angry. The waste. The exploitation.
Mind you, Hong Kong's just as bad. I work in the refugee camps,
the Boat People, and I can't get anybody to empty the bins! I can't
get bins! Last month, the month before, March, I went to a charity
dinner at the golf club, black tie, puddings in the shape of the
Island, you know, in the shape of Hong Kong, fifty dishes, and at
my table half the people who administrate the camps, OK, and so I
brought up this subject of bins, because they were all there and I
was pig sick of writing memos – I hate memos – I hate
bureaucracy. So I just said – 'What about these bins then?'

FRANCES. And what happened?

EDWARD. I got them. I got the bins. Next day. But I also got
completely ignored for the rest of the dinner and it was made clear
to me I wouldn't get another invitation. Ignorant. Underneath the
black ties they're all ignorant bloody apes.

NET *ushers in* STEPHEN *and tea and a dish of something for* EDWARD.

NET. See! (*He's been* STEPHEN's *guide.*)

STEPHEN. Hello darling, the waiter told me you'd be here.

FRANCES. Hello.

NET. I bring extra cup. Mr Edward enjoy nice sweet things.

EDWARD. Thank you.

STEPHEN *terribly conscious of* NET, *waits until he has exited before elaborating on his deception.*

STEPHEN. I'm soaked. Am I late? Everybody's fighting for a cab. Madness. I got you a present.

FRANCES. Did you? Can I see? How was the meeting?

STEPHEN. Oh OK. It's something you'll have to try on.

FRANCES. Really?

STEPHEN. Not here.

FRANCES. Right. I didn't get to the market. I got a headache.

STEPHEN. So what did you do? What a drag.

FRANCES. I went to bed.

STEPHEN. Did you sleep it off?

FRANCES. A bit. I feel better now.

GARY (*enters*). Hi.

STEPHEN. Oh hello. How are you?

GARY. Fine. How are you?

STEPHEN. (*A beat.*) Wet.

GARY. Right. Seen Adrian around?

FRANCES. No.

STEPHEN. I haven't. No.

GARY (*to* EDWARD). Have you?

EDWARD (*compromised*). No I don't think so.

GARY. Fair enough.

STEPHEN (*very uncomfortable*). Let's go upstairs and I can show you your present.

FRANCES. Have your tea first, eh?

STEPHEN. Oh yes.

GARY. Well I don't know about anybody else but I'm absolutely shagged out. (*Pause.*) Mmm? (*He looks around mischievously.*)

EDWARD. It's the humidity, I expect.

STEPHEN. Why don't you go on up ahead and try this thing on?

GARY. What's this? (*He massages STEPHEN's shoulder.*)

STEPHEN. I've bought Frances a present.

GARY. That's nice. Isn't that nice?

FRANCES. I think so. (*To STEPHEN.*) OK.

STEPHEN. Gary's teasing. He knows what it is. He helped me sort it out.

FRANCES. I wondered what was going on.

GARY. That's right. I'm just winding Stephen up. It's so easy, isn't it?

FRANCES. I will go on up.

STEPHEN. I'll come with you. I'll just gulp down my tea. I might even ask him to send it to the room. (*Hands her the parcel.*) Anyway, hope you like it, my darling.

FRANCES. Thank you. See you in a minute. (*She exits.*)

　　STEPHEN *glowers at* GARY.

GARY. What's the matter?

　　STEPHEN *refuses to join in.*

GARY. Did you think I was going to tell her you'd been *round the world*?

STEPHEN. Don't Gary, for God's sake, not even as a joke.

　　STEPHEN *is half-terrified of being found out, half-delighted at his exploits.*

GARY. Just geeing you up.

STEPHEN. Well don't.

GARY. My lips are sealed, said the tart to the elephant.

NET (*returns*). Tea for sir. (*Going to EDWARD.*) Also coffee for my friend.

EDWARD. Thank you, Net.

NET (*to GARY*). Did you want a drink, sir?

GARY. Yes, a Singha, cold.

NET. Cold beer: Singha; no problem.

GARY. If it's not cold I don't want it.

NET. Understand.

GARY. Hey, listen: well done this afternoon. We were very impressed, eh Steve?

NET. Thank you. I hope so.

GARY. Oh yeah, brilliant.

STEPHEN (*conscious of* EDWARD). There's no need to . . .

GARY. I have this friend and this friend would like to know how much it would cost to have two Thai girlfriends for an evening.

NET. Two girlfriends?

GARY. That's right.

STEPHEN. Gary . . .

NET. Talking about nice girls?

GARY. Very nice.

NET. Very nice girls maybe not too old?

GARY. Very nice young girls.

NET. Which evening? This evening?

GARY. Tomorrow evening? (*Looks at* STEPHEN.) Tomorrow evening?

STEPHEN *doesn't respond, but he's listening.*

NET. All night?

GARY *looks across, amused, as* STEPHEN *raises his eyes.*

GARY. Probably not.

NET. Still talking about a lot of baht.

STEPHEN (*muttering*). Certificates.

GARY. What?

STEPHEN. Certificates.

GARY. (*Hears.*) What?

STEPHEN. Certificates.

GARY (*to* NET). I think this friend would want to see certificates.

NET. What kind of certificates?

GARY. Like this afternoon: no AIDS, no clap.

NET. Understand. No problem. All certificates. Clean girls. Just come up country.

GARY. So how much?

NET. Maybe three thousand baht.

GARY. Come on, we're not thick.

NET. Good price.

GARY. I said two girls not twenty-two.

NET. Twenty-two! Twenty-two many thousand baht! Twenty-two!

GARY. My friend was thinking more in the region of two thousand baht.

NET. Net sorry but three thousand baht special price because you friends.

GARY. I see. It's a shame because I could have put some more business your way because I might also want some empty company tomorrow.

NET. So talking about altogether three nice girls?

GARY. That's right.

NET. I go get Singha beer for my friend, also speak. (*Mimes telephone call.*) Come back with special price. Like today: always special price.

EDWARD, GARY, STEPHEN *alone*. EDWARD *transfixed by the negotiations*. STEPHEN *too*.

GARY. I think we would expect to pay say four thousand for all three, eh? 3,800.

STEPHEN. I have to go upstairs.

GARY. What do you want to do, then?

STEPHEN. Look, I'm not sure I . . . I really have to, Fran'll wonder where, what I'm playing at.

GARY. You could help us. (EDWARD.) He could help us.

EDWARD. I'm sorry?

GARY. Don't pretend you weren't listening. Your ears were flapping like . . . (Looks at STEPHEN.) I thought he was going to take off.

EDWARD. I think that's rather an exaggeration.

GARY (*cutting in*). The fact is the guy obviously fancies you or something the way he oils all over you – if he tossed you you'd be a salad. Does he?

EDWARD. Don't be ridiculous.

GARY (*cutting in*). That's my guess – a shirt lifter – beat him down for us, do us a favour.

EDWARD. If you want to buy women, that's your business. Don't involve me.

STEPHEN. I really do have to go.

GARY. Come on, I've got to think it's a bargain. I can't bear paying top whack. Try and get him down to three thousand baht. I'll come to you for my fillings. 'Cause he took us to a massage place this afternoon and I'm sure we paid too much.

EDWARD. Net did?

GARY. Yeah.

EDWARD. If you really want my opinion and to be quite honest with you I hate the way you behave. I despise it actually.

GARY. You can't say fairer than that.

EDWARD. (*Flustered.*) I despise your mock, your mock, your facetiousness.

GARY. My mock, my mock, my facetiousness?

EDWARD. Because Net is a good man compromised by his circumstances. Because otherwise he wouldn't have to procure for you, he wouldn't have to bring you cold beer or be insulted by you.

GARY. Who's insulted him? I haven't insulted him. I said he fancies you. Is that an insult?

STEPHEN. I think we should just drop this, I wasn't really serious.

NET *reappears.*

NET. OK. Net have very good deal. Special rate for friends. Cold Singha beer for my friend, no charge.

GARY. Lovely.

NET. For these girls tomorrow night come 8:00 and leave 12:00.

GARY. Cinderellas.

NET. (*Doesn't understand.*) All clean girls. Three thousand four hundred baht. Best price I can do. Two thousand now, rest tomorrow.

GARY. 3,400? What's that? 80 quid?

STEPHEN. Yes.

GARY. That would be say fifty-five for you: twenty-five me. What do you reckon?

STEPHEN. I'll have to think about it. I'll have to cash a travellers' cheque. I'll have to . . . (*Hesitating.*) It'll be quite awkward, whichever. (*To GARY.*) *55/25, it's not exactly proper . . . (He thinks it an uneven split.)*

GARY. We'll give you three thousand baht now, cash.

STEPHEN (*protesting*). I haven't.

GARY. Yes or no?

NET. Three thousand cash now?

GARY. Now.

NET. OK. For Net nothing, but OK because all friends. Here. Cash now please.

GARY. Great. Magic. I've got 700, 900 baht. What have you got?

STEPHEN. Not enough. I've only got, I haven't got 2,000 baht. Look I've only got 1,700 baht. Shit this is taking ages.

GARY (*to* EDWARD). Lend us four hundred baht.

EDWARD. I'm sorry. I can't.

GARY. Of course you can, come on. Lend Stephen four hundred baht until the morning. Otherwise you're going to cause a real domestic rift, real problems. Four hundred baht.

STEPHEN. I can pay you at breakfast.

EDWARD. I'm sorry, I can't, I said. It goes completely against the grain. I don't think I can actually help you to exploit women, girls. It's disgusting, you're disgusting.

GARY (*to* EDWARD). No, you're disgusting! Because all we want to do is fuck them. You want them to kiss your arse. It's like school. It's like the fucking black babies. See your little flag go up the stairs. That's what we had at school . . . a little chart with stairs and a picture of God at the top. Each time you gave a penny, a flag with your name went up a stair. (*Disgust.*) Well 'Edward, you have given me 400 baht for the pagan babies. Go straight to heaven, do not pass go.'

NET. No problem. Net take two thousand now, rest tomorrow. No trouble, please.

EDWARD. Here you are. I'll give you your four hundred baht.

NET. No kid, Mr Edward: tomorrow fine.

EDWARD. Just take it. (*Gives him the four hundred baht.*)

STEPHEN. Honestly, you'll have it back by breakfast.

EDWARD *exits*.

STEPHEN. Listen, I wonder if I could sign my bill for the tea, and for my wife's? It's just that I'm cleaned out.

NET, *who's quite disturbed by the unpleasantness, just hands him the bill.*

STEPHEN. Thank you.

NET. Tomorrow, girls come reception eight p.m.

STEPHEN. Uh. (*To* GARY.) Couldn't we have them sent up to your room?

GARY. Yeah, OK, have them sent up to me. I'll check them out for you.

NET. Understand. Your room. Eight p.m. (*Exits*.)

STEPHEN. Right. I wish you hadn't tormented that bloke. He's already liable to tell Fran.

GARY. No, he's much too frightened. He'll go to his room and have a wank and *imagine* he's told her.

STEPHEN. I'm glad you're so sure.

GARY. He's frightened we'd make him cry. I keep thinking he's going to anyway. Well go on then, and see you tomorrow. At the ball, Prince Charming, eight p.m.

Scene Four

The bedroom. FRANCES *and* STEPHEN.

FRANCES. What happened? Where've you been?

STEPHEN. I got talking. Sorry. With Edward.

FRANCES (*guilty*). Oh, what did he say?

STEPHEN (*guilty*). Just on his hobby-horse, I don't know.

FRANCES. I see.

STEPHEN. Gary's right. He thinks – Edward – thinks if you make enough noise about something then you're absolved. If you blame enough people you're let off.

FRANCES. And what: who was he criticizing? Gary and Adrian?

STEPHEN. Not Adrian. I mean Adrian wasn't there. Why?

FRANCES. Oh darling, I haven't modelled my dress. Or said thank you. How did you get my size?

STEPHEN. Gary helped. I had a look inside your blue dress. Is it all right?

FRANCES. It's wonderful. I'm so touched you even, and that it's silk. Let me show you. (*Having held up the dress, she begins the process of modelling it.*)

STEPHEN. Well, you said you wanted silk.

FRANCES. I know I said. I wasn't sure you listened. It's beautiful, Stephen. You never bought me a dress before.

STEPHEN. I've paid for dresses.

FRANCES. Well, there's a difference. How was your meeting?

STEPHEN. Yes, OK. I'll have to go to the main factory tomorrow. To say I've been.

FRANCES. Shall I come?

STEPHEN. If you'd like to.

FRANCES. Would you like me to go?

STEPHEN. Yes, of course. We may have to eat with some of them.

FRANCES. Lunch or dinner?

STEPHEN. Perhaps both.

FRANCES. Not both, Stephen.

STEPHEN. Well listen, come with me, have lunch and if they insist on my stopping for supper then you can come back.

FRANCES. Or the other way round.

STEPHEN. Or the other way round, you mean you come later and have supper? Yes, fine. Would you prefer that? (*Kicks off his shoes.*)

FRANCES. Whichever you like, darling. Although actually I would rather come with you, have lunch and then go off. I still haven't got anything for Christopher.

STEPHEN. You won't be lonely in the evening?

FRANCES. No, I expect I'll join one of the tours. I haven't seen any Thai boxing.

STEPHEN. OK.

FRANCES. Can I wear my new dress?

STEPHEN. Yeah. It's beautiful. You look beautiful.

FRANCES. Thank you.

STEPHEN. You're soft today.

FRANCES. Am I? You're soft, too. (*They embrace*). And you smell nice.

STEPHEN. What do you mean.

FRANCES. You smell nice!

STEPHEN. Are you teasing me because I'm sweaty or something?

FRANCES. No!

STEPHEN. You're only happy when I'm in the bath.

FRANCES. True.

STEPHEN. I went for a massage today. (*They stay embracing, except stiffly.*)

FRANCES. Oh?

STEPHEN. I was curious.

FRANCES. What sort of massage? I thought you were visiting Mr Thinsa?

STEPHEN. On the way. On the way back. Before I collected your dress I had some time to kill. I went with Gary.

FRANCES. Right.

STEPHEN. That's why I smell clean, I expect. They give you a bath, there's a bath. You should be happy.

FRANCES. A woman gave you this massage, I take it?

STEPHEN. You don't get offered a choice.

FRANCES. And of course if you had been . . .

STEPHEN. It wasn't sexual. I'm not saying I didn't expect it to be. I'm saying it didn't turn out to be sexual. I had a really vigorous massage and that was it. (*Pause.*) I mean, of course, it was quite, I'm not pretending it wasn't, the fact is I'm telling you and I didn't have to.

FRANCES. I spent the afternoon with Adrian.

STEPHEN. Meaning?

FRANCES. As we're talking about what we did this afternoon.

STEPHEN. What do you mean you spent the afternoon with him?

FRANCES. What do you mean you had a really vigorous massage?

STEPHEN. Are you serious?

FRANCES. I am, yes.

STEPHEN. Where? Where did it happen, this spending the afternoon? In here?

FRANCES. No.

STEPHEN. Where then?

FRANCES. Don't get aggressive, Stephen, please.

STEPHEN. Christ.

FRANCES. Please don't.

STEPHEN. It's brilliant, isn't it? Because I go for a massage, which is what thousands of men do when they come to Thailand on holiday. A harmless massage, which I'm meant to be guilty, feel guilty about, have this big confession over and I feel like some sort of pervert – and my wife – because it's practically perverse not to go to one of these places we go to the Reclining Buddha and buy silk and take pictures of the squalor and all the painted men lifting up their skirts which is all fine, and all the time my wife is, it's fucking brilliant, isn't it? In this bed, was it? (*He rips the duvet off the bed.*)

FRANCES. I didn't say I went to bed with him. Stephen, if you're going to get agitated I'm going to have to leave the room.

STEPHEN. Yes, do, fuck off, go and see your friend, Adrian. He's old enough to be your father, it's pathetic.

FRANCES. It was actually something I wanted to talk to you about. I thought we could talk about things, what's missing between us, why someone like Adrian could even begin to be a threat, why I can't give you a massage if it's a massage you want: I like massaging you . . . I keep trying to talk, please talk to me, Stephen. Because just now we were close, weren't we and I was so happy about the dress and now I see it was just something to wrap your afternoon in.

STEPHEN. You think everything will yield to chat, Frances. Well it won't.

FRANCES. OK.

STEPHEN. Because there's no logic.

FRANCES. OK.

STEPHEN. That's all. Particularly for men.

FRANCES. Why particularly for men? (*The ceiling has begun to leak.* FRANCES *examines it.*) Oh Christ.

STEPHEN. Because you think it has to be love, don't you? Or nothing. There can't be just, but in fact (*Can't tell her.*) I can't even tell you. I don't think there's anything I can ask you to do. You find a magazine, just photographs, and there's an inquisition.

FRANCES. I just don't happen to think it's on for women to . . .

STEPHEN. Exactly. You won't – when was the last time we had, (*Embarrassed.*) if I come in your mouth it's like I'm supposed to think it's Christmas. You don't even like our son now. The house is a tip, I can't invite people back because I don't know how, what the place will look like: people get fired or . . . I happen to know Howard got the Manchester office on the strength of a conversation at a dinner party at their house. You want to think about what it feels like for your wife to tell you she doesn't like your son.

FRANCES. Not very nice, I expect.

STEPHEN. That's right. Not very nice.

FRANCES. This rain is ridiculous. Can't we do anything about that drip, it's driving me . . . (*She shoves the waste bin under the drip. It only serves to exacerbate the noise, and what follows is punctuated by a sporadic beat.*)

STEPHEN. It just doesn't yield to chat.

FRANCES. No.

STEPHEN. Well let me tell you – there's a cellar, inside me, inside . . . no, there's, I can't think of a word, it's got things even I don't want to look at and I'm not alone in this and I don't see why I should have to feel, I don't even want to talk about it.

FRANCES. I'm actually missing Christopher very badly today. For the record. I wanted us to call him this evening. I don't like dinner parties, I never did. I never have. Your friends, the people you work with – which is a different thing, it's a farce the – you've said this – 'They invited us so we invite them' that's a farce, Stephen. And you excel in liking what you don't do yourself like tidying up which is OK, but in fact I didn't see it – so don't accuse me. I've never left my clothes on the floor: you both do. Women were not born bent double and . . . (*Embarrassed.*) I've, we discussed this. It's not that I don't want to and you said you understood, it feels as if I'm choking, it can feel that and you're never very . . . oh anyway let's have supper shall we or just, not stay in here? The window's leaking as well. Can we call someone? The drains can't cope with all the water: did I tell you there was a condom in the bathroom this morning?

STEPHEN. Yes.

FRANCES. Ugh. I hate those things.

STEPHEN. Frances, you hate rubbers, you hate the cap, you hate the pill.

FRANCES. Yes I do hate those things.

STEPHEN. Just think about it . . . maybe it's something else you hate.

FRANCES. No. I hate those things. Whereas you hate the womb.

STEPHEN. Oh yes, that's right!

FRANCES. Whereas you hate the womb.

STEPHEN. It doesn't get any more true by repeating it.

FRANCES. Whereas you hate the womb, Stephen.

STEPHEN. I'm going to have to leave the room, Frances, because otherwise I could hit you, really hit you: not what you think is hitting.

FRANCES. Then leave the room. Or I will.

STEPHEN. OK. (*Going.*) I'll see you later.

FRANCES. Where are you going?

STEPHEN. I don't know. Oh shit, I haven't got any money.

FRANCES. Haven't you? You must have.

STEPHEN. Have you got any cash? Or the travellers' cheques?

FRANCES. Well I've got a bit. I've got the rest of the travellers' cheques. I hope it was the dress which was expensive. (*She goes to her bag.*) Is this enough?

STEPHEN. I expect so, I can't go without money.

FRANCES. You should take the umbrella. It's in the bathroom. I'll get it.

STEPHEN. It's all right. I'll go.

He exits. FRAN sits on the bed. He comes back with the umbrella which has been opened to drain off in the bath. He can't work out how to close it. Somehow everything has become slightly comic.

FRANCES. Let me.

STEPHEN. It's OK. It's a stupid design. (*Fiddles.*) Bloody thing. (*He half closes it.*) I'll see you later.

FRANCES. Stephen, you haven't got any shoes on.

STEPHEN. Where are my shoes?

FRAN picks them up, goes to him, kneels down and helps him put them on. She bends down in front of him. She puts his shoes on. She puts her arms around his knees. STEPHEN hits her: very hard.

Scene Five

Scene: *The Coffee Shop. The next day.*

At Rise: ADRIAN *and* GARY *are being led to a table by a waiter carrying their drinks.*

GARY (*appreciatively*). You're a bastard, aren't you.

ADRIAN. Now what?

GARY. Back there, at the factory. It was brilliant. The way you do business. That guy was so aggravated.

ADRIAN. (*As they sit down.*) No he wasn't. He was delighted.

GARY. Could have fooled me.

ADRIAN. He did. He did fool you. Listen, the man's just got a big contract. He's delighted.

GARY. He might have a big contract . . . He doesn't have a big profit.

ADRIAN. You reckon? Gary, think a bit. (*Points to his head.*) Exercise this other muscle. He was happy, our friend. He'll re-stitch old styles, remake, just labour. What does labour cost here? No, he was happy all right.

GARY. And what about the factory in Hong Kong? What will you say to them?

ADRIAN. Nothing.

GARY (*chortling, admiring*). Brilliant!

ADRIAN. It's business. It's not brilliant. It's business. If you think about it for five minutes it stinks.

GARY. I don't think so. They want the work. We want the clothes. Everyone makes a little bit. What's the problem?

ADRIAN. That's all right, then.

GARY (*proudly*). But did you notice? I drank tea.

ADRIAN. Yeah. I noticed.

GARY. I never drank it without milk before. (*He makes a face, then proudly.*) The things I do for love.

NET *is approaching. He's with three* THAI GIRLS.

NET (*approaching table*). Mr Gary, sorry disturb you.

GARY. It's all right. (*As he gazes lasciviously at the* GIRLS.) It is no problem at all . . . (*As he speaks to all* THREE GIRLS.) Hello, hello, hello. Oh dear. Sometimes a boy could get so greedy.

NET (*not understanding*). Excuse me.

GARY. Still, at least I get to choose, eh?

NET. Sure. Choose. No problem.

GARY. Well, it's quite a problem. Can they turn around?

NET. Turn round? Sure.

GARY (*giving instruction, with a gesture*). Turn round, turn around.

TWO GIRLS *oblige.* SHEILA *doesn't understand and stays still.*

NET (*instructing her in Thai, quite sharply*). Turn around.

GARY. No, that's all right, I like a bit of . . . sparky, suits me. (*To* SHEILA.) Come here. What's her name?

NET. Sheila.

GARY. Hello, Sheila. Is that her real name?

NET. No. But easy to say Sheila.

GARY. Fine. Sit down, Sheila.

SHEILA *doesn't understand.* GARY *demonstrates.*

GARY. Come and sit down. This is Adrian.

ADRIAN. Hello.

GARY (*to* NET). Pretty girls. I mean really. Well done. (*To* ADRIAN.) You're missing out.

ADRIAN. Yeah.

GARY. Oh yes.

NET. Net's problem is – Net off-duty, follow? – he arrange take Mr Edward out this evening.

GARY. And? What's the problem?

NET. Can you tell your friend Mr Stephen I take his girlfriends upstairs in room?

GARY. His own room?

NET. No, no, not Mr Stephen's room!

GARY. Good, 'cause I was going to say that would have been a bit dim.

NET. Sure, but small problem . . .

GARY. Which is?

NET. See, Net get this room not official, special favour, so many things in room not working: air-conditioning, telephone . . . you follow?

GARY. Yeah.

NET. But sorry, best Net can do without more charge.

GARY. So nothing works in this room? Is there a bed?

NET. Two beds. Beds no problem.

GARY. That's all right, then.

ADRIAN. What's all this?

GARY. Stephen's having a little party. Actually, two little parties, eh Net?

NET. Two girlfriends, very nice.

GARY (*to* ADRIAN). Want to join in? Net could fix you up.

ADRIAN. No thanks.

GARY. Suit yourself. (*To* NET.) So where's Edward? Brushing his teeth?

NET. Upstairs. Wait for Net.

GARY. Sweet.

FRANCES has appeared and makes her way toward ADRIAN.

ADRIAN. (*Quickly and discreetly as* FRANCES *approaches*.) Gary shut up now, eh? See if you can be a bit, try and be a bit tactful, will you? Make a real effort. (*Stands up to greet* FRANCES *as she approaches*.)

GARY (*winding* ADRIAN *up*). Be a bit what? (*Then standing up himself*.) Hello Frances.

FRANCES. Hello Gary. (*To* NET.) Hello Net. (*To* GIRLS *and* SHEILA.) Hello.

NET. Hello.

GARY. Don't mind us. I'm just going upstairs – with Sheila here – for a bit of tact. And Net's . . . (*Evil*.) What are you doing, Net? Oh that's right, you've got a dental appointment. Tee hee.

FRANCES. You're not going for my benefit, I hope?

GARY. Oh no! I'm going upstairs entirely for my own benefit. Where's Stephen?

FRANCES. He's visiting a factory. I just left him. Why?

GARY. No. Just wondered.

FRANCES (*levelly*). I came away to see Adrian. Is that OK?

GARY. That's fine.

FRANCES. Good.

GARY. Good.

NET *exits*.

GARY (*mischievous*). Well aren't we all just doing our own thing? Ta-ra. (*Mouths a kiss. Then full of wisdom to* FRANCES.) Listen, it's none of my business, but have a good time. You know.

FRANCES. You're right, Gary. It's none of your business.

GARY (*of* ADRIAN, *his fellow indulger*). And he's OK. Under the bark. He's OK. (*Goes into the elevator, holding* SHEILA's *hand, singing a snatch of 'One Night in Bangkok.'*)

There's a beat. FRANCES *sits down.*

FRANCES. Hello.

ADRIAN. Hello. (*Referring to dress.*) That looks nice.

FRANCES. I know – by the way – I know what all that's about with Gary.

ADRIAN. OK.

FRANCES. He took Stephen to a massage parlour yesterday.

ADRIAN. Right.

FRANCES. Stephen told me. Did you know about that?

ADRIAN. I had an idea, yes.

FRANCES. And I told him I was with you.

ADRIAN. How did that go down?

FRANCES. He hit me. God, I'm raging. I must have a drink.

ADRIAN. Let's get you one.

FRANCES (*brittle*). I'm raging. Oh God.

ADRIAN. Has this happened before?

FRANCES. What?

ADRIAN. Stephen hitting you?

FRANCES (ADRIAN *has misunderstood what she's saying. Explaining her rage*). No, not about that. I've just left Stephen at his firm's factory. Have you been to one of those places?

ADRIAN. A computer factory? No.

FRANCES. You should. You should go to one. Because they have to be seen to be believed. Because it puts the ping pong balls into a perspective.

ADRIAN (*spots a* WAITER, *flags him over*). What will you drink?

FRANCES. (*Distracted, agitated.*) I don't know. Just a drink. In fact I don't want a drink. I'm sorry. I don't want a drink.

ADRIAN (*to the* WAITER). I'll have another one of these. Thanks.

The WAITER *goes off.*

FRANCES. They have these women in rows glued to their microscopes. Row after row, destroying their eyes. We wouldn't tolerate it at home. Would we? It's a slave trade. I mean it is quite . . . (*Sighs.*) Oh and listen, they have a Miss Lovely Legs Competition. You know, a competition to see who has the best legs. 'Where are the men?' I said. We were being taken round by this woman. That's ironic, isn't it? A woman runs this factory.

(*Exhales sharply.*) 'Where are the men?' I said 'And their lovely legs?' 'They get a bit bored you see, men, if they're cooped up like chickens.' Oh yes, oh yes, oh yes. (*A beat.*) Anyway.

ADRIAN. The place I'm doing business with, the factory, it's probably just as bad, Frances. It's probably worse.

FRANCES. Then don't use it!

ADRIAN. I can't sell cheap clothes if they're expensive to buy.

FRANCES. Then sell expensive ones!

ADRIAN. It doesn't make any difference.

FRANCES. Yes, there's always an answer.

ADRIAN. Frances, changing one business isn't going to change anything.

FRANCES. Isn't it? Then everything must change.

ADRIAN. Ah.

FRANCES. Everything must change.

ADRIAN (*pause*). It's a beautiful dress.

FRANCES (*angry*). Is it?

ADRIAN. Where did it come from? Who made it? You know? (*Beat.*) I was in India once. I saw a rug being woven. Children on the floor in the dark. I used to love those rugs. Their tiny patterns. Now I can't look at them. What do we do? One day you can't look at the rug. Then you can't look at yourself. (*Pause.*) Let's go out. Let me take you out somewhere.

FRANCES. No. I want you to take me to bed. I want you to take my dress off.

ADRIAN. OK.

FRANCES. Do you want to? Say if you don't want to.

ADRIAN (*gently*). Hey. I would like to take you to bed. There's never been anyone I've more wanted to take to bed.

FRANCES. Thank you for saying that.

ADRIAN. You're very welcome.

FRANCES. You're good fun. You're good fun to talk with, to listen to, to touch.

ADRIAN. And so are you.

FRANCES. Notice I say good fun. I do not mention the word love. (*They move toward the stairs.*) Half-way up the elevator, of course, who knows what I'll say. (*They move toward the elevator, step in, the doors close.*)

Scene Six

GARY *is shutting and locking the door behind him. He surveys the room. Then he surveys SHEILA.*

GARY. I expect you've seen plenty of these before? (*The room.*) Do you speak English?

SHEILA *shrugs.*

GARY. Doesn't matter to me. (*Looks at floor.*) Excuse my socks. (*Gathers them up and rolls them with the discarded knickers into a ball.*) Got wet. You either get wet with sweat, don't you, or you get wet 'cause it's raining or a bit of both. Ridiculous place. Sit down. (*Pats the bed.*) Sit down. Make yourself comfortable. We can watch videos. Get a few clues, eh? You hungry? We can get food sent up. Want a hamburger? (*Blank.*) McDonald's?

SHEILA (*nods happily*). Donald's!

GARY (*delighted whenever they communicate*). Thought you might. We can do that. Coming up. (*He picks up the phone.*) Hello. Room service? Room service? Hello? (*Speaks to SHEILA.*) I am Gary. Gary. OK?

SHEILA (*nods*). Charlie.

GARY (*to phone*). Yeah. Three hamburgers please with everything on it. Yeah. Three. Uh: one seven. Thank you. That's done. Everything is hunky dory on the hamburger front. Do you know 'How Much is That Doggie in the Window?' Yeah? Well anyway it's a song. Well today we passed a hamburger shop . . . a McDonald's: understand.

SHEILA. Donalds!

GARY. Good! It wasn't a McDonald's, but anyway.

SHEILA. Donalds.

GARY. Great. But anyway, there is this beautiful doggie. (*Does a mime of a dog as he explains.*) Doggie. Dog. (*Goes to all fours, excessive impersonation.*)

SHEILA. Wo-wo!

GARY. Right! Wo-wo! A Wo-wo is looking at this McDonald's.

SHEILA. Donalds.

GARY. Good. Window, all sad and mournful, you know, and I thought of this great commercial they could do, you know, like – (*Sings to the tune of 'How Much is That Doggie in the Window?'*) 'How much is that burger in the window?'

SHEILA. Wo-wo.

GARY (*continues singing*). Wo-wo . . . da dee da dee da . . . I do hope that burger's for sale! Fab, eh?

SHEILA *chuckles*. GARY *beams*.

GARY. You like my singing, eh? What else do you like? Do you like this?

HE *does a rather impressive sleight-of-hand using his lighter. The lighter disappears and then* GARY *produces it as if from behind* SHEILA's *ear. She laughs.* GARY *finishes his magic. Stares at her as a sexual object for the first time.*

GARY. Do you have your book of, you know: the clinic thing, the VD thing? VD book?

SHEILA *nods and produces what looks like an old driving licence from her handbag.* GARY *gives it some scrutiny.*

GARY. Ta. How anybody's supposed to be able to read this writing. (*Referring to the Thai script.*) Legible! Right, so you're (*Very slowly.*) Khin-Thi-Da Phitpricha.

SHEILA *corrects pronunciation.*

GARY. And you have been to the clinic every Monday and it says you were OK this week and last week and the week before and for many Mondays. Oh, see you had a small problem last year, eh?

Points at entry in the booklet. SHEILA *nods.*

GARY. Khin-Thi-Da: yeah?

SHEILA *nods.*

GARY. I am Gary.

SHEILA. Jary.

GARY. *Ga–*

SHEILA. Ga–

GARY. Ray.

SHEILA. Ray.

GARY. And you're . . . born . . . (*Looks at date.*) . . . makes you: you must be seventeen. Seventeen. Khin-Thi-Da seventeen.

Counts on his hands. She repeats age with her fingers.

GARY. Right! Right! You seventeen: me twenty-three. Do you want to have a bath first? Eh? Bath?

Points to bathroom. SHEILA *shakes her head.*

GARY. No, not the bog . . . a bath! (*Mimes taps etc. Points at her groin.*) Give pussy a good clean, eh? A good scrub. (*Goes to bedside table and gets out his antibiotic supplies. Continues singing his 'Burger in the Window' invention.*) See you in a minute. Ciao.

She exits obediently.

GARY. And I'll take a pill while we're about it.

Scene Seven

NET *and* EDWARD *return to Edward's room prior to going to Net's cousin's house.*

EDWARD (*going straight to the bathroom*). Won't be long, hang on. These bloody lenses, they're new, they're not right.

NET. No problem.

EDWARD (*off*). There are about eight different things you have to put on them. It's a complete con, Net. If I had the nerve I'd wash them in Fairy Liquid.

NET. Good boxing, eh?

EDWARD (*off*). Very interesting.

NET *does a few Thai boxing routines: a kick, a punch, etc.*

EDWARD. (*Off.*) Very violent.

NET. No kid?

EDWARD (*off*). No, I said, the boxing was very violent, lot of blood.

NET. See what you mean.

EDWARD (*off*). That last boy's nose was broken.

NET. Very great kick. (*Gives the bed a sample.*)

EDWARD (*off*). What are you doing out there? Kicking my bed?

NET. Just fool around.

EDWARD (*emerging*). I've put my specs back on . . . I can't be doing with those bloody things. It's just vanity, eh?

NET. No problem.

EDWARD. Net, I don't think you understand English. I just think you've learned some phrases like 'I understand' and 'no kid' and whatever else it is you say: 'No problem' and those are the only words you actually know. Or is that not fair?

NET. Half-half!

EDWARD. Half-half! Good! You're a bright little bugger, aren't you?

NET (*expecting to go*). OK?

EDWARD. Hang about, I can't rush in this weather. Not when it's so close. Do you want a glass of water? (*As he pours himself one.*)

NET. No. Late for cousin's house.

EDWARD. I don't know about that Net. I can't enjoy too many people at once.

NET. OK, OK.

EDWARD. I have enjoyed the evening so far though. Thank you.

NET (*shrugs happily*). Edward, Mr Net's friend.

EDWARD. Net, Edward's friend. (*They shake hands, comfortable then uncomfortable. A beat.*) So, off tomorrow, Hong Kong.

NET. Hong Kong. Very nice?

EDWARD. No. Yes, nice place. Many problems.

NET. Chinese come in make everybody unhappy.

EDWARD. Not everybody. Not me for a kick-off. It is China anyway. Well, no, actually it's Hong Kong. I mean it's not England. It's not a colony.

NET. Don't follow.

EDWARD (*looking at NET's incomprehension and laughs*). Why should Hong Kong be under anybody's foot? Britain's or China's? Like the bloody Falklands. Do you know about the Falklands?

NET (*he doesn't*). Expect so.

EDWARD. Well, it doesn't matter, Net. It's impossible. The things people have stolen. The countries countries have stolen. (*Mimes.*) Lunacy. I tell you, if it could happen, if things were given back to their rightful owners – if there are natural owners, if we agree to ownership – what a bloody wind there would be, eh? The paintings and jewels and gold and stuff that would fly across the world, bloody marvellous . . . this stuff all flying home . . . and in the West, in my country . . . or in America . . . the fat that would come off! The fat that belongs to other people clawed off . . . earrings yanked off, rings, bracelets, wallets emptied, the banks cleared, clothes stripped, every bloody thing until the skin itself would rip open and the fat and the entrails scoured until . . . until, well I'll tell you England would be stubble. The rest we pinched from somewhere. (*A beat.*) Eh? What do you think? You think shut up, Edward, shut up, Edward.

NET *shrugs*.

EDWARD. How do you think our friends are getting on?

NET. Cousin?

EDWARD. No, I mean Gary and Stephen and their girlfriends.

NET. Good time, I expect.

EDWARD. It doesn't bother you, does it?

NET. Edward sad maybe want girl, too?

EDWARD. No. Just something else we've stolen, isn't it? Say: 'Shut up, Edward.'

NET. Shut up, Edward.

EDWARD. You should add that to your vocabulary.

NET. Maybe go now? Net have videos.

EDWARD. What videos?

NET. Bumsin videos.

EDWARD. Blue films?

NET. Sure. Very filthy. Show everything. No kid.

EDWARD. Men and women?

NET. Boy/girl sure.

EDWARD. Always boy/girl?

NET. No. Some two girls.

EDWARD. Two boys?

NET. Possible. You want see two boys?

EDWARD. So easy, isn't it?

NET. Also have one video: she boys.

EDWARD. She boys? Transvestites?

NET. Kra-Toeys. (*Shrugs in amusement.*)

EDWARD. Who goes with them?

NET (*shrugs*). All crazy, you ask Net. Net drive past. Blow horn, all lift up skirts. (*Holds his crotch to demonstrate their gesture.*) Whoo! Crazy!

EDWARD. So is everybody for sale in Bangkok?

NET. Guess so. Except maybe King.

EDWARD. So, is Net for sale?

NET (*shrugs*). Guess . . . (*Nods.*) Guess Net for sale everyday. (*He means his job.*)

EDWARD. I mean . . . as boyfriend . . .

NET. Net as boyfriend? No! (*Laughs.*) No one want Net as boyfriend! Not so pretty! Crazy.

EDWARD. What if I wanted Net as boyfriend tonight?

NET. Crazy.

EDWARD. How much?

NET (*laughs*). My friend kid Net.

EDWARD. No.

NET (*serious*). No kid?

EDWARD. No kid. How much?

NET (*shakes his head*). Edward my friend, not *boy*friend.

EDWARD. So I can't buy you? (*Pause.*)

NET. How much you pay?

EDWARD. How much do you want?

NET. How much do you give?

EDWARD. I don't know: eight hundred baht? One thousand baht?

NET. Net find pretty boy, very cheap. Net arrange now, no problem. Very sexy.

EDWARD. Two thousand baht.

NET. See, really Net not fucking boy.

EDWARD. Are you saying you want more than a thousand baht?

NET. Net unhappy.

EDWARD. Five thousand baht.

NET (*a huge sum to him*). Five thousand baht?

EDWARD. You must never say anything.

NET. For five thousand baht, Net find two pretty boys. Three boys! Stay all night. Do anything. No kid. Make Mr Edward very happy. OK?

EDWARD. You don't understand, Net. You would make me very happy. I can't offer more than five thousand, it's practically all the cash I have left. You can have my watch as well, if you want. Please.

NET. See, Net and Mr Edward good friends. Problem. Net bit unhappy.

EDWARD. Edward also very unhappy. Now Net Mr Edward's friend.

NET. Sure! Very good friends!

EDWARD. I can't offer you anything else – my money and my watch. I haven't got anything else except toothbrushes. (*He goes to his bed and from his pocket and wallet produces all of his cash, emptying the notes onto the bed. He throws his watch down with the money.*) 5,200 baht.

NET *walks slowly across to the bed, lights a cigarette. Such a lot of money.*

EDWARD. Come on! It's more than you charge for three girls!

NET *picks up the money, then the watch.*

EDWARD. Thank you, Net.

NET. Also toothbrushes, please.

EDWARD. What?

NET. Also toothbrushes.

EDWARD. Come on, Net, they're not even really mine.

NET. Also toothbrushes.

EDWARD. OK.

NET. What you want Net to do?

EDWARD. Come here. Sit down.

He beckons NET *to the bed.* NET *dolefully walks over. Sits next to him. Unbuttoning* NET's *shirt.*

EDWARD. I've been writing a poem about you. Take off your shirt. Take off your shirt. Somebody ruined their fingers sewing it. Take off your watch, somebody's eye's got ruined making it. Take off your jeans, take off your shirt, the cigarette is ruining you, it's killing you. (*He throws* NET's *cigarette into the waste bin.*) Everything we've done is ruining you. (*He's unzipping* NET's *trousers. He tries to turn him around.*) Turn around. Turn over.

The cigarette smokes from the waste bin.

Scene Eight

Scene: *The Coffee Shop.*

At Rise: STEPHEN *comes out of the elevator looking for a* WAITER.

STEPHEN. Hello! Hello! Service!

WAITRESS (*appears*). Sir?

STEPHEN. I want some drinks to take up to my room.

WAITRESS (*helpfully*). Room service?

STEPHEN. Yes, I know. But the telephone's broken.

WAITRESS (*helpfully*). Can tell reception fix for you.

STEPHEN. I'm quite happy just to take the drinks up. Can you get me a drink?

WAITRESS. Sure.

STEPHEN. I want some cold beer and some Coke . . . two Cokes. (*Explaining.*) There's a group of us, a little party.

WAITRESS. One beer, and two Cokes. OK. (*Helpfully.*) Tell me room number, I tell reception fix phone.

STEPHEN. I'll do it myself. It's OK. In fact they know, actually. They know. So.

WAITRESS. You want me to take drink to room?

STEPHEN (*edgy*). No. Look, just bring the drinks here, will you, and I'll carry them up. I'm quite happy.

The WAITRESS *exits.* STEPHEN *sits down, blows. He's very hot and flushed.* FRANCES *and* ADRIAN *emerge from the elevator.*

FRANCES (*simply*). Our key's not in reception and the room's locked. I didn't know where you were or if you were back.

STEPHEN (*aggressive*). Right, I mean otherwise you wouldn't be upstairs with your chum.

FRANCES (*over this*). Otherwise I would have known where you were, Stephen. Because I thought you were staying over for dinner.

STEPHEN. Yes. I just got back from dinner. I thought you were going to watch Thai boxing.

FRANCES. We decided not to go.

STEPHEN (*facetious*). Is that what you decided?

FRANCES. We went shopping for Christopher, and then we . . . anyway, I'm not going to make excuses.

ADRIAN. I said I'd come down with Frances and wait until you got back. I didn't want her to have to sit here alone.

STEPHEN. Great. Terrific. Yes, I must have gone off with the key.

FRANCES. How?

STEPHEN. I don't know. But obviously I must have as you clearly have no faults.

FRANCES. No, I just meant . . . because the key was here when I first got back. That's all I'm saying. I can't understand where it went if you haven't been . . .

STEPHEN (*pressing for the elevator*). I said I've got it. (*He reaches into his pocket. For a split second it dawns on him he has two keys. He pulls out a key and examines it nonchalantly as he can.*) Here it is. This is our key. OK? (*He dangles it in front of her.*) So, I'll leave you to your little . . .

FRANCES. I'll come with you.

STEPHEN (*presses again impatiently*). Come on, come on . . .

FRANCES. I said, I'll come with you. You don't have to stomp out.

STEPHEN. Because it's amazing isn't it? It's all fine, it's all wonderful as long as it's romantic. As long as you know the person's name before you take their pants off, that's tickety-boo. Oh yes. (*Pressing again.*) Where is the fucking elevator?

ADRIAN. If Frances does go up, if you do go up, I don't want there to be any repeat of yesterday's . . .

FRANCES (*flustered*). Adrian, don't . . .

STEPHEN (*dangerous*). What's this?

ADRIAN. I think you know what I'm talking about.

STEPHEN. Oh yes: I can just imagine your little chats. About your terrible husband. Well don't bother, you know, please . . . just . . . (*As if dismissing them.*) I've been pressing this bloody button for hours, quite astonishing.

The WAITRESS *appears with the drinks. This coincides with the elevator arriving.*

WAITRESS. Want drinks downstairs now?

STEPHEN. What?

WAITRESS. Drinks.

STEPHEN. Drinks? Great. Yes. Here's fine.

FRANCES. Who are these for?

STEPHEN. Us, I suppose. There's no one else about. Thanks.

WAITRESS. Don't want in room now?

STEPHEN. No.

FRANCES. Why have you ordered Coke?

STEPHEN. I want Coke. Do you want Coke?

FRANCES. No.

STEPHEN. Then there's a beer. Adrian?

ADRIAN. No thanks.

Fire alarm sounds. Piercing noise.

FRANCES. What's going on?

ADRIAN. I don't know.

EVERYONE *is shouting to be heard.*

STEPHEN. Oh God.

ADRIAN. It's the fire alarm!

STEPHEN. What?

ADRIAN. It's the fire alarm.

The WAITRESS *rushes in, speaking in Thai. A lick of smoke appears from the elevator shaft. There's some activity on the mezzanine level.*

WAITRESS (*tugging at* FRANCES *and* STEPHEN. *Garbled*). Outside, please, outside by swimming pool.

FRANCES. What's she saying? Stephen?

STEPHEN (*appalled*). Oh God!

ADRIAN (*looking on*). Stephen, what is the situation upstairs?

FRANCES. What?

ADRIAN. Stephen, what is the situation upstairs?

WAITRESS (*tugging at* FRANCES). Come with me please. Hurry.

FRANCES (*over this*). What situation?

Some PEOPLE *hurry past and out. A lot of shouting and chaos.*

ADRIAN (*low, to* STEPHEN). Have you left those girls upstairs?

STEPHEN. What girls?

ADRIAN. You know what I'm talking about. Where are they?

STEPHEN (*distracted, paralyzed*). I've not – actually – idea, I really don't know – I'll have to think what you're um . . .

FRANCES *comes over to join this exchange. All of this is going very fast.*

FRANCES. What's going on? (*To* ADRIAN.) What's wrong with him? (*To* STEPHEN.) Stephen?

ADRIAN (*decisively*). Go outside, Frances. Just in case. Go out by the pool.

FRANCES. What about you? Where are you going?

ADRIAN. Upstairs. Where am I going, Stephen?

STEPHEN *holds up the room key.*

FRANCES. Will somebody please tell me what is happening? That's not our key. (*Dawning.*) Am I being dense? Adrian? Oh God, am I being very dense?

ADRIAN. Just go outside. Take him with you. I'll be right back.

ADRIAN goes to the stairs. PEOPLE rush past him on their way out. The fire alarm howls away.

FRANCES. Stephen, come on! What's happening? Say something. Say something to me!

STEPHEN (*dully*). What?

WAITER (*appearing, shouting*). Everyone outside! Everyone outside!

GARY and SHEILA run on, dressed in hotel-issue towelling robes.

GARY. What's going on?

FRANCES. I don't know. Is there a fire? Is there smoke upstairs?

GARY. I don't know. I thought I could smell smoke.

WAITRESS and SHEILA exchange stories in Thai.

GARY (*to SHEILA*). What's she saying?

SHEILA (*to GARY in Thai*). Mistake. Probably a false alarm.

GARY. What?

WAITRESS. Mistake probably.

GARY. What the fuck is going on? Where's Adrian?

FRANCES. Upstairs.

GARY. You're joking? Where? Stephen? (*To FRANCES.*) What's the matter with him?

FRANCES. I don't know.

GARY (*to STEPHEN*). Well where are your two? Stephen? Where are your two? Fucking hell! Are they still upstairs? Give me the key!

FRANCES. I think Adrian's got it.

Over these last two exchanges, EDWARD and NET make a slightly dishevelled entry onto the mezzanine floor and shout down as they join the rest of the group.

NET (*running*). False alarm! Stop! False alarm! False alarm!

The alarm ceases as abruptly as it began. Everyone registers the silence for a beat, then EDWARD and NET explain simultaneously.

NET. False alarm. Sorry. No problem. Net have cigarette, set fire to rubbish bin and catch curtain – (*Mimes.*) lot of smoke but small fire no problem.

EDWARD. It's quite ridiculous. We were in my room and Net was smoking and there was an accident with the cigarette – (*Commenting on* NET's *explanation as he hears it.*) Yes, Net's cigarette, it was in the rubbish bin and there was obviously some paper and so on and it caught fire to the uh, that's all . . .

GARY. What? You mean you were in –

EDWARD (*interrupting.*) Yes, and didn't notice at first and then one of the drapes, it caught one of the drapes and there was a lot of smoke and it set the thing off.

NET (*partially over this*). Every week fire alarm. Nobody else pay too much attention. (*To* FRANCES.) For Thai people no problem.

GARY. (*To* EDWARD, *over* NET.) Bit odd, isn't it?

EDWARD (*brittle*). What's odd?

GARY. Not noticing the bin was on fire.

EDWARD (*violently*). No, and we did notice eventually, but by then it was too late. What are you trying to say?

GARY (*evil*). I think a few questions, mate, wouldn't you? Eh? (*Moving straight on to* STEPHEN.)

EDWARD (*over this*). No, come on, come on! I'm not having you just, I can't stand it when people make remarks and then just, come on!

The elevator opens, interrupting this, spilling out STEPHEN's *girlfriends, one wrapped in a sheet, the other in a towel. One of them still has a ripped and knotted sheet dragging around her ankle. Smoke has found its way into the elevator shaft and wisps out.* ADRIAN *walks out of the elevator behind the* GIRLS *and goes to* STEPHEN, *dropping the key at his feet.*

FRANCES (*shocked*). Will you tell me please what has happened here, please? Were these women with Stephen?

GARY *is investigating as* SHEILA *talks animatedly to the two* WOMEN *who are themselves very distressed.*

GARY. He's tied them up hasn't he? (*To* ADRIAN.) That's right, isn't it? (*To* FRANCES.) Your husband has tied these girls up and left them when . . . (*Walking over to* STEPHEN, *very close.*) Do you know what that means? – They couldn't get out, could they? – If there had been a real fire?(*With heavy irony.*) How much would that cost, Net? To burn a couple of girls to death? What's Stephen's special price on that one?

Scene Nine

Scene: *Outside the hotel. Morning.*

At Rise: NET *appears, burdened by as much luggage as he can manage. It's all clearly labelled with Eastern Promise tags. He dumps his load as EDWARD appears carrying a flight bag and a paper package. NET immediately walks past EDWARD without acknowledging him.*

EDWARD. Net . . .

   NET *stops, but doesn't turn around.*

EDWARD. Net, I've wrapped, I've put the toothbrushes in this . . . you didn't take them last night in all the, but anyway, I hope you get a good . . .

NET (*turns, but without warmth. Refusing*). Take toothbrush Hong Kong. Best thing. Net have toothbrush already.

EDWARD. No they're yours.

NET. OK, Net give toothbrush Hong Kong.

EDWARD. Then I'll send you money.

NET. No.

EDWARD. I haven't slept.

NET. No kid?

EDWARD. No kid.

NET. Big storm.

EDWARD. Buddha taking bath . . . isn't that what you say?

   NET *shrugs.*

EDWARD. Anyway, the rain's good, it — I think — it's, I was going to say it cleanses, it feels cleaner this morning, but that's a bit obvious, isn't it? Net, I'd like to take a photograph of you.

NET. No.

EDWARD. Please.

NET. No.

   EDWARD *raises camera.* NET *turns his back.*

EDWARD. Please, Net, turn around.

NET. No, don't want turn around.

EDWARD. I'll take the picture, anyway.

   No effect. NET *keeps his back turned.* EDWARD *takes a picture of the back of his head.*

EDWARD. Well.

NET *still facing away.*

EDWARD. How's the watch? Are you pleased with it?

NET. Sure.

EDWARD. I'm happy you're wearing my watch.

NET. May sell sometime. Who knows?

EDWARD. Net, I wanted to explain about last night, before I go. It wasn't how, I, I, I, I, I know I – you can't buy friendship, can you? I'd like to write – (*Going back.*) Love, I mean, I'd like to write to you anyway. Can I?

NET *says nothing. Busying himself with the luggage.* FRANCES *and* STEPHEN *enter with their hand luggage.* EDWARD *recovers himself.*

FRANCES. Hello.

EDWARD. Good morning.

NET. Morning.

FRANCES. Has anyone turned up yet, do you know?

EDWARD. No, it's early yet, I think. And I expect Net will be driving us to the airport? Yes?

NET. No. (*To* FRANCES.) What you want? Eastern Promise Tour Rep?

FRANCES. No rush.

NET (*happy to go*). Net go look. No problem.

EDWARD (*upset*). Net. Net. Net!

NET *exits. The others stand, uncomfortable, subdued.*

EDWARD (*to* FRANCES). I've offended Net somehow and now I'd like to write and what have you but I don't know his full name or address or, and of course, he won't tell me! (*Laughs.*) He won't even let me take a photograph of him, which is sad, isn't it? Really.

FRANCES. I'm sorry.

EDWARD. A letter wouldn't hurt, would it?

FRANCES. Do you always do this? Stop off in Bangkok?

EDWARD. Have done, yes.

FRANCES. Do you find it's worth more than one visit?

GARY *and* ADRIAN *enter with their bags.*

FRANCES. Hello.

ADRIAN. Hello.

GARY (*to* FRANCES *of* STEPHEN). How's the psychopath? (*To* STEPHEN.) Something of a struggle on the old pervert front. (*To* FRANCES *with some feeling*.) How can you stay with him? No, really, I'm fascinated.

ADRIAN. Shut up Gary.

GARY. Certainly, sir. (*To* EDWARD.) And what about your little friend? Has he lubricated the front step this morning?

EDWARD. I've seen him, yes.

GARY. Little twat owes me some money.

EDWARD. Net does?

GARY. And I intend to get it off him before we go. 'Cause I got ripped off last night, in all the commotion, didn't I? Lost my watch, which was not a cheap watch, and some cash. Bitch had it away, didn't she?

ADRIAN. Gary, I suggest you shut your mouth.

GARY. Why should I?

ADRIAN. Well, let's start with Jeannie, shall we?

GARY. What?

ADRIAN. Because she's going to be very interested in what we did on our holidays, isn't she?

EDWARD (*to* GARY). I can write you a cheque if Net owes you money, although I can't quite see that he does.

ADRIAN. He'll live. (*Horn sounds*.)

FRANCES (*to* ADRIAN). Is this us?

ADRIAN. It's you, I think, probably.

FRANCES. What does that mean?

ADRIAN. Gary and I are going back to London, or rather we're going to sign a contract this morning – we're getting a taxi – and then we're going back to London.

FRANCES. What about Hong Kong? Are you joking?

ADRIAN. No.

FRANCES (*shocked*). I see. (*Takes a breath*.) Can you do that then? Just get on a plane?

ADRIAN. If they've arranged the tickets, yes, but that's not what you mean, is it?

FRANCES. No. That's right. That's not quite what I mean. Well.

TOUR OPERATOR *appears, brisk efficient and late. She reads from her clipboard.*

TOUR OPERATOR. Ah Mr Britter, Mr West, Mr Alexander, Mr Grover –

EDWARD (*correcting her as she reads*). Gover.

TOUR OPERATOR. – Gover, please board bus, have all bags ready and check have ticket and passport before leaving hotel. Also check you have no bill outstanding at the hotel of your stay. Hurry please, thank you.

ADRIAN (*over to her*). Well, actually, yes, I called your company yesterday and explained that we we – this is Mr West and Mr Alexander – I explained that we were returning to London and –

TOUR OPERATOR. Sure, OK, no problem. I remember. I have written down somewhere. (*Searching through her clipboard.*) OK, everyone on bus, please.

NET *has appeared with more luggage and now begins to move it in the direction of the bus.*

GARY (*of the luggage*). Not ours!

EDWARD. Net!

GARY. And where's my watch?

EDWARD. Net, I can carry my own case.

NET, *head down, pushes off the* BRITTERS' *luggage.*

FRANCES. Yesterday?

ADRIAN. Yesterday what?

FRANCES. You changed your plans yesterday?

ADRIAN. Yes.

FRANCES. I don't want to be completely uh, but what time yesterday? No, don't answer that.

ADRIAN. Yesterday afternoon.

FRANCES. Ah, then you should have told me in the afternoon before you took me to bed.

TOUR OPERATOR. On bus, please. (*Over this. Insistent, exiting.*) Please hurry on the bus!

NET (*returning having taken off all the Hong Kong luggage. Approaching* ADRIAN). You want taxi, sir?

ADRIAN. Yes, please.

EDWARD. Net, I have to go.

GARY. Is he going to answer me about that watch?

EDWARD. Will you shut up about your bloody watch! (*To* NET.) He says he had his watch stolen last night.

The horn sounds, long, insistent.

STEPHEN. I'll see you on the bus. (*He exits.*)

FRANCES. I'm coming now.

NET *takes off the watch* EDWARD *has given him.*

NET. No problem, take Net's watch.

EDWARD. No!

GARY (*dropping it on the ground*). I don't want your crappy watch, I want my own!

NET *stomps off angrily.*

GARY. Oy! Where are you going? What about our cab!

EDWARD (*anguish*). Net! (*Then rounding on* GARY.) You're rubbish, aren't you!

GARY. Be careful, lovey.

ADRIAN (*powerful*). Gary, go and find a cab, now!

GARY. I can't wait. It is a fucking rip-off this place. What a fucking rip-off. (*Exits, passing* EDWARD, *mouthing him a kiss.*)

EDWARD, ADRIAN *and* FRANCES *stand in silence.* EDWARD *realizes they're waiting for him to go.*

EDWARD. I'll say goodbye then.

ADRIAN. Right.

FRANCES. Bye.

EDWARD *goes.* FRANCES *and* ADRIAN *alone.*

ADRIAN. You could come back with us.

FRANCES. No, how could I? Do you want me to? Tell me.

ADRIAN *can't tell her he does.*

FRANCES. Yes, I can see I'm a liability.

ADRIAN (*meaning it*). No, I think you're great.

FRANCES. But not irresistibly great. That's the problem.

ADRIAN. I bought you these. (*He produces a small jewelry box.*) They're sapphires. I had an address. Supposed to be good.

FRANCES. Adrian, my ears aren't pierced.

ADRIAN (*mortified*). Let me see. (*He pushes back her hair.*) You're right. They're not pierced. (*Laughs*.) You could keep them as a souvenir.

FRANCES (*laughs*). No, you keep them as a souvenir. But thank you.

They understand each other. A short laugh.

FRANCES. (*Warm.*) Thank you.

They kiss a nice kiss.

ADRIAN. Frances.

The horn, insistent.

FRANCES. I must go.

ADRIAN. Will you stay with him?

FRANCES (*simply*). I don't know. Nothing can stay the same now can it. (*Then suddenly bleak.*) I hate this kind of weather so much.

STEPHEN (*reappears. Off the minibus*). If you don't come now, I think we'll . . .

FRANCES (*cutting him off*). Right. (*To* ADRIAN.) Goodbye.

ADRIAN. Goodbye.

They turn and exit in opposite directions.

Scene Ten

GARY's *bedroom.*

Two chambermaids enter. They set about changing the sheets with an elegant, practised ease. One of them turns on the wireless which is pumping out Thai pop, a hybrid of Western disco and Thai ballad. The girls know this song and join in.
In the process of stripping the linen from the bed, one of the maids comes across GARY's *watch. It spills on to the floor. She picks it up and she and her friend discuss it. She laughs and pockets the watch.*

The song finishes and after a rapid announcement is replaced by some ethnic Thai music of the kind which accompanies classical dancing. The music is pure, strange. One of the girls has obviously studied this form of dancing at some stage, and clowning around with a sheet to amuse her friend, she performs the briefest, most beautiful dance.